Cheese:

A Guide to the World of Cheese and Cheesemaking

Bruno Battistotti   Vittorio Bottazzi
Antonio Piccinardi   Giancarlo Volpato

Cheese:
A Guide to the World of Cheese and Cheesemaking

Facts On File Publications
New York, New York • Bicester, England

Drawings by Vittorio Salarolo

Cheese: A Guide to the World of Cheese
and Cheesemaking

Copyright © 1983 Arnoldo Mondadori Editore S.p.A., Milan

Translated from the Italian by Sara Harris

English translation copyright © 1984 Arnoldo Mondadori
Editore S.p.A., Milan

First published in the United States by
Facts On File, Inc.
460 Park Avenue South
New York, N.Y. 10016

Library of Congress Cataloging in Publication Data
Cheese: a guide to the world of cheese and cheesemaking.
   Translation of: Formaggi del mondo.
   1. Cheese   2. Cheese—Varieties.   I. Battistotti,
Bruno.
SF271.F7613   1984   641.3'73   84-7960
ISBN 0-87196-981-5

Printed and bound in Italy by Arnoldo Mondadori Editore,
Verona

Contents

9
Introduction

10
The story of cheese

25
The making of cheese

41
The great cheeses of the world

93
Dictionary of world cheeses

157
Wine with cheese

160
Cutting cheese

162
Cheese defects

163
Soured milk products

165
Glossary

167
Index

Key to symbols used in the Dictionary of Cheeses

Type of milk used to make the cheese

Cow's milk   **Buffalo milk**   **Ewe's milk**   **Goat's milk**   **Mixed milk**

Heat treatment (if any) of the curd

Uncooked-curd   **Scalded-curd**   **Cooked-curd**

This classification of cheeses as raw, scalded or 'cooked' is based on the maximum temperature reached during the process of cheesemaking and the extent to which whey is released by the curd (this in turn depends on the duration of the heating process; this does not take into account heat treatment such as pasteurization to destroy harmful bacteria). As a very general guide, to which there are many exceptions, uncooked-curd cheese will not have been heated to temperatures in excess of 100–104°F (38–40°C) nor scalded-curd cheese to beyond 104–120°F (40–48°C). Cooked-curd cheeses are heated to temperatures in excess of 120°F (48°C).

Consistency of the cheese

Soft   **Semi-hard**   **Hard**

The consistency of a cheese is directly related to its moisture content. As a general rule, soft cheeses will have a moisture content of 45–50%; semi-hard, 40–45% and hard, less than 40%. Classification is according to a cheese's resistance when cut.

Internal appearance of the cheese (the paste)

Even, dense, without holes

Small, oval or round holes ('eyes') up to ¹⁄₁₀ in (2 mm) in diameter

Oval or round holes measuring up to ⅕ in (5 mm) in diameter

Large, round holes measuring ⅜ in (1 cm) or more

Blue cheese (greenish-blue and/or white internal mould)

Spun or plastic-curd cheese, in which the curd has been spun, drawn or kneaded

Where the same cheese may vary in consistency and appearance depending on whether it is fresh, matured for a short time or aged, the symbols refer to the most popular and widely-manufactured type.

Introduction

Throughout history and into the present day, cheese has remained one of the most popular, varied and nutritious foods. For our ancestors cheese often replaced meat as the basic animal protein for those too poor to own animals or to slaughter those they did own. At the same time, the richest milk and cream were turned into cheese for the tables of the wealthy and privileged. Those who lived close to the land relied on the sheep or goat rather than the hungrier cow and there are few traditional cheeses that were not made with ewe's or goat's milk. The variety was infinite. Numberless farmers' wives made their own cheese as a matter of course and altered and adapted their methods according to the season and what was at hand.

The Industrial Revolution changed these traditions. As more and more people migrated from the farms to the cities, the centuries'-old tradition of home-made cheesemaking declined. It was easier to have milk brought to the factories and have the work done indoors. From then on only the great pressed cheeses were assured a future. Few were left on the farms to make the sweet, soft, short-lived cheeses.

However, pockets of resistance remain. In France (and in Greece and Spain, where a large proportion still live as genuine peasants) there has been no influence strong enough to shake the foundations of tradition. While some cheesemaking peasant families have prospered and become large suppliers and some of the old cheeses are now made in factories and sent abroad, much of the cheese in these countries is still made locally on the farm. For example, there is almost no central commercial manufacturing of French goat cheese and the yield to marketers of this cheese is mercilessly dependent on the inclination of both animal and owner.

How should cheese be served? Except for soft cream cheese, all cheese benefits from being served at normal room temperature – but is harmed by being allowed to "breathe." Air is the worst enemy of cheese and should be in contact with cut surfaces as little as possible. All cheese should be stored in tight plastic wrap in a refrigerator. Bring it out in time to let it warm up before a meal, but unwrap it only seconds before serving. Cheese exposed to the air is also exposed to bacteria that make it rot rather than ripen.

When do you serve cheese? In the United States cheese is often served as part of the hors d'oeuvre before a meal; in Britain it is generally served as the last course; and in France it is often eaten between the main course and the dessert to accompany the end of a bottle of wine before a different wine is served.

But it is really up to the individual. The variety of cheese is so rich and the occasions for its use – both by itself and as an ingredient in many dishes – so numerous, that most people don't have much trouble figuring out when to serve it. They just eat it and enjoy it!

The story of cheese

None of life's great culinary pleasures is more simple than cheese. The varieties of flavour and complexities of appearance are little short of miraculous when you consider that man only has to leave milk alone for cheese to form. It must have been that very simplicity which stimulated the sages of the ancient world to credit the origin of cheese to some divine gift from the gods or goddesses. The priests of the great, gone civilizations of Nineveh and Greece, the Brahmins of India, the Norsemen and the Saxons all felt obliged to explain cheese, and did so in the way they accounted for everything else – in terms of another world.

Yet, once you have even the most rudimentary understanding of cheese, it is clear its discovery would be inevitable amidst any community which husbanded milking animals.

Essential protein

Once discovered, cheese became one of the great foundation stones upon which hunting and gathering clans came to build their early settlements and civilizations. Cheese was a reliable source of protein available in some form throughout the seasons, virtually regardless of drought or flood. It kept well, indeed improved with keeping. And if you really had to move camp, for purposes of migration, meadows or massacre, it could be transported: either you carried a chunk of it, or you drove its source ahead of you on its own four legs, or, like the hordes of Mongolia and the Scythians, you rode your equestrian source by day and made cheese from its milk by night. To relieve any tedium in your diet, cheese could be enjoyed hot or cold and as a sweet or savoury food. It was as well to give thanks to the gods – in case they really did exist, for without cheese Western Man, or many of his number, simply could not have survived as long as he has.

Cheese in the ancient world

Cheese has always been the staple of the peasant and the serf throughout what might be called the ancient western world – Scandinavia, Europe, the Mediterranean, and parts of Asia. In Britain, it was known as 'white meat', and you were grateful to have it – if you wanted red meat you had to kill the single goat or sheep you owned or shared, and then there would be neither red nor white meat. For although it was the long-horned auroch, ancestor of all our modern cattle, that was first domesticated as a milking animal, most countries came to rely upon the more self-sufficient sheep and goats until the Vikings came to spread their superior husbandry throughout the known western world and improved cattle strains. Even then, ewe's or goat's milk was more likely to have been used to make cheese than milk from the hungrier cow.

Considering the reliance of this area on milk and milk products, it is a considerable surprise that the magnificent Inca, Aztec and Mayan civilizations, and those of the Indians of North America, had no knowledge or tradition of cheesemaking. Animals such as the llama and the buffalo could have been milked, but were not. There never was cheese to be eaten in the Pacific for there were no large milking animals. And in China, which complacently considered itself the Middle Kingdom, the thought of drinking milk or eating rotten milk (as they considered cheese) was thought disgusting. It is said that some Mongolians still milk their mares, but this is regarded by the majority of Chinese with the same revulsion as the Englishman feels for the Scots' habit of eating stuffed stomachs – the haggis.

Permanent settlements were first made in the West so that plants could be grown and reliable crops of grain

harvested. The most useful or companionable of the animals which once had only been hunted were now domesticated, a process which began about 6000 BC in Macedonia, northern Greece. It clearly made sense to rely on milk and milk products rather than to kill an animal and have the bother of hunting for a replacement. Gradually, the dietary

The Dairy Frieze is a Sumerian bas-relief which dates from between 3500 and 3000 BC, and is now in the Baghdad Museum, Iraq. This interesting relic shows the Sumerian priests milking their animals and curdling the milk.
Opposite, below The Ancient milking method described by Homer in his *Odyssey* and still used today by Sardinian shepherds. Pushing a suckling under its mother encourages her to release milk.

balance of grain, flesh and milk meant that people became masters of their environment and, to some extent, of their destiny. But inevitably communal ambition became individual competitiveness; some became rulers, some were ruled.

Conspicuous display of power or wealth was vital if you had either – to discourage the others. Not only were you to be seen with more food, but with better food, and thus was born the basic division of society – those who laboured and those who ate well. From the beginning, the rich ate meat and soft cheese while the poor ate no meat and hard cheese. It was a situation that existed well into the twentieth century in Britain, and in European countries which still have a peasant population it remains endemic. France, Spain and Greece would have no peasants if there were no cheese; many cannot afford meat, while for others the land is too poor to sustain animals to be reared for meat purposes alone.

Today, ironically, it is the travelled and the prosperous who consume and display cheese as a mark of sophistication, whilst those lower down the scale enjoy the new status of being able to afford conspicuous quantities of flesh. In the last century, it was largely those unable to eat meat who led the great migrations to colonies in the southern hemisphere and to the New World. Nowhere else in the world will you see such quantities of meat served or such quantities of cheese made as in North America, Australasia and Southern Africa.

Types of early cheeses

The very first cheeses enjoyed were universally sharp and acidic, for acidity is what converts milk into cheese naturally. In all milk there are bacteria which feed upon its natural sugar, lactose. A by-product of this action is the formation of lactic acid and once the level of acid passes a certain point, the milk protein, casein, will separate from the watery content of milk, giving solid curds and liquid whey. The acidity of naturally curdled milk can be very refreshing, but has another important advantage, quickly discovered. Few dangerous germs can live in a high-acid environment, and thus acid-curd cheese is safer to consume than either milk directly from an animal or meat which cannot be chilled.

Ancient methods of coagulation

Acid-curd will form when any milk is left to sit, but it doubtless took a little time for someone to discover that milk could also be solidified more quickly by the addition of an acid – a citrus juice or vinegar for instance, which speeded up the process but still left you with a sharp-tasting product. Whether by the observation of what had happened to milk in the stomach of a suckling animal which had been slaughtered, or by the storing of milk in an improperly cured container made from an animal stomach, the next step was the discovery of enzymic curdling which could be done with sweet milk. The best known medium for this is rennet, which is made from the fourth stomach of young, cud-chewing animals. But the ancients used vegetarian products, too, including fig juice, thistle, safflower, and in Britain a variety of wild flowers including Ladies' Bedstraw, called 'cheese rennet' by country folk. It is said monks in Denmark once used the digestive juices of the carnivorous Venus Flytrap plant. In Spain and Portugal cheese is regularly made with non-animal curdling agents and, of course, all cheese made for orthodox Jewish consumption must be, for dietary law expressly prescribes the mixing together of milk and meat products.

Once cheese could be made with the choice of either acidic or sweet curd there was no limit to the possibilities. Every year scientists and historians find new evidence of cheese's extraordinarily long history and early importance. The tomb of the dynastic Pharaoh Horus has been found to contain traces of what is believed to be cheese, and the Sumerians left us a magnificent bas-relief, aptly known as the Dairy Frieze. Now almost five thousand years old, it demonstrates the complete cheesemaking process and confirms they were only too aware of its special status, for only priests were privy to the more sophisticated techniques of cheesemaking.

Ancient Greece and Rome

In the city states of Ancient Greece, cheese was chosen as part of the controlled diet of athletes, but in the scant pastures where most people lived, there was no such choice for here only a few sheep and goats could survive and meat was a rare treat. Cheese played its part, too, in the sustenance taken by monarchs, for when Alexander the Great defeated Darius at Damascus in 331 BC, the vanquished Persian king fled leaving behind his 500 cooks, 13 of whom were experts at processing milk to make cheeses for his tables. Fresh soft cheeses, though, did not form part of an ordinary soldier's diet: he carried hard cheeses, indeed could hardly have travelled without these reminders of home to sustain him.

Every market in Greece sold cheeses to those who could not make their own, and by the fourth century BC the popular fresh white Greek cheeses were being flavoured with herbs and spices and baked into all manner of cakes and pies. Cheese was combined with other foods, too, particularly with fish, something which survives in the ever-popular dishes of fish with mornay sauce. But it was the Romans who took cheesemaking on its next great leap forward. In Imperial Rome there were at least 13 different styles being made and cheese was imported from as far away as Britain and the Pyrenees.

In the early days of Roman civilisation ewes and goats were the most domesticated of the animals later to become exploited for wool, meat and milk. The tribes of Latium, later to become the Romans, were shepherds who lived in small settlements in clearings. Their diet was gruel and milk eked out with cheese made by curdling their milk with fig juice. Only much later did techniques improve and rennet was then extracted from the lining of the stomachs of calves, kids and hares and used for coagulating milk.

Once the Romans conquered the Greek colonies of Magna Graecia, south of Naples, cheesemaking acquired a far higher level of expertise and the choice was considerably widened when cow's milk was introduced as a basic material. Cheese production became a commercial activity of great economic importance. Columella, an ex-army officer of the first century AD, was the first ancient writer to describe the treatment of the milk for cheesemaking in great detail and the first to acknowledge that the temperature of the milk and of the atmosphere are of vital importance. In his treatise on farming, *De Rustica*, he writes:

'But the milk tub, when it is filled with milk, ought not to be without some gentle warmth. Nevertheless, it must not be brought so near as to touch the flames, as some people are of the opinion, but be placed not far from the fire: and presently, after it is curdled, the liquor must be transferred into wicker baskets, cheese vats, or moulds; for it is of great importance that the whey be strained and separated from the condensed substance as soon as possible: for which reason, the country people do not indeed suffer the moisture to drop slowly from it of its own accord; but, when the cheese becomes a little more solid, they put weights upon it, that thereby the whey may be squeezed out: then as it is taken out of the moulds or frails, it is laid up in a dark and cold place, upon the very cleanest boards, that it may not be spoiled; and it is sprinkled with bruised salt, that it may sweat out the acid liquor; and when it is hardened, it is pressed more vehemently, that it may be conspissated; and it is sprinkled again with toasted salt, and condensed again with weights. After this has been done for nine days, it is washed thoroughly with sweet water, and placed in such a manner under a shade, upon hurdles made for that purpose, that one cheese may not touch another, and that it may be moderately dried. Then, that it may keep the tenderer, they put it close together in several stories, in a close place, not exposed to winds. Thus it neither becomes spongey and full of holes, nor salt, nor dry: the first of which faults used to happen, if it be pressed but a little; the second if it be seasoned with too much salt and the third if it be scorched in the sun.

This kind of cheese may also be exported beyond sea. For that which is designed to be eaten in few days, while it is new, is made up with less care: for, being taken out of the wicker baskets it is put into salt and brine, and soon afterwards dried a little in the sun.'

In the *Moretum*, attributed to Virgil, a cheese is celebrated which must have been basically very simple but has earned praise because of the subtlety and intricacy of its flavouring with coriander, pepper, garlic, peppermint

Detail from a pastoral scene found in Agrippa Postumus's villa in Boscotrecase in Campania, Italy, now part of the collection of the *Museo Nazionale* in Naples. Originally painted as a mural, this 1st century AD scene shows shepherds with goats. Goats and sheep were the most important source of milk and cheese in the ancient world.

and thyme. Columella admits of the advantages of a discerning flavouring of cheese in some cases. He tells us that goat's cheese was flavoured with must and also with green pine kernels or with bruised or chopped thyme put through a sieve, and also mentions a variety of cheese called *manupressus* (hand pressed) – a cheese of which the Ancient Romans were particularly fond. When the milk had coagulated and the cheese was still warm in the tub, it would be cut, sprinkled with boiling water and either shaped by hand, or the whey would be squeezed out of it in boxwood moulds. It would then be salted and smoked and eaten straight away; this was the fresh cheese which the Romans served at almost any time of day or night, whether as an appetizer or first course, or dessert.

Dietary habits in Ancient Rome

Cheese and grain-based foods were the basis of everyday life throughout the Roman Empire during the time of the Republic. The pattern of food in most households was probably like this: a light morning meal of bread, cheese and milk, and bread and milk for children. A mid-day meal would usually consist of some mixture of cheese and vegetables, and the more substantial evening meal would include a hot porridge or hash of flour cooked in milk or in water and oil, then sprinkled with cheese. Meat was only eaten by most people on high days and holidays. The Romans were later influenced by the cooks they imported from Greece and Byzantium – their foods became more elaborate and rich, yet cheese remained essential, sometimes mixed with honey as a condiment and always served with the customary desserts of figs and fresh fruits and olives.

Cheese in cooking

The Roman Empire used cheese a great deal in cooking. In Cato's *De Agricultura*, a number of the most important dishes are mentioned, including *libum* (a sacrificial cake) which was also one of the poet Ovid's favourites. This was made with crumbled or grated cheese, flour, eggs and oil, covered and cooked in the hot ashes and coals in the hearth. *Placenta*, also described by Horace, was made by blending cheese and honey, and covering it with a type of puff pastry. This mixture was wrapped in bay leaves, placed in a large, wide cooking pot, sprinkled with oil, and baked slowly. *Scriblita* was another cheese pie served as a dessert, but was made without honey.

Cato mentions a sauce based on salt which was used to preserve cheese and gives the recipe for a celebration wedding cake, in which the main ingredient was cheese,

Against the spectacular backdrop of Alpine peaks, a cheesemaker carries freshly-made mountain cheeses on his shoulders. Little has changed in this type of cheesemaking for centuries, and it was in the Alps (particularly that part known as the Raetian Alps in ancient geography) that the Italian cheese industry was revived and developed in medieval times.

spiced and flavoured with grape must, fat, aniseed and bay leaves; this was also baked on top of bay leaves which imparted their agreeable aroma to the concoction. We no longer use bay with cheese, but custard flavoured with bay leaves was a British favourite until Victorian times. Apicius, the foremost Roman gastronome, included a very elaborate dish among his recipes, served

rarely goat's milk. From the writer Virgil we know that the famous Roman legionnaire was issued with about one ounce of cheese a day, and it is also possible that soldiers with an agricultural background were responsible for introducing improved cheesemaking techniques across Europe. Certainly Roman governors of Britain were impressed enough with Cheshire cheese to have it sent

world to come. For the Barbarians were not cheese eaters: instead they preferred to make butter from their cream. Gradually knowledge of specialist cheesemaking techniques was lost all over Europe – the exception was in monasteries. Once again, as we have already seen in the Ancient Egypt of the pharaohs, it was the priests who were the guardians of the secrets of cheese.

cold, in which the cheese was blended with honey, peppermint, water melon, vinegar and many other ingredients; he also lists a number of homemade sweetmeats and *melcae* or honey titbits, as he rather endearingly calls them. In all these preparations cheese is inevitably one of the ingredients and it is always made with cow's or ewe's milk by now, and

back to be sold on Rome's food stalls and markets.

There were movements of cheese to and from Rome and an export trade was particularly concentrated in the northern part of the Italian peninsula. But as the Roman Empire declined, so did standards and once the Barbarians arrived cheese became an early victim of the harsh new

The Dark Ages

From the beginnings of the eclipse of the Roman Empire until about 1000 AD, little advance was possible in the making of specialist cheeses, although soft, fresh cheeses were undoubtedly made and enjoyed as a staple by peasants everywhere – indeed there was no reason why cooks in cities could not also do precisely

This detail of a painting dating from 1406 by an artist known as the *Maestro dei Mesi* (the 'Master of the Months') depicts the tasks which the inhabitants of the mountains had to carry out in May and June. A woman is shown milking cows while others busy themselves with making cheese.

the same thing. But in most places these simple cheeses were forbidden you if you were poor, for they needed the richest and best milks. The pattern of many a society was for the lord alone to enjoy cream and soft cheeses on his table, allowing only skimmed milk, which made hard bland cheeses, for his followers. In Britain even this could not be relied upon, for here there was a belief that hard cheeses aided your digestion by sealing the stomach whilst you slept.

The main meal was taken around the middle of the day and only a little beer was drunk with it. Englishmen drank wine after meals, unlike the French who drank it with food. In the evening a light supper was taken and this was always finished with a little hard cheese, for digestion's sake. Gradually the large mid-day meal was taken later and later until that meal, wine-drinking and the cheese supper were combined. Thus was born the British habit of finishing an evening meal with cheese: almost every other society has eaten cheese before the sweet course to finish their main wine, or instead of a sweet.

With some exceptions, the further away you were from the marauding barbarianism of central and southern Europe during the Dark Ages, the better your chances of finding more complicated and sophisticated cheeses. In particular, any country or area with a Celtic connection could be relied upon to have maintained a healthy interest in both old and new cheesemaking traditions. The inhabitants of Scandinavia, loosely called the Vikings, were also isolated enough to continue developing cheeses specifically for their own needs. They needed sweet, simple, delicate flavours to balance the rigours of their diet of salted fish and meat. Today, Sweden alone makes over 200 types of cheese, all rather similar to one another but recognizably direct descendants of

much earlier requirements.

In the politically isolated and unruffled wilderness of Ireland's west coast, Catholic monks treasured what they considered the most authentic links with pre-Christian and Romanic cheese styles. By the eighth century, these monks began barefootedly to take Christianity and civilization back into Europe, in-

troducing or reintroducing important cheeses at the same time – Swiss Appenzell has precisely this pedigree. In 1976–7, when the British explorer Tim Severin sailed his open leather boat across the Atlantic to prove the American continent was first discovered by the sixth century Irish monk St Brendan, he asked me to help plan food supplies that were as close as possible to the original. Modern food in plastic packs had been a disaster on the first leg of the voyage from Ireland to Iceland. On the second leg they ate smoked meats and sausages, grain and dried fruits – and Appenzell cheese; and they made it, feeling stronger and healthier than on their carefully-planned, but unsuccessful, twentieth century diet.

Not surprisingly, the one exception to universal Dark Age boorishness was the Christian ruler Charlemagne, first Holy Roman Emperor. He clearly instructed his minions that the highest standards of butter and cheese production were to be encouraged. But he was the exception, and the only encouragement most travelling Irish, or any other, cheese enthusiast might have found was a general improvement in the types of cattle to be found in Europe – a sign that an interest in dairying, and perhaps in cheesemaking, had survived, albeit rudimentary.

The contribution of the Vikings

It is little realised how far and wide were the travels of the Vikings or that they gave quite as much as they pillaged. Vikings plied their various trades by land and by sea, some reaching as far away as modern Istanbul, where the bigger, blonder ones found even newer horizons open to them as bodyguards and status symbols amongst the shorter, darker, bored rulers of Islam.

In the ninth century Vikings caught by the Moors of Spain are said to have passed on everything they knew about cheesemaking to their captors but their most valuable contribution was in breeding new types of cattle throughout Europe. Quite why these inveterate travellers transported bulls and cows in their long ships is beyond modern comprehension, but it is as well they did. The great brown cow of Normandy owes its existence to such bloodlines and without it, Brie

or Camembert are unlikely to have developed as they did. Normandy cattle, or some close relatives, became the favoured type amongst Breton monks who in turn bred the smaller Guernsey during the Middle Ages. Together with the related, but even smaller, Jersey cow, it provides amongst the richest and most highly coloured milk of all, giving the natural golden glow to butter and cheese from Australasia where they still predominate in most herds. In Britain, the high-yielding Friesian, Ayrshire and Dairy Shorthorn breeds now predominate but demand for richer flavours means single herds of Jersey and Guernsey cattle are kept. Their milks are usually mixed and sold as Channel Island milk.

A number of breeds the Vikings helped create or improve – or would have recognized – have today disappeared or lessened in importance. The British White, Welsh Black and the Kerry exist only in pocket-sized populations but the truly magnificent Gloucester, almost certainly bred by the Vikings and only true source of milk for single and double Gloucester cheeses, has recently found some champions and a few herds are being husbanded. A particularly successful cross-bred stock resulted from breeding the ancient auroch with a now-forgotten alpine breed to give the great Brown Alpine or Braunvieh cow. It is still the sturdy backbone of the thriving Swiss dairy industry and of equal importance in northern Italy which tenuously held on to a few traditions of Roman cheesemaking after the fall of the Empire. Indeed, wherever you find a combination of mountain and valley pasture in Central Europe you are liable to find flocks of grazing Braunvieh.

The ancestors of today's cheeses

As the Dark Ages ended and the light of learning slowly spread back

through Europe, many of the cheeses we know today started to emerge. In Britain, a sense of co-operation meant that large cheeses of the semi-hard variety began to become established as men pooled both milk and resources. Cheese made from cow's milk was certainly established at Cheddar in Somerset by Tudor times and, probably, in the surrounding areas of east Devon and parts of Dorset and Wiltshire.

Cheddar must at first have been made with ewe's milk and at times it would also have been made with skimmed cow's milk – perhaps that is why it was sometimes dyed with marigold – to give an appearance of richness. Throughout the centuries Cheddar has kept its popularity and its market prices remained firm whilst others rose and fell; indeed the degree with which it has been copied is a fair guide to its position as the world's number one cheese. Cheddar has even become a verb, for a vital part of manufacturing such a cheese is the milling of the curd so it settles more evenly into the mould – this is now known as cheddaring and together with a double scalding of the curd is essential to all types which use this name, however dissimilar their flavour and appearance.

The development of European cheeses

After 1200, the Po Valley in Italy became one of the main production and commercial exchanges for cheese in Europe. By the fourteenth century, cheeses from Lodi, Piacenza and Parma were already much sought after by foreign buyers, while at the same time Lombardy butter was sent to Rome and to the south of Italy, and cattle of many breeds were exported, together with quantities of sausages and smoked meats and cheeses. The most famous cheeses of the time were Gorgonzola, Parmesan and Marzolino from Tuscany, a mixture of

From the Middle Ages onwards, Roquefort-sur-Soulzon in the south of France has been producing blue cheeses which have gradually become world famous. This photograph shows some of the utensils once employed by the local cheesemakers.

goat's and cow's milk.

Brie was one of the first famous French cheeses and available far from its home in Normandy; Maroilles cheese from the Vexin, Brenne cheese from Touraine and Cancoillotte from the Franche-Comté were also liked.

Early Italian cheese

In Italy, religious orders carried on a thriving cheesemaking business in the northern mountain pastures, and their products provided them with a substantial income, recorded in many documents of the time. For example, when a register of land and property was drawn up for the purposes of levying taxes in Casentino in 1427, the lands belonging to the Abbey were included, giving details of the numbers of cattle and sheep which were being reared by the Camaldolite monks: their flocks of sheep amounted to 500, from whose milk the monastery made a considerable quantity of cheese, some of which was kept for the brothers' own consump-

tion and the rest regularly sold in Florence and the Ravenna region. To complement their dairying activities the monks extended the use of land as water meadows to provide lush grazing for their animals and thus increase their milk yield.

Cheesemaking, though, had yet to become an industry in its own right, and was still part of general mixed farming, which gradually evolved and improved. The new availability of rich pastureland led to a growth in the size of flocks and herds, and this in turn meant that there was a great quantity of milk to be used. The development of efficient Italian dairying and production of cheese and other milk derivatives coincides with the late-medieval Renaissance mainly in the region of the fertile river valleys and plains. With irrigation and pastureland which could be grazed in rotation as well as such rich pastures as the water meadows of Lombardy, and the draining of the Po Valley, communal cheese manufacture came

into existence, especially in the Bergamo region of Italy.

Swiss, Austrian and Dutch cheeses

Switzerland was already producing Gruyère in the Canton of Fribourg and Bohemia supplied several regions of Germany with cheese. In French-speaking Swiss Jura co-operatives had been formed, and this practice subsequently spread to other mountainous regions, since a reliable source of labour was vital to ensure enough workers for efficient processing of large quantities of milk for various types of Gruyère cheeses. Switzerland produced great quantities of cheese, the majority emanating from the monasteries in the mountains. The well-known Gruyère was soon joined by other varieties – Sbrinz, Appenzell and Emmental – which were exported to Italy, over the St Gotthard pass.

Medieval Austria was still producing her oldest cheese, the sharp and acidulated Sauerkäse, known to have been made since late Roman times. Medieval Holland's most popular cheese was known familiarly as 'dead man's head' and sold in the great market at Alkmaar, where Edam and Gouda are still auctioned.

Cheesemaking in medieval France

Specialist cheesemaking in France, though, was confined to relatively few places during the medieval period, and Italy was to remain the world's great cheesemaking hub for several more centuries. (Even by 1777, only about 30 varieties of French cheese had made a name for themselves: nowhere near the 400 or so we now know.) The most popular French cheeses in medieval times were Brie, Cantal from the Auvergne, Roquefort, and early versions of Comté.

This absence of the variety which we associate nowadays with French cheese production should not obscure the importance of cheese to the medieval French. Alexander Neckam, an Englishman visiting France around 1178, described at length the willow baskets used for pressing curds into cheese; these, he wrote, were among the most important items of the average peasant's equipment. In Montaillou, the Pyrenean village described so minutely from clerical records in the book of that name by Emmanual Le Roy Ladurie, the chief source of protein for nearly all during the period around 1300 was cheese, made by the shepherds from ewe's and goat's milk in the mountain pastures and uplands.

By the late 1300s, the anonymous author of the *Ménagier de Paris* included a little verse warning against buying cheese with too many eyes like Argus, weepy like Mary Magdalene, or pale like Helen – so some variety was available, in the capital at least. And an early French cookery book, the *Viandier de Taillevent*, includes in one edition a recipe for pancakes (*crespes*) rolled up around sticks of cheese as thick as a finger: these were set in a hot place to dry and crisp. Throughout the medieval period it had been a custom in courtly French society to send gifts of cheese to people one admired: Blanche de Navarre, at the end of the twelfth century, sent 200 cheeses to Phillippe Auguste every year, and the poet Charles d'Orléans, in 1407, sent several to 'ladies to whom he was attached'. International co-operation began to play a part in cheesemaking, too: Froissart, the medieval French historian, is one of the first of his countrymen to mention the importing of buffaloes to make cheese. Buffalo milk was already being turned into cheese in Sicily and southern Italy, where the animals had been introduced in the sixth century.

Early Scandinavian cheese

Denmark had also earned a reputation for good cheeses: Tybo was marketed and this country had developed a highly sophisticated cheese industry which was well organized, the peasants being taught the finer points of cheesemaking so that they in turn could instruct their families and neighbours. Edam, a Dutch cheese, was famous and was also made in Denmark and eaten in Sweden and Norway; these two latter countries had not yet managed to develop a significant cheese industry of any great variety, the only cheeses of any note being Nokkelost and the sharp-tasting Gammelost.

Towards the end of the Middle Ages, in 1477, a scholarly work on cheesemaking was written by Pantaleon, a Dutch physician working in Confienza, a market town near Vercelli. The author deals with the production of milk, describing how the quality varies depending on the type of fodder the animal eats and how it is processed once the animal has been milked. Pantaleon was specially fascinated by English cheeses, not only because of the abundant quantity and variety produced, but also because of 'the flora and fauna' on their rinds. In his writings, he seemed disconcerted by the cheeses from Flanders and Switzerland, which he finds insipid and immature, besides lacking good keeping qualities and having an 'earthy' and coarse character.

Cheesemaking in the sixteenth century

After a long gap without any significant literature on the subject of agriculture, interest revived in this topic during the sixteenth century, and authors again discussed techniques and explored scientific theories which related to husbandry.

It was not, though, until 1569 that anything new was published on the art and technology of cheesemaking.

In that year, Agostino Gallo from Brescia wrote his *Vinti giornate dell'agricoltura e de' piaceri della villa* ('Twenty-one days devoted to agriculture and the pleasures of country life') and devoted most of the 11th day to a dissertation on cheesemaking. Gallo's work is interesting because it highlights the change which had come about since previous writers had published works on the subject: cow's milk had now taken the place of sheep's milk in the production of cheese, the latter being used only in a few specialized products and even then, usually mixed with cow's milk. This revolution in the industry had come about as a result of greatly increased numbers and size of cattle herds which could now thrive because of the efficient production of forage and fodder and a greater understanding of breeding methods. Animals were now being reared which were healthy, hardy and gave good milk yields; Friesians and Brown Swiss were considered the best milch cows.

Advances in techniques of milk production

The most important innovation was the technique of heating the milk and the use of vats, unknown to the earlier generations of cheesemakers; pressing was now no longer carried out with stones or other similar weights, but with wooden presses and weights. Salting had increased in importance and the cheeses were no longer simply sprinkled when they were removed from their moulds; a preference is shown for the curd undergoing a gradual and progressive salting as it slowly hardens and firms up. Gallo also refers to the addition of small quantities of saffron to add colour and the covering of the finished cheeses with linseed oil which he liked for the reddish tint it imparted to the rind of a cheese, making it look more attractive than the traditional

The plates below are taken from the famous *Encyclopédie*, partly written by and published under the editorship of Diderot and D'Alembert in France from 1751 to 1772. They show how cheese was made in a contemporary dairy. The various items of equipment so painstakingly and accurately drawn were in common use at the time.

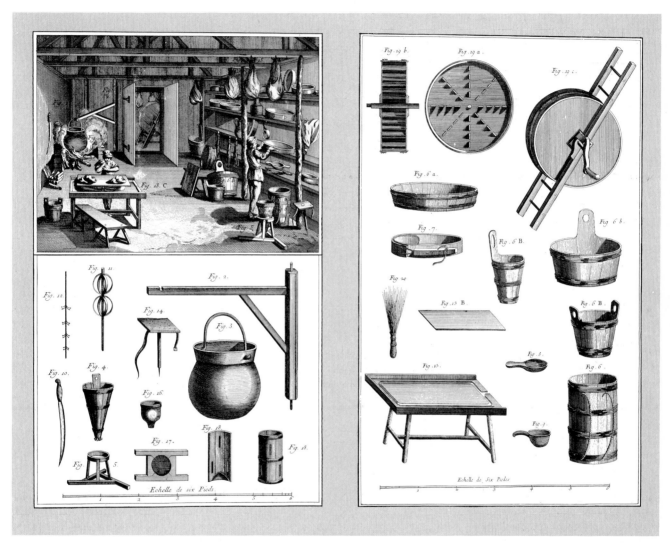

olive oil or rancid butter which had the effect of making the cheeses look pale and insipid.

The method of producing cheese as described by Gallo has remained almost unchanged until relatively recent times in the remote mountainous regions where small producers of cheese, often family-run, made their cheeses in mountain huts. Machines were developed to save time and manpower. Improvements were introduced to churns and cheese presses and the first attempts to separate cream from milk by centrifuge were

made. The discovery was made of lactose, milk sugar, as one of the ingredients of milk but there was a tremendous amount of basic information still to be discovered. It was not until the eighteenth century, in what has come to be known as the Age of Enlightenment, that cheese technology really began to develop and become more of a commercial proposition. The eighteenth century launched the trend towards industrialization, although it was not until well into the 19th century that this assumed great commercial import-

ance, for this was when the cheese 'industry' proper was born.

European cheese technology in the Age of Enlightenment

By the first half of the eighteenth century it was no longer a practical proposition to make dairy products in small quantities in isolated communities. It was suggested that these products should be made in specially equipped creameries situated in the centre of dairying zones, so that the forage could be brought to the animals, rather than vice versa. The

Swiss were the first to try out this new method with Emmental cheese and now many cows were no longer taken up to the high pastures because they were fed in cattle sheds in the valleys. The number of village creameries increased rapidly as soon as the cheese dealers realized what a difference there was between cheeses made in the mountains and those made in the valleys.

In the early eighteenth century, cheesemaking was still considered a craft and a skill, but by the latter half it had become rather more of an industrial process. Napoleon, who was particularly fond of cheese, was one of its greatest popularizers, and had a particular weakness for those from the Lomellina district of north Italy, which benefitted greatly from his fame and patronage.

The origins of modern cheese technology

Modern cheese technology can be said to have been launched with an observation made by an English innovator of the nineteenth century, Joseph Harding, who asserted that the crucial part of cheesemaking depended on how the procedure was handled in the dairy and advocated the strictest standards of hygiene and perfected various stages of making Cheddar cheese. His scientific approach to the production of cheese represented a great step forward: each process was of equally vital importance needing to be carried out correctly and under controlled conditions. The growing understanding of methods whereby fertile, rich pastures could be ensured complemented the newly-understood chemical processes involved in cheesemaking and quickened the already far from slotheful pace of industrialization.

In 1836 Justus von Liebig was able to explain the process of fermentation in cheese, and the work of Louis

Pasteur and the Russian biologist Metchnikov rendered milk pure and safe by treating it with heat. The Irish physicist Tyndall discovered heat-

resistant spores and this led to the development of the first industrially produced rennets. Refrigeration was introduced into dairies and machines were brought in to replace manual labour. The curd was now cut by mechanical rotary curd knives and presses became far more sophisticated and could be minutely controlled to apply very gradual pressure to the cheese forms. With the understanding of how to encourage the growth of the desired surface flora, the quality of Camembert and Gervais cheeses was standardized. European countries have industrialized their cheese production to a great extent, the most conspicuously successful among them being Denmark; soft, fresh and sliceable, table cheeses are gaining in popularity as a convenience food which is replacing other items in people's diet.

The making of cheese in the nineteenth century

By the end of the nineteenth century cheesemaking had become an up-to-date industry and the mechanization of production had swept away many of the old traditions. In 1856, Norway had set up the first modern and

profitable cheesemaking factory and the idea of forming co-operatives rapidly found favour in Italy. In 1881, at Collina, in Friuli, the first communally-owned cheese factory was opened, its most successful product being Montafa. The new railway systems meant the opening up of greater commercial horizons than ever had been imagined in those pioneering days – the country was coming to town, at last.

British cheeses in the twentieth century

Compared with Cheddar, the fortunes of other British cheeses were mixed. Caerphilly, for instance, once the mainstay of Welsh miners and at the height of its popularity in the 1800s, isn't even made there any more but across the border, in Somerset. In the 18th century Gloucester cheeses were already being exported. It is interesting to reflect on whether the tough skin and wheel shape of these cheeses came before or after the local custom of rolling cheeses downhill annually. The Second World War, during which most cheesemaking was officially banned, was responsible for the disappearance of most real Gloucester making, but efforts are now being made to revive it. In a few places both traditional methods and Gloucester cattle can be found.

Cheshire is Britain's oldest named cheese, made well before Roman times and unique for being made only with cow's milk since the beginning. In 1914 over 200 farmhouses still made Cheshire; today it is perhaps only one per cent of that figure, but all farmhouse Cheshire uses unpasteurized milk and methods are largely unchanged compared with those of the eighteenth century.

One of Britain's newest cheeses is Blue Cheshire. Originally known as Green Fade, blue cheeses were rarely encouraged to turn blue but the process was welcomed when it happened spontaneously. Until early this century Blue Cheshire cheeses remained a prized rarity, particularly popular in London's gentlemen's clubs and with shipping companies. In 1922 an enthusiast called Hutchinson began storing likely cheeses in beer cellars and sold the successful results as Old Blue Cheshire. He died in 1961 and in 1968 the first purpose-made Blue Cheshire was created by a Mrs Hutchinson-Smith. The taste described by a French gastronome as 'fit only for heroes' became more generally available. Some say it is greater than Stilton and certainly its golden colour and rich acidity make it difficult to ignore. Shropshire Blue is even newer, created in the 1970s to bridge the flavour gap between Stilton and Blue Cheshire. This keeps appearing and disappearing from the market but is eminently worthy of support if you are fortunate enough to come across it.

Lancashire cheese, still mainly consumed in the county of that name, was probably a variety of Cheshire when first mentioned (as long ago as the Domesday book), but once its unique manufacturing method was adopted so was a new name – true Lancashire is always made from unpasteurised milk and from the mixed curd of two days. There were softer cheeses made in the area but they were banned by a government edict in 1940 and we are now left with the white, crumbly but buttery Lancashire only, a robust cheese that is specially suited to winter and is, undoubtedly the best English cheese when it comes to using for melting and toasting.

The Dales cheeses

Honey Wensleydale is the only survivor of a range of Dale cheeses and this particular name seems first to have been used generally about 1840. The style of cheese is said to have been made first by monks acquainted with the methods of Roquefort soon after the Conquest by William I in 1066; Saxons had been making cheese here of a different kind but which did not meet with the approval of the new Norman soldiers or their masters. Ewe's milk Wensleydale was usually blue – the Roquefort connection – and even when it came to be made with cow's milk was appreciably more spreadable than the newcomer, Stilton. At the turn of this century, factory cheesemakers, impatient with the long waiting time for natural blueing to occur, and at the variations involved, began to salt the curd and to press it more heavily, both of which inhibits the growth of mould: White Wensleydale was born. Blue Wensleydale is available in limited quantities but is drier and harder than the original; it has been suggested it should really be given another quite different name.

Stilton – King of Cheese

In general, the names by which the most famous English cheeses are internationally known were established early in the 18th century – at about the time they were being joined by the one that would become feted as the King of British Cheese: Stilton. Never made in the town after which it took its name, this aristocrat of blue cheese seems first to have been made at or near a house called Quenby Hall, a few miles from Leicester. First actually called Quenby, it was made famous by being sold at the Bell Inn at Stilton, an important coaching house on the Great North Road. By the 1870s, soon after the first co-operative cheese factory had been established in Derby, Stilton was being made on a more or less commercial basis, yet the tradition of making it in farmhouses managed to survive until the 1930s. By 1969, so many disparate types of Stilton were being made that a High Court judgement was required to protect its reputation. Today a Stilton must be a 'blue or white cheese made from full-cream milk with no applied pressure, forming its own coat or crust and made in cylindrical form, the milk coming from English dairy herds in the district of Melton Mowbray and surrounding areas falling within the counties of Leicestershire, Derbyshire and Nottinghamshire...'

Pasteurized or unpasteurized?

In *The Great British Cheese Book* Patrick Rance, perhaps the foremost cheese expert in Britain, regrets the fact that unpasteurised milk was not specified, and today only one of the dairies that makes Stilton regularly uses unpasteurised milk. Mr Rance's fascinating book also gives a sensible explanation of the origin of the horrid habit of pouring port wine into Stilton, often to disguise the all-too-common inferior cheese. It seems in the early days of manufacture, when science was equally infantile, that wine was often dribbled into the new curds to encourage the growth of the necessary mould. Now the mould growth can be controlled, the urge to muck up Stilton with any sort of liquid should be, too. We must also be grateful for the passing of another custom associated with Stilton,

The story of cheese

Above How milk is turned into cheese. Bacteria or rennet causes the milk to coagulate and from then on the exact process differs from cheese to cheese. Beneath the diagram is a table showing how the constituents of milk change and in what final form they are present in cheese.
Below These diagrams illustrate the proportions of the most important constituents present in milk, and comparative proportions for those also present in cheese.

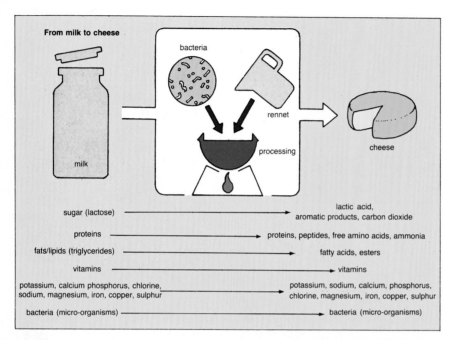

From milk to cheese

bacteria

rennet

milk

processing

cheese

sugar (lactose) ⟶	lactic acid, aromatic products, carbon dioxide
proteins ⟶	proteins, peptides, free amino acids, ammonia
fats/lipids (triglycerides) ⟶	fatty acids, esters
vitamins ⟶	vitamins
potassium, calcium phosphorus, chlorine, sodium, magnesium, iron, copper, sulphur ⟶	potassium, sodium, calcium, phosphorus, chlorine, magnesium, iron, copper, sulphur
bacteria (micro-organisms) ⟶	bacteria (micro-organisms)

which even Mrs Beeton once used to call 'English Parmesan'. Stilton was once considered unfit to eat unless the skin was infested to the point of being a moving coat of cheese mites and Daniel Defoe wrote, 'they bring a spoon for you to eat the mites with, as you do the cheese.'

A modern Stilton exemplifies the way in which science and tradition can sometimes combine to make a product which is relatively true to its origins but has none of the drawbacks. You will still find good and bad Stiltons, some with too much blueing and some with not enough. Neither are they good only at Christmas time – the use of pasteurized milk largely erases seasonal differences. Choose a Stilton that is cream to yellow-coloured and with veins noticeably greenish-blue rather than blueish-grey, enjoy the difference in blueing from middle to edge, cut it rather than scoop it, drink with port or any other sweet wine and you will discover at once why this is indeed the King of Cheeses. The French may protest that their Brie de Meaux was

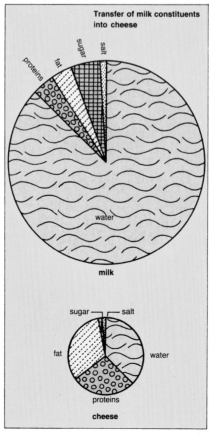

Transfer of milk constituents into cheese

proteins

fat

sugar

salt

water

milk

sugar — salt

fat

water

proteins

cheese

awarded the title at the Congress of Vienna in 1814. But most authorities accept that that was because no Stilton was present.

British cheesemaking today – an optimistic view

Statistically speaking, British cheese-making, and British cheese-buying, is still in the slough of monotony that has existed since 1940. Over half the cheese bought in Britain is factory-produced block cheddar, and around a quarter of that is produced elsewhere than in England, let alone anywhere near Cheddar.

The farmhouse cheeses (some ten per cent of total UK production) do represent a step in the right direction, and are increasingly popular with consumers, though it is slightly misleading to think of them as wholly traditional cheeses. For example, out of the 23 Milk Marketing Board registered farms making 'Farmhouse Cheddar' in 1980, only 11 were making it in traditional forms, and only three of these used unpasteurised milk. Furthermore some of the biggest farmhouse creameries rely on milk from up to 20 different sources, which makes for factory-scale production by any other name.

Yet there is real cause for optimism, and every indication that over the coming years we may reclaim a substantial proportion of our cheese heritage. The variety and range of foreign cheese in our shops now is an indication of the public's lively interest in cheese, and shows, too, that we are prepared to pay for quality if we can get it. And real, unpasteurised, wholly traditional cheeses of the highest quality are being made in every corner of the United Kingdom: what follows is only a very brief guide.

Some 25 farms in the southwest of England make traditional Cheddar, and a smaller number of other farms throughout the country produce tra-

Two very different ways of making cheese.
Below The simple, traditional techniques of mountain cheesemakers. Here production takes place in the Alpine herdsman's hut in the high pastures: we see the curdled milk being heated.
Bottom Preparation for laboratory testing of milk in a university department which specializes in carrying out research designed to improve the cheese industry's products and achieve greater efficiency.

The story of cheese

ditional versions of the other most famous British cheeses: Single and Double Gloucester, White and Blue Stilton, White and Blue Cheshire, Lancashire, Leicester, White and Blue Wensleydale, and Caerphilly. In addition, an enormous variety of near-extinct British cheeses is once again being produced, as well as new cheeses based on traditional cheesemaking methods and ingredients. Of particular note is the great revival of ewe's milk cheese.

In the English Dales, a number of goat's milk cheeses are made, as well as Swaledale and Cotherstone (semi-soft or soft whole milk cheeses). In Cheshire, the Blue Cheshire cheese is the most exciting recovery of the past few years. In the Midlands and East Anglia, goat's milk cheeses are again being produced in both soft and hard versions, as well as the cow's milk cheeses Cambridge and Colwick. Cambridge is a soft, unripened, medium-fat cheese with a coloured orange layer (or sometimes a sage-flavoured green layer) in the middle; and Colwick is either a skimmed or full-fat lightly salted cheese, the full-

fat version sometimes being called Slipcote. Derby cheese is again being produced in North Yorkshire, near Ripon. In Dorset, the famous Dorset Blue Vinney, unavailable or inauthentic for so long, at last shows signs of coming back onto the market, but most sold under this name is unquestionably Stilton which has not made the grade – true Vinney is clouded rather than veined.

Scottish Dunlop is still difficult to buy, though it should become easier to find over the next few years; and Barac (a semi-hard ewe's or goat's milk cheese), Crowdie (a cottage cheese), and Caboc (an oatmeal-rolled, double cream cheese) are once again available. Orkney and Islay cheeses, firm and either plain or smoked, are on sale both on the islands and elsewhere.

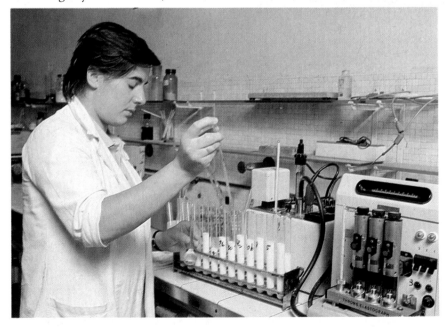

The story of cheese

The table on the left, *below*, compares the chemical composition of cow's milk with ewe's, goat's and buffalo milk. The quantity of the various constituents is shown in grammes per 100 ml. The table, *below right*, shows the constituents of 220 lb (100 kg) of cow's milk and the resolution of these constituents, also in percentage terms, into cheese (dotted left-hand area) and into whey (clear area on right). *Opposite, top* The practical side of studies on feeding dairy cows. *Below* Making Ricotta in a dairy in Puglia, southern Italy.

An exception to these positive trends is that there is still no traditional Caerphilly made in Wales, though a semi-hard cow's milk cheese – Llangloffan – and a pressed goat's milk cheese called Haminiog are made in Dyfed, as well as a soft lactic cheese at the Abbey on Caldey Island. Across the South of England a wide variety of cow's and goat's milk

both the hard and soft varieties.

Flavoured cheeses are also available, and they have been an area of considerable growth in production and consumption over the last few years. Some excellent examples of this new though not entirely untraditional style of cheesemaking are produced in Ilchester (Ilchester – Cheddar with beer and garlic; Ap-

Distribution of constituents of 220 lb (100 kg) of milk in cheese (on left) and in whey (on right)

6%	Water 191–194 lb (87–88 kg)	94%
48%	Dry matter 26–28 lb (12–13 kg)	52%
96%	Casein 5–6 lb (2.3–2.8 kg)	4%
4%	Whey proteins 1 lb 5 oz–1 lb 8 oz (0.6–0.7 kg)	96%
94%	Fat 7 lb 12 oz–8 lb 13 oz (3.5–4 kg)	6%
6%	Lactose 9 lb 12 oz–10 lb 8 oz (4.4–4.8 kg)	94%
62%	Calcium 3½–4 oz (100 g–120 g or 0.10–0.12 kg)	38%
94%	Vitamin A 30–40 mg	6%
15%	Thiamin 40–45 mg	85%
26%	Riboflavine 160–180 mg	74%
6%	Vitamin C 1700–1800 mg	94%

Average chemical composition of milk of various dairy animals				
	Cow's milk	Ewe's milk	Goat's milk	Buffalo milk
	g/100 ml	g/100 ml	g/100 ml	g/100 ml
Water	87.5	80–84	86–88	78–86
Fats/lipids and related substances	3.4–5 of which: 3.4–3.9 triglycerides 0.007–0.04 phospholipids (1) 0.03–0.04 associated substances (2)	5–7	4.05	6–9
Nitrogenous substances	2.9–3.5 of which 2.3–2.8 casein 0.5–0.7 albumin (3) 0.04–0.8 globulins 0.03–0.05 enzymes 0.02–0.03 non-protein nitrogen (4)	5.6–6	3.75	4.7–4.9
Carbohydrates	4.4–4.8 lactose (5)	4.5–5	4.5–5.5	4.6–4.9
Salts	0.9	1–1.2	0.9–1	0.8–0.9
Water soluble vitamins (6)	traces	traces	traces	traces
Gases (7)	traces	traces	traces	traces

(1) Lecithins, cephalosporin, phosphatilserine, sphingomyelin, cerebrosides, silicones (waxes) and monoglycerides.
(2) Free fatty acids, cholesterol, various sterols, carotenoids, vitamin D, vitamin E, vitamin K, hydrocarbons, squalene.
(3) β lactoglobulin and α lactalbumin, whey albumins.
(4) Ammoniacal, uric and amino acid nitrogen; creatine, creatinine, uric acid, orotic acid, hippuric acid, indigo and thiocyanides.
(5) Traces of glucose and galactose.
(6) Thiamin, lactoflavine, vitamin B$_6$, pantothenic acid, biotin, folic acid, choline, vitamin B$_{12}$, inositol, niacin, ascorbic acid.
(7) Carbon dioxide, nitrogen and oxygen.

cheeses is produced: as well as English types, Feta, Pecorino, Ricotta, Labna and Coulommiers are all made using traditional artisanal methods. In Cheddar country, finally, other traditional types of cheese made include Caerphilly and Double Gloucester, as well as Beenleigh Blue (an unpasteurised ewe's milk cheese), Chittlehamholt White and Devon Garland (both Cheshire types, the latter with the addition of a centre layer of herbs), and a wide range of spiced soft cheese and goat's milk cheeses,

plewood – paprika-coated smoked Cheddar; Cheddar with port, sage, or pickle; and Double Gloucester with onion, chives, or mustard pickle), and in the Vale of Belvoir at Tythly Farm Dairy (Charnwood – similar to Applewood; Cheviot – white Cheddar with chives; Cotswold – Double Gloucester with chives and onions; Huntsman – two layers of Stilton sandwiched between three of Double Gloucester; Nutwood – Cheddar with raisins, cider and hazlenuts; Rutland – Cheddar with beer, garlic and

parsley; Sherwood – Double Gloucester with pickle; Walton – Cheddar and Stilton with chopped walnuts and a nibbed walnut coat; and Windsor Red – Cheddar curd washed with elderberry wine, giving a marbled effect).

But as some measure of what we have lost, where can we now find Berkeley, Guildford, North Wiltshire, Banbury, Cottenham, Essex, Newmarket, Reading Yellow, Suffolk, Warwickshire? Sadly the answer is nowhere: all are extinct.

The making of cheese

Although animals have been milked by man since the earliest days of civilization, thousands of years had passed before the composition of milk was fully understood and it consequently became possible to produce – by design rather than chance – a wide range of milk products which differed from each other in nutritional value, appearance, taste, texture and aroma. Ancient cheesemaking skills, painstakingly acquired and handed down from generation to generation, were complemented and in some cases superceded by the new scientific approach to the fabrication of milk

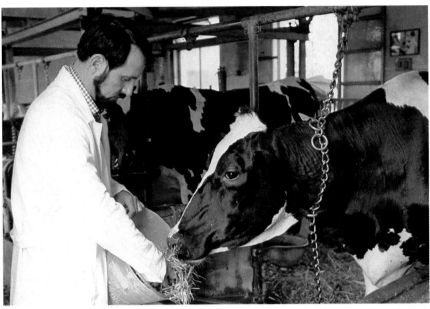

products. Cheeses which proved particularly popular have been adopted – and adapted – by industrial producers to satisfy mass markets, and while farmhouse cheeses continue to be made, this is on a sadly reduced scale.

The challenge of producing quality cheese in enormous quantities brings together the traditional craftsman, the microbiologist, the chemist and the engineer. The fact that our cheese consumption has doubled in the last 20 years suggests that the public by and large likes what the cheese indus-

try has to offer, though connoisseurs have until recently been ill-catered for.

Cheese consumption is highest in Europe, where half the world's cheese is produced, and it is particularly impressive in those countries where rural cheesemaking has continued uninterruptedly for hundreds of years, like France and Italy. Continued expansion is forecast for this section of the food industry: a growing percentage of liquid milk production is likely to be processed into other dairy products, of which cheese is the most important.

The table below, based on International Dairy Federation statistics, shows the changing uses to which milk has been and is being put:

World Consumption of Milk in Percentage Terms   Source: I.D.F.

	1965	1980	1990
Butter	35%	35%	33%
Cheese	15%	30%	34%
Tinned and powdered milk	4%	6%	6%
Liquid milk	46%	29%	27%

The swing towards cheese revealed by these figures is easily explained by the public's increased awareness of comparative food costs, world food shortages, and the growing realisation that milk is one of our most complete foods, meeting nearly all of our nutritional requirements, while three of its constituents (milk fat, lactose and casein) are found in no other natural food substance.

The composition of cheese

Cheese is a solid derivative of milk produced by the process of coagulation of the protein matter in milk (casein), and the draining off of the liquid or water constituents of milk (whey). The curdling of the milk and the separation of whey from the solids are the two fundamental processes of all cheesemaking. A more technical definition is that 'cheese is the product of whole, partially skimmed or fully skimmed milk, or of milk enriched by the addition of cream, which has been coagulated by lactic acid or by the addition of rennet, leading to the release and draining off of whey'. The separation of the whey is therefore the key dif-

The making of cheese

Below left Ewes being machine milked, for Roquefort cheese. As soon as a space is left free, the next animal will step into it of its own accord so that all the dairyman has to do is affix the teat cups. The pipeline system goes direct to a central collection point and thus the milk is processed without delay. Hundreds of ewes are milked in this way twice a day.
Bottom Production of Grana Padano; adding the lactic ferment (starter) culture to a vat full of milk.

ference between cheese and other coagulated milk products such as yogurt or junket. Experts maintain, however, that a further technical distinction should be made between true cheese and other curdled milk products, based on the fact that cheeses undergo a ripening process during which they change in taste, texture and appearance, and during which each cheese variety will take on an individual character of its own.

In order to grasp the theory of cheese production and the physical, chemical and biological processes involved, we have to understand exactly what milk is, and how one milk may differ from another. Milk's quality and condition will determine whether a satisfactory curd will form, how much curd there will be, and the quality of the finished cheese.

Types of milk

The appearance and constituents of mammal's milk are similar whatever the species, but the percentage of the substances contained in different types of milk varies, and further variations are produced by climate, surroundings, and feed. As far as mass production of cheese is concerned, the only types of milk which need concern us here are (in descending order of importance) cow's, ewe's, goat's and buffalo milk. These dairy animals can all give commercially satisfactory yields so long as they are provided with the correct climate, soil and pasture, and are reared and husbanded properly. Since cheese made from cow's milk is the most widely produced and known, I will concentrate on this type and only make passing reference to other milks, where they differ markedly from that of cows.

Both in the illustrated section and under each heading in the dictionary of cheeses, the type of milk used and the difference each species' milk makes to the character of the individual cheeses is clearly indicated.

The chemical composition of milk is shown in the table on page 22. It is mostly water, with other constituents held in suspension. Some of these constituents, like fat, are present in minute globules, as they are not soluble in water; while others, like the protein and minerals, are contained in still smaller particles, uniformly distributed, and invisible to the human eye unless viewed through an electron microscope. Still more substances are present which are soluble and therefore totally dissolved in the water content of milk, such as milk sugar (known as lactose), water-soluble vitamins, and other trace elements.

Most of these constituents remain present in the curd, although in differing quantities and proportions. Once the cheese ripens, however, many will undergo chemical changes, resulting in the substances that determine the acidity, flavour and aroma of the finished cheese. (The percentages of the constituent parts of milk present in the curd and whey are shown in the table on page 24).

The composition of milk

Milk Protein (*Casein*). Out of the several different proteins in milk, by far the most important is casein: it accounts for 78 per cent of all milk protein. Other proteins are present in smaller quantities, but as these are totally soluble, they are expressed in the whey (the group name for them is 'whey proteins'). Casein, therefore, is the only protein present in quantity in cheese made from curds – as vir-

In the photograph, *below right*, an old countrywoman prepares rennet in time-honoured fashion, using the dried lining of a pig's or ewe's stomach which is crumbled and then macerated in vinegar in a bottle.

tually all cheese is. A very little cheese is made from whey: Italian Ricotta, for example, and the brown Norwegian Gjetost.

Milk Sugar The type of sugar that is found in milk is called lactose – indeed milk is the only substance in which lactose is found. When milk ripens, it is the conversion of lactose into lactic acid that leads to the natural curdling of the milk, forming curds and whey. Curds formed by lactic acid are used for acidic-tasting soft cheeses, like Quark. The majority of cheeses, though, are not produced from lactic acid curd, as we will see in a moment or two.

Milk Fat There are a number of different fats in milk, all of them known under the group name of lipids. The lipids in milk include both saturated and unsaturated fatty acids, in a tolerably healthy ratio of 60 per cent saturated to 40 per cent unsaturated. During cheesemaking, nearly all of the fat is precipitated into the curd, and thus into the cheese.

Milk Minerals There is a wide variety of minerals present in milk, of which the two most important are calcium and phosphorus. In addition to enhancing the nutritive value of the finished cheese, these minerals are very important to the cheesemaking process itself, for without their presence the curd would never separate from the whey.

Milk Vitamins The most important milk vitamins are Vitamin A and members of the Vitamin B group, particularly B2. Vitamin D is also present in smaller quantities in the finished cheese.

The technology of cheesemaking

The transformation of milk into cheese involves some or all of a series of separate processes, each of which serves a clearly defined purpose:

* ★ Preparation of the milk, which may include heating, pasteurising and the addition of cultures of lactic bacteria.
* ★ Coagulation
* ★ Cutting or breaking up of the coagulated curd mass, sometimes including 'cooking' or 'scalding' the curd and draining off the whey. This is often accompanied by pressing, moulding or turning to encourage or slow the release of the whey.
* ★ Salting
* ★ Ripening

Preparation of the milk

In the case of some varieties of cheese, the milk may not be left to sour or ripen at all, but instead is simply heated to the temperature at which it is to be coagulated with rennet. This gives a very bland, sweet curd, containing a high amount of lactose.

In traditional farmhouse production, raw milk only was used, either straight after milking or when it had been left to ripen and/or slightly sour at room temperature. Nowadays, raw milk is mainly used for those cheeses which undergo a fairly long or very protracted maturing process, with the emphasis on high-quality cheese; where the cheeses are only ripened for a very short time, pasteurized milk is used.

One more noticeable change brought about by the growing interest in cheese is the rebirth of cheeses made with raw milk. The unpasteurized Brie de Meaux and a variety of Camembert-style cheeses are being joined by a variety of British farmhouse cheeses made in the traditional way. Pasteurisation involves heating milk to just over 70°C (160°F) for 15 seconds in order to destroy those disease-bearing bacteria which could be contained in milk. However, this process also kills off most of the microflora which play a vital role in milk's transformation into cheese, and renders inactive milk's natural enzymes. So cheese made with pasteurized milk that is not treated further can never achieve any great quality or character. Nowadays some of the lost microflora and enzymes are replaced with a standardized lactic bacterial culture known as a cheese 'starter'.

Long-maturing cheeses

In cheeses with long or very long maturing periods, any disease-bearing bacteria which may be present in raw milk are spontaneously attacked and destroyed during the ripening. So cheese made with raw milk will be

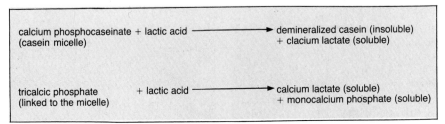

calcium phosphocaseinate + lactic acid ⟶ demineralized casein (insoluble)
(casein micelle)   + clacium lactate (soluble)

tricalcic phosphate   + lactic acid ⟶ calcium lactate (soluble)
(linked to the micelle)   + monocalcium phosphate (soluble)

The various stages of the manufacture of Pecorino Romano in a large industrial creamery are shown below and on the facing page. The first two photographs show the cutting of the curd(1), and the transfer of the curd to the cooler (2). Having been allowed to rest the curd is cut into blocks (3), which are removed (4), rounded off by hand and placed in moulds (5).

safe in terms of hygiene; they may, however, be subject to abnormalities casued by other bacteria which are harmful to cheese, leading to 'off flavours'. As the milk sours or ripens, some of the microflora will disappear and new enzymes will form; these, together with those enzymes originally present in the milk, will act as agents or catalysts to promote the separation of the protein, lactose and fat from the rest of the milk, thus enabling a curd of the desired type to be formed.

Controlled fat content

Many industrial producers of cheese at present control the fat content of milk, adding or removing cream to ensure a constant fat/protein content in their cheese. Most cheeses are made with whole milk, but for some, partially skimmed or even fully skimmed milk is necessary, depending on the cheese variety concerned. A minimum fat content must, however, be guaranteed to comply with

1

2

3

6

7

8

The bottom row of photographs illustrates subsequent phases. The curd is pressed in the moulds which are perforated to allow easy drainage of whey (6); after a few hours the cheese form is given its first piercing (7), followed by the first salting, (8). Subsequent saltings are carried out by removing and then replacing the moulds (9); after 90 days at most, the cheeses are finally removed from their moulds and are stored in caves to undergo curing (10).

legislation covering various types of cheese. Once the 'starter' (the laboratory-grown culture of cheesemaking bacteria) has been added and the milk is ready, it is heated to a temperature ranging from 20°C–40°C (68°F–104°F), depending on what type of curd is to be produced during the next phase: coagulation.

Coagulation of the milk

Clotting of the milk, or coagulation, is the basis of cheese production. This change of state is brought about by physical and chemical modifications to the constituents of milk, and leads to the separation of the whey from the curd. The curd, which is the embryo cheese, will vary in flavour, composition and appearance, depending on the clotting or curdling agent used and on the conditions under which the coagulation is brought about. In particular, the method of coagulation through either acid or enzyme (i.e. natural souring, or the use of rennet), will result in a sharp or a sweet-tasting curd.

In cheese making, we are concerned with both lactic acid coagulation and with clotting induced by the addition of enzymes. The former is adopted in the production of such milk derivatives as yogurt and all soured milks, as well as lactic cheeses, such as Quark or Petit Suisse; the latter is adopted in the production of most firm cheeses. However, the combination of both lactic acid and enzyme-induced coagulation is called for in the production of many varieties of cheese.

While lactic coagulation occurs naturally in milk, a special substance called rennet is needed for enzyme-induced coagulation. This contains enzymes found in an extract obtained from the stomach of suckling animals such as calves, kids and lambs. Traditionally, rennet was prepared in cheese factories, or by farmers and shepherds, using the dried stomach linings of these animals, soaked in salt water or in whey. Today, though, it is produced on a very large scale in industrial laboratories which manufacture a reliable, consistent product whose enzyme activity and hygiene can be guaranteed.

Various forms of rennet are made: liquid, dried liquid, or solid, and each is particularly well-suited to certain types of cheesemaking. Even some of the most elusive enzymes can now be artificially isolated, and this has enabled the cheese industry to react more sensitively to public demand than ever before, tailoring cheeses to fit precise market needs.

Acid curds and rennet curds differ

4

5

9

10

Two stages in the production of Parmesan cheese. *Below left* Cutting the curd, using a special tool called a 'thornbush'. *Below right* Lifting out the curd in a coarsely-woven hemp cloth.

both in texture and in flavour, the former being crumbly and porous, the latter firmer, denser, elastic and impermeable. A 'combination' curd shares some of the characteristics of both, and is produced by using only very small amounts of rennet at a low temperature, giving a slow clotting period that enables the milk microflora to develop of their own accord by lactic activity.

The curd: cutting, release of whey, 'cooking', kneading

Separation of whey from the curd is encouraged by breaking the curd up when it is still a junket-like gel, and this slow and progressive cutting process continues until the pieces of curd are only about the size of rice grains for very dry cheeses (such as Parmesan) or into walnut-sized pieces for soft cheeses with a high moisture content (such as Saint-Paulin or Taleggio).

With these soft cheeses, the curd is placed straight into moulds after having been cut and partially drained of whey. The curds which are destined to form harder cheeses with a lower moisture content are heated to between 46-56°C (115-132°F), depending on the type being made. This operation leads to more whey being expelled, and is adopted for cheeses which are aged for a long time (Par-

mesan again), or for very large cheeses (like Emmental or Comté). This process is helped by the development of lactic bacteria which increase the acidity of the curd.

Salting

This process follows that of draining the curd and, depending on style and size, is done before or after the curd has been placed in moulds. When salted, the cheese releases more whey as it is gradually impregnated by the salt, forcing the whey out.

There are three usual methods of salting: sprinkling salt into the draining curds; sprinkling it onto the surface of the cheese; or immersing whole cheese in brine baths. Adding some or all of the salt to curd before it has been placed in mould typifies the way certain cheeses are made (Cheddar is an example), but is confined to relatively few varieties. Dry salting is still fairly widely used (as, for example, with Gorgonzola and Pecorino): it allows the salt to penetrate quickly, thus speeding up the whole salting process. This is the oldest way of salting, and is gradually being replaced by salting in brine, or by a combination of both methods.

The length of time required for soaking in brine depends on the type of cheese and ranges from a few minutes to a number of days; with

certain cheeses like Feta, it lasts for the whole of the ripening period. The salt penetrates the cheese gradually by osmosis (the process of diffusion through more or less porous matter). By the time that the cheese is fully ripe, both the outer layers and the heart of the cheese should have the same concentration of salt.

Besides improving the taste of cheese, salt inhibits the development of certain bacteria which would be harmful to the cheese and cause spoilage, especially on the surface. It further assists in the process of dissolving the casein, in rind formation, as well as in slowing down enzyme activity. The salt content of a cheese will, of course, vary as it is modified by several factors: the strength of the brine solution, the weight and shape of the cheese, and the way in which it is salted. The salt content is usually between one per cent and three per cent, but it is lower for quick-ripening soft cheeses and higher for long-maturing hard cheeses like Parmesan.

Ripening

This is the stage when different cheese varieties acquire their own unique, typical texture, aroma and taste, through complex physical and chemical changes. These are in part determined by the constituents of milk, but can be mainly attributed to bacteriological action. The curd is subject to a varying number of these actions, depending on the type of microflora present, the method of cheesemaking, the moisture content of the curd, the amount of salt in the paste or body of the developing cheese, its particle size, and the temperature and humidity of the curing room. Bacteriological development may affect the whole of the paste of the cheese, or only certain areas of the cheese such as the surface.

Another interesting aspect of

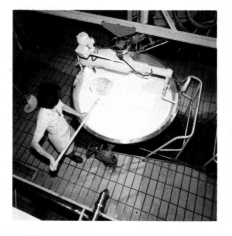

The diagram below represents the process of homolactic fermentation in a bacterium cell in the whey of the curd. The red arrows signify energy exchanges.
Right The curd for Mozzarella cheese being 'drawn' or 'spun' in a southern Italian dairy.
Below Salting Grana Padano cheeses in a brine bath.

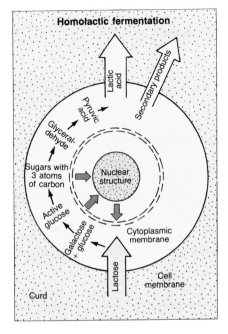

Homolactic fermentation

Lactic acid
Secondary products
Pyruvic acid
Glyceraldehyde
Sugars with 3 atoms of carbon
Nuclear structure
Active glucose
Galactose + glucose
Cytoplasmic membrane
Lactose
Cell membrane
Curd

ripening is the breakdown of the protein (casein) into other, simpler proteins, which confer a specific aroma and taste on a cheese. It is this process which, when allowed to continue for too long, can result in a powerful ammonia smell in some cheeses, such as over-ripe Camembert. The new proteins produced, however, are more easily digested than casein.

Ripening takes place under conditions where the temperature remains at about 4.5°C (40°F) for soft cheese and 18°C (64°F) for harder cheese, given medium or long periods of ageing. The humidity also has to be carefully controlled to suit the variety of cheese, varying from 75 per cent to 85 per cent for hard, dry-rind cheese to over 90 per cent for soft, rindless cheese or surface-ripened soft cheese. The importance of these conditions means that most manufacturers have curing rooms where the temperature and humidity are automatically controlled with regulated ventilation.

Most cheeses have a rind or crust, part of the cheese's surface which comes into direct contact with the surrounding atmosphere, but some cheeses have no rind in the traditional sense of the word (such as fresh cheeses, those ripened in brine or in a keeping fluid, and those which are vacuum-packed in plastic). The rind varies in appearance and function, depending on the type of cheese. It first makes its appearance as an outer layer of curd which is denser and less moist than the rest of the curd, while the curd is being drained in moulds, but only after salting and curing does the rind achieve the characteristic texture and appearance demanded for that variety of cheese. It will be hard and dry in 'cooked', aged cheeses; soft and moist or sticky in certain soft cheeses and will develop a flourishing layer of surface flora or mould stemming from aerobic (oxygen dependent) bacteria, all of which will ensure that the finished cheese possesses the characteristic features that we associate with that type. The rind should always be thin and well-defined so that a clear distinction can be made between the rind and the paste, without an intermediate layer beneath the rind.

The presence of rind controls the progression of moisture from the internal part of the cheese towards the outside and thus regulates evaporation and the escape of gases released by the cheese during the ripening period. The successful maturing of any cheese is dependent to a very large extent on the rind, and so it is this that the cheesemakers watch and monitor carefully while the cheeses are in the curing rooms, undergoing such treatments as oiling, brushing, turning, periodic saltings, mould-inhibiting treatments of the surface, waxing, washing the rind with brine, smearing the surface with mould cultures, or covering the surface with ashes to reduce acidity in the case of some farmhouse cheeses.

Some cheeses rely wholly on surface bacteria or mould for their curing or maturation, and these are called 'surface-ripening cheeses'. They fall into two categories. The first is the Camembert and Brie group, which develop white surface flora (a mould that belongs to the penicillin family) all around their exterior. When ripe, these cheeses should smell of fresh mushrooms: an ammonia smell indicates over-ripeness.

The other group of surface-ripening cheeses are those that rely on bacteria rather than mould – cheeses like Pont l'Évêque and Munster. They are

Diagram illustrating the process of proteolysis in a bacterium cell contained in the curd, taking place during ripening (the broken lines stand for secondary reactions).

known as washed-rind cheeses, as frequent washing facilitates the growth of bacteria. This group, easily recognized by the orange-red surface colour, also smells much more pungent than the first group, of anything from dirty socks to drains, but strangely enough these cheeses tend to be sweet on the palate. Surface-ripened cheeses are usually relatively small to increase the ratio of surface to total weight.

Varieties of cheese with a slow ageing process that takes place evenly through the paste rely on enzymes trapped in the curd when coagulation occurred to accomplish the curing. They are further assisted by micro-organisms produced within the cheese during the ripening process. Here the rind will be kept dry, covered with a watertight wrapping, or may be cleaned, scrubbed and brushed at frequent intervals.

Between these widely differing categories of total surface-ripening and negligible surface-ripening there is a third group that partly relies on surface-ripening in the curing process: this group includes the Swiss cheeses Emmental and Gruyère.

The production of rindless cheeses that are matured while wrapped in plastic is one way of avoiding heavy curing costs and means that more of the cheese is edible. This is a recent development in cheese manufacture and is particularly widespread in countries where cheese technology is very advanced.

Plastic wrapped cheeses never 'mature' in the fullest sense, as they are stored at too low a temperature, and the airtight seal prohibits any osmosis or gas exchange, so vital to proper curing. Any distinctive flavour they do have will come from the starter used. More traditional practices like covering the surface with ashes, with paraffin wax, or with ordinary wax are different from plastic wrapping for the purpose here

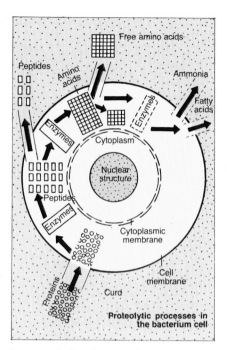

Proteolytic processes in the bacterium cell

is to seal the cheese after the curing has finished. In some cases, cracks or holes develop within the paste during the curing: these are caused by the gases produced as the cheese matures, and are important features of cheese like Emmental.

The nutritive profile of cheese

Milk is sometimes described as our most 'complete' food because it contains such a well-balanced combination of various nutrients. Cheese shares this nutritive richness to some extent, although we must remember that milk's water soluble nutrients are expressed in the whey, rather than in the curd from which cheese is made, so the final cheese product will not have quite as complete a nutritive profile as that of milk.

Cheese provides important amounts of calcium and phosphorus: as a general rule, the harder the cheese, the greater will be the concentration of these minerals. The vitamins in cheese (A, B_2, D), on the other hand, are present in greatest quantities in softer, whole-milk

cheeses in which some whey remains unexpressed from the curd.

Cheese is a useful source of protein, most of it casein, though we noted earlier the process of casein breakdown during ripening, to produce a number of other, simpler proteins, easier to digest than casein. This is, of course, in comparative terms only: casein is a first-class, complete protein, and no healthy person used to eating cheese should have any difficulty in digesting it.

The fat content of cheese

The fat in cheese is not only nutritionally but legally very important, as cheese legislation in many countries is based on a certain minimum percentage of fat *in dry matter* for each cheese. This does not mean a fat percentage of the total cheese, but only of what remains after all moisture has been removed. So, for example, if a cheese says '45% fat in dry matter' on its wrapper, it does *not* mean that just under half that weight of cheese is fat, but rather that, if it were to have all the water squashed out of it, what remains would contain 45 per cent fat. It follows from this that, if you want to monitor your fat (or cholesterol) intake while still enjoying cheese – and the two are in no way contradictory – you should remember that weight for weight the wetter, moister cheeses (like Brie and Camembert) will contain less fat than harder cheeses (like Cheddar or Parmesan – even though the latter is made with skimmed milk). It's also worth noting that cholesterol levels vary surprisingly, even in cheeses with identical fat contents: a 45 per cent fat Brie will contain 60 mg of cholesterol every 100 g, whereas a 45 per cent fat Gouda will contain 80 mg of cholesterol per 100 g. There is, though, the same rational explanation for this: Brie, weight for weight, has a greater proportion of water in it than Gouda, and this explains the

Below right One of the famous Roquefort caves which form a subterranean town twice the size of Roquefort-sur-Soulzon above ground. The cheese, which takes its name from the town, matures in these caves under perfect conditions due to the air currents which keep the temperature and humidity constant. The diagram below shows how one of these enormous subterranean caverns deep in the rock has been organized; the currents of air penetrate through natural fissures in the rock known as *fleurines*.

apparent anomaly. Out of the 100 g of Gouda, a greater proportion of it is dry matter, and therefore fat, and therefore cholesterol, than is the case with the wetter 100 g of Brie.

Criteria for classifying cheese

There are many ways in which cheese can be classified but no single set of criteria has been universally adopted. Cheese can be classified, as indicated above, by the fat content of the finished cheese in dry matter, giving a tripartite division into fat, semi-fat, and low-fat cheeses. These terms, though, should never be regarded as anything more than a rough guide: semi-fat cheeses, for example, may contain in some countries anything between 20 per cent and 40 per cent fat in dry matter; in other words, one semi-fat cheese may have twice the fat content of another.

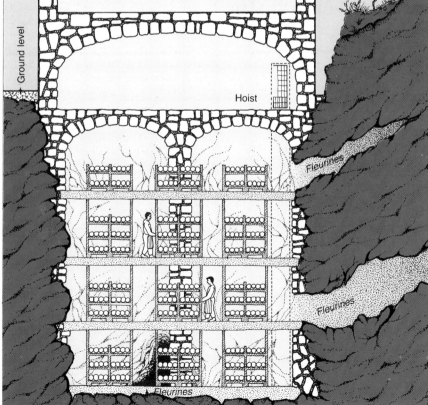

Another commonly used system for classifying cheese is based on the consistency of the finished product. Soft cheeses have a water content of 45 per cent to 50 per cent; semi-hard cheeses have a moisture content below 40 per cent: these percentages are calculated for the whole of the cheese.

A third classification is based on the method of preparation and production used: soft cheeses then become those that retain quantities of whey, and whose coagulation temperatures are the same as the final treatment of curd in the vat (between 20–40°C, 68–104°F). Semi-hard cheeses undergo more draining, and the curd is heated to 42–48°C (107–118°F); and hard, 'cooked-curd' cheeses are well-drained and are heated to 52–55°C (125–131°F) in the vat.

Within these large groupings of cheeses other subtypes can be distinguished and classified. One such category is soft, fresh cheeses which can be consumed just after the whey has been released and after salting, if any, has been completed. They can be

The making of cheese

Diagram showing the various methods and production sequences which are involved in making different types of cheese. In some cases lactic bacteria may or may not be added and the curd may or may not be cooked: these alternatives are shown.

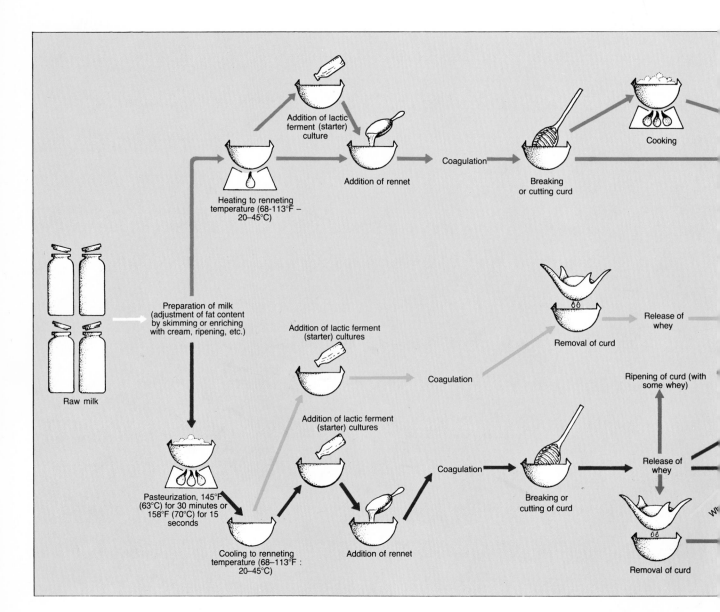

Addition of lactic ferment (starter) culture

Heating to renneting temperature (68–113°F – 20–45°C)

Addition of rennet

Coagulation

Breaking or cutting curd

Cooking

Preparation of milk (adjustment of fat content by skimming or enriching with cream, ripening, etc.)

Addition of lactic ferment (starter) cultures

Coagulation

Removal of curd

Release of whey

Ripening of curd (with some whey)

Raw milk

Addition of lactic ferment (starter) cultures

Release of whey

Pasteurization, 145°F (63°C) for 30 minutes or 158°F (70°C) for 15 seconds

Cooling to renneting temperature (68–113°F : 20–45°C)

Addition of rennet

Coagulation

Breaking or cutting of curd

Removal of curd

classified as follows:

* Acid-curd cheeses coagulated at low temperatures such as Quark
* Acid-curd cheeses coagulated at a higher temperature, such as Ricotta
* Rennet-curd cheeses, such as curd cheese
* Lactic acid rennet-curd cheeses which are kneaded or spun, such as Mozzarella

These cheeses usually contain 60 per cent or more water and have limited keeping potential: a few days at most, even in a refrigerator.

Next come the soft cheeses which ripen only for a short time, and in which the development of acidity and protein breakdown has not progressed very far. Delicate on the palate, they are matured for a few weeks in refrigerated curing rooms. These cheeses have thin, soft rinds,

with a smooth, even, buttery paste: examples include St-Paulin and Reblochon, or the Italian Taleggio.

Another category embraces those soft cheeses which develop a very decided, sometimes sharp taste due to enzyme action produced by the surface bacteria: these are the surface-ripened cheeses described above. They must be eaten as soon as they are ripe or they deteriorate and produce unpleasant odours and tastes.

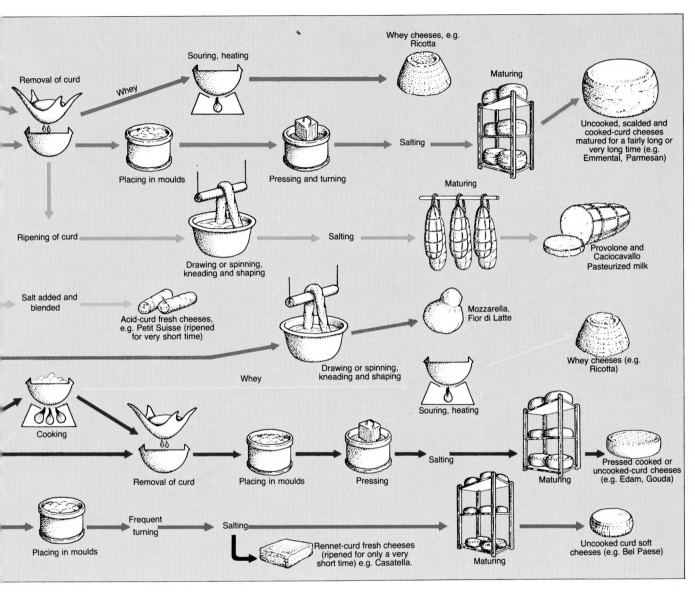

Souring, heating

Whey cheeses, e.g. Ricotta

Removal of curd

Whey

Maturing

Uncooked, scalded and cooked-curd cheeses matured for a fairly long or very long time (e.g. Emmental, Parmesan)

Placing in moulds

Pressing and turning

Salting

Maturing

Ripening of curd

Drawing or spinning, kneading and shaping

Salting

Provolone and Caciocavallo Pasteurized milk

Salt added and blended

Acid-curd fresh cheeses, e.g. Petit Suisse (ripened for very short time)

Mozzarella, Fior di Latte

Whey cheeses (e.g. Ricotta)

Drawing or spinning, kneading and shaping

Whey

Souring, heating

Cooking

Removal of curd

Placing in moulds

Pressing

Salting

Maturing

Pressed cooked or uncooked-curd cheeses (e.g. Edam, Gouda)

Frequent turning

Salting

Placing in moulds

Rennet-curd fresh cheeses (ripened for only a very short time) e.g. Casatella.

Maturing

Uncooked curd soft cheeses (e.g. Bel Paese)

Other examples in addition to the cheeses mentioned earlier include Livarot and Romadour.

Among full-flavoured, mature cheeses, the blue cheeses are very popular. These cheeses develop moulds and greenish-blue veining (from which they get their name) which penetrates and develops right through the cheese, growing along the spaces between the curds left after only a light pressing or by special steel needles used to puncture the cheese and allow the air access to it. Among the most famous and typical cheese of this type are Blue Stilton, Roquefort, Danish Blue, Gorgonzola, and Bleu d'Auvergne.

Next come the semi-hard, pressed cheeses, with thin rinds, the paste being supple or firm, sometimes with evenly spaced holes, and fairly mild in taste. Ripening lasts for 2–6 months in temperatures of 10–20°C (50–68°F). A number of goat's milk cheeses belong to this group, as do Tilsit and the Danish cheese Havarti.

Finally, we come to the hard, dry cheeses which are matured for a long time and which have a dry rind. Some of these, such as Parmesan and Pecorino, are used as grating cheeses. They are medium to large in size, with a grainy texture, and they tend to be slightly salty with a pronounced taste which makes them ideal for

Below right Scamorza cheese, the distinctively shaped cow's milk cheese made by the spun or kneaded-curd method.
Below left Two views of Parmesan cheese, magnified 7000 times through a microscope. *Above* Calcium phosphate microcrystals and, *below*, calcium lactate microcrystals. Parmesan contains a high percentage (70–80%) of the calcium and phosphorus content of the milk.

flavouring or finishing cooked dishes. Other hard cheeses are widely used as table or dessert cheeses, cut into pieces or sliced: among the most well-known are Emmental, Cheddar and Cheshire.

Processed cheeses

These cheeses cannot be classified under any of the previous headings since they consist of finished cheese which then undergoes further treatment. Several varieties may be combined for the basic 'mix'; emulsifying salts are always added; and powdered milk, whey, cream or butter and water may be added. The mixture is heated and stirred and produces a stable, homogenous emulsion in which the water, fat, and salt are evenly distributed. The addition of certain salts is vital if a stable emulsion is to be formed: if cheese and water are subjected to the same treatment without these salts, the water will

evaporate, the fat separate, and the protein become a rubbery mass.

Once the mixture has partially cooled, it is shaped into blocks, slices, put into cartons or cut into segments, according to market requirements. Processed cheeses are available all over the world and serve various needs: the creamy, soft varieties can be used as spreads and the firmer ones used as sliceable dessert cheeses, or cooked in snacks like Welsh Rabbit. Storage of processed cheese is considerably easier than that of proper cheese, as processed cheese is sterile and not a 'living' product. It also makes a good introduction to the world of cheese for young children, who like its mild taste and chewy texture. But it is not, in the best sense of the word, a 'real' cheese, and it stands to reason that no manufacturer will ever turn his best cheese to this uninteresting end.

Certification of type and origin

The cheese industry has for some time been trying to protect the consumer and safeguard the reputation of its own products by classifying certain types of cheese and stipulating that they must only bear that variety's name if they are produced in a certain area and are made according to recognized, traditional methods. This task was undertaken by the International Dairy Federation, which drew up reports on the subject in 1933 and 1937, and in 1951 an agreement was signed at the Stresa Convention between Austria, Belgium, Denmark, France, Italy, Norway, Holland and Switzerland which defined certain cheeses and stipulated the conditions for using certain names. The United Kingdom respects this convention and so, for example, if a Brie-style cheese or a Cheddar has been made anywhere other than its certified production area (in France or England), when on sale in this country the label should specify as much: 'Bavarian

Brie', for example, or 'Irish Cheddar'. This is known as certification of type. There is also a further, more exacting control on certain names: the certification of origin. This means that any cheese bearing a name 'certified in origin' can only be what it says it is: anything with 'Parmesan' on the label *must* be Parmesan from the Parma area of Italy. The tables below illustrate a selection of those cheeses whose names are certified by either type or origin:

Certification of type

Camembert (France)
Brie (France)
Saint-Paulin (France)
Emmental (Switzerland)
Gruyère (Switzerland and France)
Samso (Denmark)
Danbo (Denmark)
Svecia (Sweden)
Pinzgauer Bergkäse (Austria)
Gouda (Netherlands)
Friesian (Netherlands)
Fynbo (Denmark)
Havarti (Denmark)
Danish Blue (Denmark)
Ädelost (Sweden)

Below right Gouda, a semi-hard Dutch cheese: its manufacture is controlled by Certification of Type, and so it can be produced in other countries. Made with cow's milk, it has a fat content of 25–26%.
Bottom One of the large family of blue cheeses, so called because of their greenish-blue mould; this is Edelpilz which is made in Austria and Germany.

Certification of origin

Gorgonzola (Italy)
Parmesan (Italy)
Pont-l'Évêque (France)
Neufchâtel (France)
Brie de Meaux (France)
Munster (France)
Pecorino Siciliano (Italy)
Saint-Nectaire (France)
Roquefort (France)
Livarot (France)
Reblochon (France)
Crottin de Chavignol (France)
Bleu d'Auvergne (France)
Comté (France)

Cheese in Canada

In the past, Cheddar-style cheese has been the mainstay of the Canadian cheese industry. But recently there has been a noticeable growth in the making of variety cheeses, so much so that they are expected soon to outstrip the overall production of Cheddar on an annual basis.

Canadian Cheddar is world renowned for its 'bite', due to long, carefully-controlled ageing, usually at least 9 months. Although the variety cheeses are more expensive to make and sell, consumption in Canada has increased by 37.9 per cent in the four years 1975–79 whilst that of Cheddar decreased by 30 per cent; the remainder is covered by an increase of almost 10 per cent in the eating of processed cheese.

The most common variety cheese made in Canada is, surprisingly, Mozzarella, accounting for almost 45 per cent of the market, a business ingeniously assisted by mechanical means of stretching and tempering the plastic curd.

The next most important product is something called Pizza Cheese, followed by Brick cheese (see American cheese, page 38), Colby, Camembert (whose sales are increasing on a phenomenal scale – over 700 per cent in four years), and, well behind, two

Italian styles: Scamorza and Caciocavallo. About 20 per cent of the market is made up of some 45 other varieties which are a mixture of foreign styles, reflecting the origin of local communities, or of Canadian varieties just individual enough to be thought of as new varieties. As expected Blue Vein, Brie, Feta, Gouda, Gruyère and St-Paulin are made but you will also

find Oka, a Canadian type of Port-du-Salut originating in a monastery; Portuguese varieties especially Vaquinha, Jowa and Lemoine; Mt. St. Benoit and Suries. Ontario produces most of the variety cheeses closely followed by Quebec and then, trailing well behind, Western Canada.

The most interesting fact about this industry is how much it depends on

A whole Parmesan cheese, its golden exterior gleaming invitingly. This world-famous cheese is protected under the Certification of Origin system and the approved production zones are strictly controlled. The words 'Parmigiano-Reggiano' are branded into the rind all the way round the cheese, guaranteeing its authenticity.

the pizza trade for its main varieties – mozzarella and pizza cheese. In 1979 these two cheeses accounted for more than 90,000 pounds out of a total market of 143,733 pounds.

American cheese

The American cheese industry began in 1851, when Jesse Williams opened the first cheddar factory near Rome, Oneida County (New York State), and today Americans consume an average of 4.5 kg of cheese per person per year. The United States of America is the world's largest producer of cheese, and the majority of cheese there is made in Wisconsin. The American cheese industry makes up in volume for what it lacks in variety: 80 per cent of all cheese produced is a cheddar or cheddar-derived type of cheese and, of that, 67 per cent is marketed under the name of American Cheddar.

Many of the native American cheeses – Colby, Coon, Cornhusker, Monterey, Pineapple, Tillamook, Washed-Curd, Soaked-Curd, Stirred-Curd and Granular – are variations on the cheddar theme, often with regional roots. Colby, for example, is a mild, semi-firm type of cheddar, traditional in Vermont. Coon is a sharper, piquant cheddar made in New York State: it has a

crumbly texture and the cheese itself is very pale with a dark rind. Cornhusker is a Nebraska cheddar, first introduced in 1940: it is similar to Colby. Monterey (sometimes known under its older name, Jack) was originally made in Monterey County, California, about 1892, and is a cheddar type that exists in different versions. If made from whole milk, it is semi-firm, creamy and pale, and is matured for three to six weeks; if made from skimmed or partially skimmed milk it is firmer and zestier: the 'grating-type' or 'dry' Monterey is matured for at least six months. Pineapple is a cheddar matured in net bags to give it a pineapple shape: the outer surface is rubbed with oil as the cheese ripens to give it a hard, shiny surface. Tillamook is an Oregon cheddar (a special, salt-free variety is also produced). Washed-Curd or Soaked-Curd are cheddars produced by a special process that increases the water content, giving a softer, moister cheese; and Stirred-Curd or Granular are names sometimes given to Colby-style cheddars.

Two native American varieties depart from this cheddar-base: Brick and Liederkranz. Brick is a sweet, semi-soft cowsmilk cheese often described as being between Cheddar

and Limburger in both taste and texture: the origin of its name is unknown, it is claimed, though the fact that it is packed in brick-like shapes, and that bricks are used to press the cheese during its manufacture, seems to point to a tolerably obvious conclusion. Liederkranz is the great exception: it was created by a New York delicatessen owner called Emil Frey in 1850, and he named it after his choral society. It is a mould-ripened, aromatic, soft dessert cheese, now mainly produced in Ohio and sold in New York.

America also produces a large number of European-style cheeses: Italian types, particularly Mozzarella, are popular, as is 'Swiss Cheese', based on Emmental and Gruyère. Processed cheese is very important – what is called American Cheese, for example, is a mild processed cheese of a cheddar type – and Cottage Cheese, also known as Pot Cheese or Dutch Cheese, is likewise produced in large quantities across the continent.

A ban on the import of many cheeses made with unpasteurized milk means the gourmets of the United States simply don't know the pleasures of many of the world's greatest cheeses. But with their usual independence they try to emulate them where they can. Just outside San Francisco, for instance, a small family business has been making Brie and Camembert cheese for some time and with varying success; if they called the cheese a name of their own making instead of invoking the revered names of French cheese, they would avoid comparison and have a most worthwhile product that could stand on its own. In some of the more established communities on the East Coast there is growing interest in cheeses which have largely disappeared. Best of these, in my opinion, is the variety of sage-flavoured cheeses, which are not marbled with green fluid but flavoured with rolled

Below A selection of French cheeses. France has a very old and vigorous tradition of cheesemaking, producing an enormously varied selection of cheeses, many of which are world-famous. In one of his speeches, Churchill remarked how impossible it must be to govern a nation which produced over 400 cheeses!

fresh or dried sage. Vermont Sage is said to be the best but all East Coast sage cheeses are worth watching for.

Australian Cheesemaking

Australia has been a great dairying country since the early days of its founding as a British colony in the late eighteenth century. Now, in exactly the same way as other ex-colonies have started to move away from an almost exclusive manufacturing of Cheddar cheese, Australia makes nearly 50 other varieties of cheese for home consumption. Migration has been the major stimulus, combining both to create the demand and to supply the know-how. Modern travel and the generally high standard of Australian life has also meant an increasing sophistication amongst young Australians, many of whom are very well travelled these days before they settle down for good.

Cheesemaking began in New South Wales about 1820 and was followed in other states in the 1830s. Even as late as 1900, half of the Cheddar was still made laboriously on farms and homesteads, but since 1960 virtually all the cheese has been made in highly mechanized central factories on an industrial scale.

The main styles of Cheddar cheese made by Australia owe their discernible differences to ageing. Mild Cheddar is usually sold after three months (a considerably longer period than allowed by many countries or manufacturers); semi-matured Cheddar is three to six months old and thus richer, without any sharpness. Mature Australian Cheddar is up to one year old and displays much of the authentic Cheddar flavour and style. Vintage Cheddar is over 15 months old and both the latter are excellent all-round cheeses and particularly good in cooking. With typical Australian individuality, mature cheeses are usually labelled as 'tasty'.

Australia has only two relatively well-known varieties unique to herself. Cheedam is a firm but open-textured cheese combining the qualities of Cheddar and Edam; Pastorello is a soft, mild and delicately flavoured variety similar to Fontina. As might be expected, the variety cheeses in Australia clearly reflect the pattern of immigration with Italian and Greek cheeses being particularly noticeable (indeed Melbourne, capital of Victoria, is said to be the world's second largest Greek city). Fetta, Mozzarella, Blue Vein, Parmesan, Pecorino, Camembert, Gouda, Edam and Swiss-style cheeses are perhaps the most commonly made variety cheeses. Together with cream and ricotta cheeses they are eaten in a wide variety of Australian homes and are being used more and more to create a recognisably Australian style of cooking – international in origin but decidedly national in actuality. One major manufacturer has recently decided to capitalize on investment and the new import and trading conditions caused by Britain's membership of the European Economic Community and so a number of English regional cheeses – Cheshire, Double Gloucester, Sage Derby, Red Leicester and Wensleydale – are now being made for national distribution.

Flavoured and processed cheeses are particularly popular with

Australians and available in startling choices. Curry-flavoured cheese is a great favourite and so, as might be expected, are garlic and spring onion cheeses. But you can also choose peanut, ginger or salami-flavoured cheese and recently a cream cheese mixed with dried fruits was put on the market with some success.

New Zealand cheeses

New Zealand's climate is perfect for dairy farming: warm and moist, with such mild winters that pasture is available the year round. The much-publicized inhibitory effect of EEC quotas for British imports of New Zealand cheese has, in fact, been a positive factor in stimulating New Zealand's rapid strides across world markets. New Zealand now exports 90 per cent of her total cheese production, and Britain takes only a small percentage of this.

New Zealand Cheddar is the best-known and most widely-exported variety, easily spotted in the shops by its bright yellow colour. This is entirely natural, and is due to the fact that the majority of cows in New Zealand's dairy herds are Jersey cows, whose rich milk has a higher carotene content than that of Friesians. While New Zealand Cheddar is always produced in blocks, it is generally aged for longer than the four weeks customary elsewhere, and nowadays a two-year old mature cheddar is being marketed as 'Vintage Cheddar'. This will never rival a cloth-bound, matured Farmhouse Cheddar, but it does offer a markedly superior alternative to standard, factory-produced blocks. Other cheeses produced by New Zealand include a New Zealand Blue Vein, a smooth, semi-soft textured cheese exported to 27 different countries and thought to be one of the most successful of New Zealand's style cheese; a New Zealand Gouda and a New Zealand Edam, the latter containing the traditional lower fat content; a New Zealand Gruyère, first produced in 1959, sweet and nutty on the palate with a good hole distribution and aroma; a New Zealand Danbo, one of the most versatile of all New Zealand's cheeses in the kitchen; a New Zealand Feta, made from cow's milk but with the strong salty flavour of the original; and a New Zealand Parmesan and a New Zealand Romano, the latter styled on the Italian Pecorino, though again made from cow's rather than sheep's milk. A New Zealand Colby is also made, similar in taste and texture to the American original, and this cheese is commonly used as a basis for kosher versions of the strict 'Cholov Yisroel' type. New Zealand also makes a wide variety of processed cheeses, among them being chive, green pepper, ham and smoked versions. Since 1974, New Zealand has had its own separate variety of cheese, recognized by the codex alimentarius of the UN Food and Agriculture Organization: Egmont. This cheese, made in a single factory only 20 kilometres from the foot of Mount Egmont, is a pliable hard cheese with a slightly sweet, nutty flavour: it has been described as lying between Cheddar and Gouda in both texture and taste. Its main export markets are the USA and Japan.

The great cheeses of the world

Munster
A soft French cheese whose label of origin is protected by law; it is made with whole cow's milk and although mild with a hint of saltiness when very young, it becomes spicy with a pronounced tangy flavour when matured. Square moulds are used to shape the curd, but once removed they round out.
Details on page 132.

Chevrotin des Aravis
Produced in the French province of Savoie from goat's milk, this firm, pressed, uncooked cheese has a fairly mild flavour.
Details on page 109.

Maroilles
This soft French cheese is protected by an *appellation d'origine*. It is made from cow's milk and has a full, creamy flavour which is tangy but not bitter; like most washed-rind cheeses, it has a pungent smell.
Details on page 128.

Port-Salut
A pasteurized French cow's milk cheese, pressed and uncooked, which is produced on a large commercial scale and can be grouped with the Saint-Paulin cheeses, the name having been sold to a large producer. It should not be confused with the original Port-du-Salut cheese, still produced by the monks of the abbey of Entrammes, and sold under the name of 'Entrammes'.
Details on page 138.

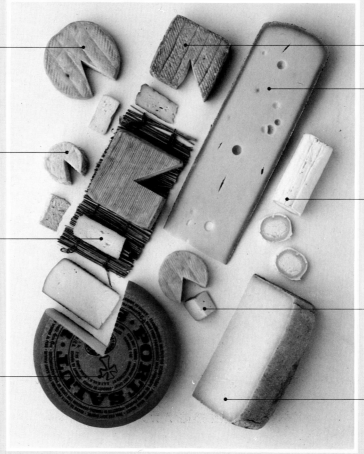

Pont-l'Evêque
This soft French cheese is made in Normandy from whole or partially skimmed cow's milk; it has a creamy rich flavour with the strong smell usually associated with washed-rind cheeses.
Details on page 138.

Gruyère de Comté
A member of the French Gruyère family of large, hard-pressed cooked cheeses, made in the Franche-Comté from cow's milk. Resembles a Swiss Gruyère with holes.
Details on page 121.

Sainte-Maure
A soft French goat's milk cheese made in Touraine. As the cheese matures the rind acquires a downy white or green mould.
Details on page 145.

Petit Munster
A smaller version of this famous cow's milk cheese, described above.
Details on page 132.

Cantal
A noted cow's milk cheese from the Auvergne in France. Cantal is thought to be the oldest of French cheeses; pressed and uncooked, it has a very pleasant nutty flavour with a hint of tartness and a pronounced bouquet. A French Cheddar, in fact.
Details on page 106.

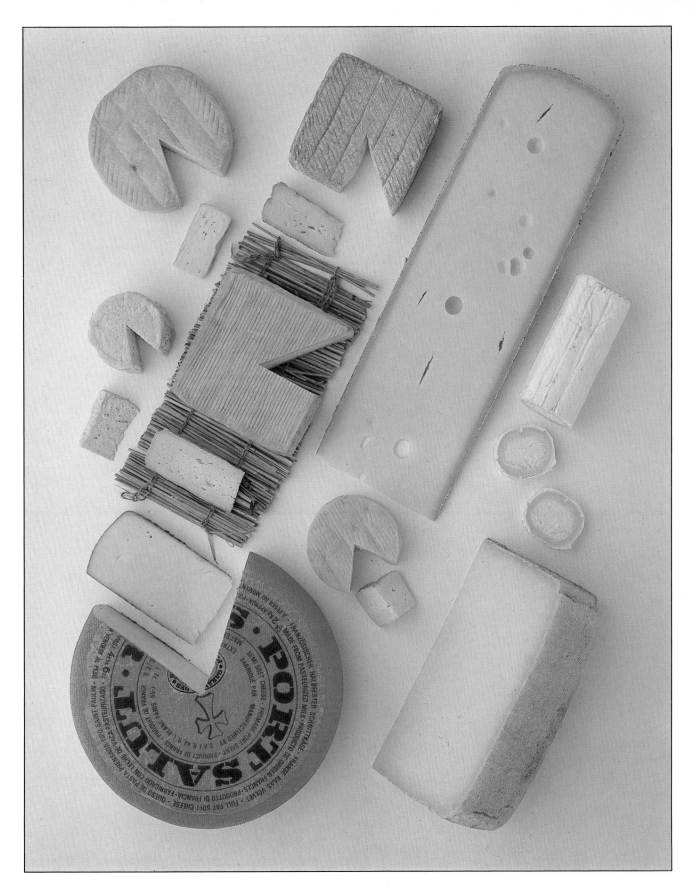

Reblochon
Made in the Haute-Savoie region of France but also in Italy, in Piedmont and the Aosta Valley. It is a soft, lightly-pressed cow's milk cheese; the flavour is subtle, fruity and delicious. Rare and expensive if genuine.
Details on page 142.

Bûche de Chèvre
A soft French goat's milk cheese which can be described as a larger version of Sainte-Maure. *Bûche* means 'log', unsurprisingly enough, and the cheese is often simply referred to as 'log'.
Details on page 103.

Tomme de Savoie
An uncooked, pressed semi-hard cow's milk cheese from Savoy in France with a lactic and pleasantly aromatic flavour. Cured for one month in damp, cold caves. An Italian version of this cheese is to be found on the other side of the Alps. Commercial copies often have black plastic coverings.
Details on page 152.

Roquefort
The illustrious French blue cheese, made only with ewe's milk and matured for three months in the caves at Roquefort, where natural conditions provide ideal surroundings for the cheeses to mature to perfection. The paste is creamy white, dense, salty but buttery, with a decided ewe's milk taste.
Details on page 144.

Pyramides
The shape of these little French goat's milk cheeses has given rise to their name – resembling small truncated pyramids. Their soft paste is mild in taste when young, acquiring character and intensity if they are matured for any length of time.
Details on page 140.

Camembert
One of the most famous of all French cheeses and certainly the most widely imitated and marketed. Although the best Camembert is still made in the Normandy region where it originated, production has spread to other parts of France and all over the world. It is a soft, uncooked cow's milk cheese with a white mould on the rind. The genuine article (*véritable Camembert*) from the Pays d'Auge has a truly exquisite flavour.
Details on page 105.

Brie
An outstanding and justly famous soft French cheese made with whole cow's milk. The interior is smooth, creamy and buttery and the taste is full and fruity, with a slight tang to it. Apart from the classic Brie, higher-fat-content variations have been developed as well as versions flavoured with herbs and mushrooms. A bonus for connoisseurs is that the unpasteurized Brie de Meaux is now common. An English Brie is successfully made in Somerset.
Details on page 101.

Babybel
A French whole cow's milk cheese whose mild, semi-hard paste is covered with a distinctive coating of red wax.
Details on page 96.

Mini Babybel
A miniaturized version of the French Babybel cheese pictured above left, and a useful size when just one small portion is required, such as for airline catering or children's lunches.
Details on page 96.

Pont-Moutier
This uncooked-curd French cow's milk cheese has a delicate, fragrant flavour and aroma.
Details on page 138.

Suprême des Ducs
A soft French cow's milk cheese produced in Normandy. The interior is very velvety, creamy and fragrant and the flavour acquires strength and character as the cheese matures. It is similar to Caprice des Dieux, produced in Champagne.
Details on page 149.

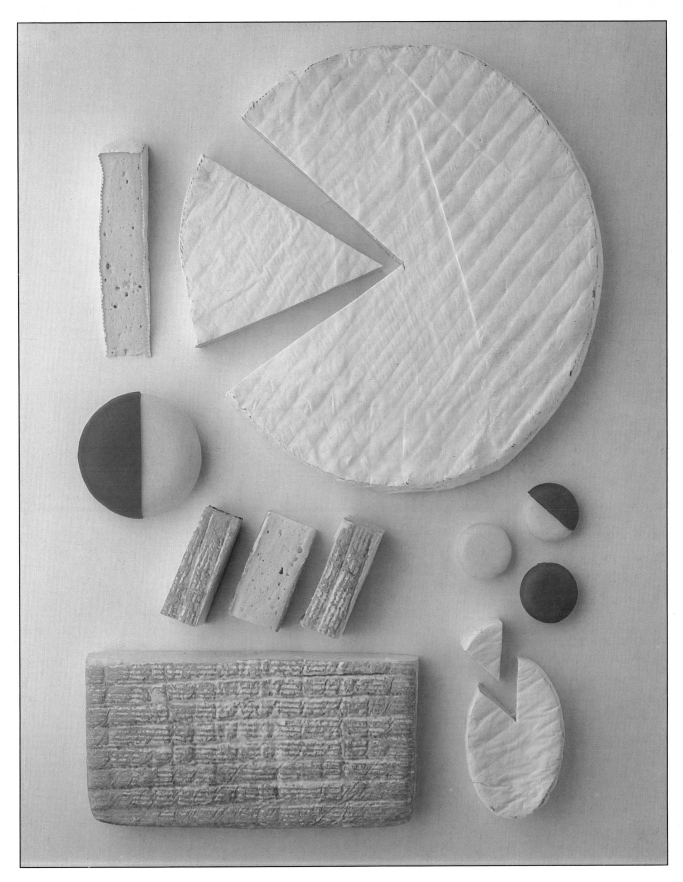

Vacherol du Port-du-Salut de la Trappe
A medium-hard, pressed, uncooked-curd French cheese made with cow's milk. The taste is mild. This cheese can be classified in the category represented by Saint-Paulin cheese and similar types, though it is markedly superior to commercial versions of these cheeses in delicacy of flavour and texture.
Details on page 154.

Margotin aux Herbes
Rich, creamy, commercial fresh cheese, to which herbs are added; produced in the Perigord region of France.
Details on page 127.

Caprice des Dieux
A pasteurized cow's milk cheese enriched with 60% butterfat which comes from the Champagne country in France. The tender crust is covered in white rind flora, enclosing the soft creamy interior. The flavour is delicate but has plenty of character. Packaged in oval cardboard boxes, with an interior wrapping of perforated plasticized paper.
Details on page 106.

Coulommiers
A soft cow's milk cheese from the Île-de-France region, covered in white rind flora. The taste is mild, slightly acidulated when fresh but growing stronger as the cheese matures. Often sold on a straw mat, it is between a Brie and a Camembert in size and flavour.
Details on page 110.

Margotin au Poivre
A fresh French cheese given added flavouring with crushed peppercorns.
Details on page 127.

Bleu d'Auvergne
A French blue cheese made with whole cow's milk in the Auvergne. The paste is quite firm yet moist, fat and creamy with evenly-distributed greenish-blue veining of mould. The flavour and aroma – neither like Roquefort – are pronounced and quite strong. The shape of the cheeses may vary so the label is one's surest guide: genuine Bleu d'Auvergne will bear the words *Syndicat du véritable Bleu d'Auvergne.*
Details on page 99.

49

Lou Palou
This cheese from south-west France can be made with ewe's or cow's milk. The dry rind with its glossy black covering makes the cheese unmistakable. The paste is pressed and made from scalded curds. The flavour has a definite tang to it if ewe's milk is used, whereas the cow's milk cheeses are mild and restrained in taste.
Details on page 126.

Fourme d'Ambert
A French blue cheese produced in the Auvergne with cow's milk. The consistency is firm but soft, and the subtle, aromatic taste leaves a faint hint of bitterness. Smaller and fatter than other French blues. The greyish-blue mould develops in the cheese's large holes.
Details on page 116.

Pyramide Cendré
This French goat's milk cheese is shaped like a truncated pyramid. The surface of the cheese is rubbed and coated with ashes which tends to dry the cheese and helps to lower the acidity of the paste, making it sweeter and, apparently, easier to digest.
Details on page 140.

Crédioux aux Noix
A French processed cheese with walnuts pressed into the surface. Cheese made with cow's milk is the basic material used by the manufacturers.
Details on page 110.

Chamois d'Or
A fragrant French cheese rather like Brie, made with cow's milk enriched with cream. The paste is velvety and the crust is covered with white rind flora.
Details on page 108.

Grana Padano
A well-known cheese in Italy, where its integrity and quality are protected by an *appellation d'origine* – the system whereby not only the origin but specific methods of making the cheese are guaranteed, to protect the consumer. Grana is a hard cheese which comes from the Lombardy Plain, towards the north of the Po Valley. Like Parmesan, it is a classic grating cheese.
Details on page 120.

Pecorino Siciliano
Another cheese which is protected by an appellation of origin, Pecorino is made in Sicily with whole ewe's milk. It is a hard, uncooked cheese, flavoured with peppercorns on occasion and has a distinct, sharp taste. It is an excellent substitute for Parmesan.
Details on page 137.

Fiore Sardo
A hard ewe's milk cheese with a sharp taste, enjoying certification when produced in traditional factories; it is made throughout Sardinia by an old process common before the production of Pecorino Romano began on the island. Good for grating.
Details on page 115.

Provolone
Typical of the hard *pasta filata* – plastic-curd kneaded cow's milk cheeses, which were at one time only made in southern Italy. Production has now spread to other regions. When matured for 2–3 months the cheese has a delicate, buttery taste which becomes sharp when Provolone is aged for six months to two years or when goat's milk is used. The aged cheese is another excellent grating cheese.
Details on page 139.

Canestrato
A south Italian cheese traditionally made with ewe's milk but cow's milk is sometimes used. Usually strong or sharp tasting, becoming stronger when aged, the cheese retains the ridges which are formed when it is pressed in a wicker mould. Another Canestrato cheese is shown in the lower centre of this photograph, to which a differently shaped reed basket has given the curd its own form and imprint.
Details on page 105.

Ragusano
A typical Sicilian example of a hard *pasta filata*, Ragusano is a kneaded-curd cheese made from cow's milk. When ripened for a short time the result is a sweet and delicately flavoured sliceable cheese; when aged the taste becomes more pungent.
Details on page 141.

Canestrato
See description above.
Details on page 105.

Parmesan (Parmigiano-Reggiano)
This is the most widely famed member of the Grana family of cheeses, with a subtle yet distinct flavour, equally delicious when eaten by the piece or grated. Produced in certain provinces of Emilia and in parts of the Mantua region. A classic cheese protected by an appellation of origin guarantee.
Details on page 135.

Friulano
A semi-cooked (scalded-curd) pressed cheese produced in the Friuli countryside near Venice using cow's milk. If ripened for only a short time it resembles Montasio (a springy, pungent cheese); when matured the taste becomes extremely piquant.
Details on page 117.

Bel Paese
This is the registered trade name of a very popular cheese manufactured on a large scale and belonging to a range of semi-soft, uncooked cheeses made with whole cow's milk, given the official designation *Italico* – Italian type.
Details on page 98.

Fontal
This uncooked dessert cheese is produced in northern Italy and eastern France using whole cow's milk. It is very like Fontina but lacks the outstanding quality that cheese has when made in the Aosta Valley. Legislation has been passed to differentiate the two cheeses.
Details on page 115.

Fontina
A sliceable cheese which has been famous for centuries, produced in the Val d'Aosta, protected by certification of origin. This full fat, semi-cooked cheese calls for whole, unpasteurized cow's milk from a single milking to give a semi-hard, smooth and elastic consistency with a delicately sweet, buttery flavour.
Details on page 116.

Taleggio
A supple full-fat cheese produced according to specified traditional methods in many regions of Lombardy with whole cow's milk, fresh from milking. It has a distinctive, slightly aromatic taste. A cooked version is also found, made with pasteurized milk.
Details on page 150.

Gorgonzola
A full-flavoured uncooked soft cheese, to which an *appellation d'origine* applies and which is made from cow's milk in Lombardy and Piedmont. It is veined with a greenish-blue mould; these fissures of *Penicillium glaucum* lend a strong, somewhat spicy element to the bland, creamy paste. Mountain Gorgonzola is considered the best of all Gorgonzolas; Dolcelatte is a younger, sweeter version of basic Gorgonzola.
Details on page 118.

Quartirolo
A soft, uncooked pressed cheese made in Lombardy according to traditional methods on a small, non-industrialized scale and as a farmhouse cheese. It resembles the classic Taleggio but is matured in caves, which gives it a faint mushroomy flavour.
Details on page 141.

Caciotta di Pecora
Sweet and creamy cheese which is semi-soft and sliceable. Produced in Sardinia and central Italy from whole ewe's milk.
Details on page 104.

Caciocavallo
Spun-curd cheese typical of southern Italy made with whole cow's milk. The dessert variety has a sweet and delicate taste; when well-aged this cheese is used for grating and acquires a piquant, more pronounced taste.
Details on page 103.

Toscanello
A semi-hard ewe's milk cheese made in central Italy and in Sardinia. The flavour is not predictable, and may tend either towards sweetness or slight sharpness.
Details on page 153.

Asiago Pressato
A pressed dessert cheese which, in common with the other cheeses belonging to Asiago family, hails from the province of Vicenza and originated on the high Asiago plateau from which it takes its name. It has a delicate and pleasing taste.
Details on page 96.

Pecorino Romano
A world-famous cheese of guaranteed origin and officially controlled methods of production, Pecorino is perhaps the most ancient Italian cheese of all. Whole fresh ewe's milk is used to produce a hard cheese, with a sharp and instantly recognisable savour, ripened for at least eight months. Can be grated over hot food in the same way as Parmesan or served as a dessert or snack cheese.
Details on page 137.

Scamorza
Resembling Mozzarella but more dense, this is a spun-curd cheese made with cow's milk or mixed cow's and ewe's milk. Scamorza comes from southern Italy and is delicious when charcoal-grilled or spit-roasted.
Details on page 148.

Castelmagno
Made in the high valleys of Piedmont and classified as a blue cheese: it is aromatic with a mild, fresh taste when ripened for a short time, becoming sharper with age.
Details on page 107.

Young Lodigiano
Flavoursome slivers shaved off a Lodigiano cheese before it has started its ageing process to become a Grana variety.
Details on page 121.

Smoked Mozzarella
A buffalo milk cheese to which the smoking process gives a pleasing extra nuance of flavour. Now often Mozzarella is made with cow's milk.
Details on page 131.

Pannerone
This unveined, rich, creamy relation of Gorgonzola is a specialty of southern Lombardy. Also known as White Gorgonzola and as Gorgonzola Dolce, it is an uncooked cheese which matures quickly and has a very delicate taste with a slight tang and a hint of sharpness. Made from whole cow's milk, it does not usually undergo the salting process.
Details on page 134.

Matured Toma (Toma Stagionata)
Toma cheeses come from the Aosta Valley and Piedmont in northern Italy and the neighbouring French region of Haute-Savoie. Made from whole or partly-skimmed milk, their fat content depends on the milk used (usually cow's milk, sometimes mixed with goat's or ewe's milk).
Details on page 152.

Fresh Toma
This is the unmatured version of the aged Toma described above; it is ripened for a short time only and has a supple texture.
Details on page 152.

Smoked Scamorza
The same cheese as at the top left of this photograph, but lightly smoked, giving it a rustic texture and flavour.
Details of Scamorza cheeses on page 148.

Montasio
A full fat cooked-curd cheese from the Carnia region in the north-eastern province of Udine for which whole cow's milk is used. When the cheese is ripened for only a short time the texture is firm though pliable: when aged for up to 2 years the texture becomes hard and brittle and the taste changes from mild and nutty to appetizingly sharp.
Details on page 130.

Buffalo Milk Mozzarella
A spun-curd soft cheese which is typical of southern Italy. It has a very mild, slightly acidulated taste and should be eaten as soon as possible after purchasing, since it deteriorates rapidly. *Details on page 131.*

Fior di Latte
The official designation for a Mozzarella-type spun-curd cheese made with cow's milk, which in this illustration has been shaped into a plait. *Details on page 114.*

Robiola Fresca
Fresh, soft cheese manufactured by coagulating cow's milk with lactic acid. The curd is often enriched by the addition of extra butterfat or cream. *Details on page 143.*

Robiolini Freschi
These small, soft cheeses are produced from cow's milk but are often referred to as *caprini* – 'little goats' – a survival from the days when they were made with goat's milk. *Details on page 144.*

Piedmont Ricotta (Ricotta Piemontese)
Traditionally a low-fat cheese made from cow's milk whey; nowadays whole or partially skimmed milk is sometimes added. *Details on page 142.*

Ricotta Romana
After the manufacture of *Pecorino Romano*, the leftover whey is used to make this by-product, often used for pasta stuffings and tart or open pie fillings. *Details on page 142.*

Robiolino Stagionato
If Robiolino is cured it acquires a more pronounced flavour, and the texture becomes crumbly. *Details on page 144.*

Tomino Fresco (Fresh Tomino)
A cheese made in Piedmont and the Aosta Valley from cow's milk, the curd being uncooked. It has a delicate, lactic taste. *Details on page 152.*

Mascarpone
This cheese, which is like very thick, velvety cream in texture, has a delectable, buttery quality with a sweet flavour. Sometimes layered with a blue cheese. *Details on page 128.*

Crescenza
Made with pasteurized cow's milk, the curd of which is not cooked. It is a spreadable cheese with a delicious, delicately creamy taste and a melting texture on the palate. *Details on page 110.*

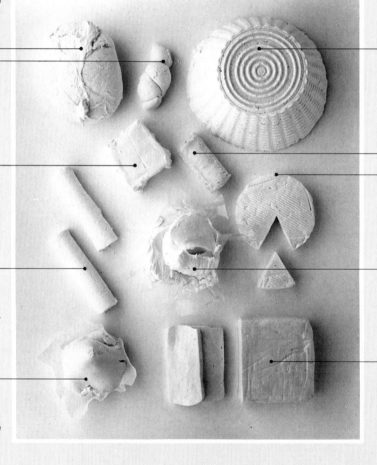

Emmental
One of the heavyweights of the cheese world, not only in size but also in its worldwide reputation for outstanding quality. Made in central (German-speaking) Switzerland with whole cow's milk. The curd is cooked and pressed during the making process and the finished cheese's texture is firm and slightly springy with large, roundish holes. Rich, golden Emmental has a well-balanced taste, being fruity without sharpness and pleasantly nutty in flavour. Genuine Swiss Emmental cheeses have 'Switzerland' stamped in red in radiating lines all round the rind. *Details on page 113.*

Appenzell
A full-fat whole cow's milk cheese produced in the Swiss canton of Appenzell and in some neighbouring areas. The rind is given several washings in a brine containing not only salt but white wine as well as pepper and spices and this makes the cheese particularly highly flavoured with a pleasant tang. *Details on page 94.*

Walliser
Belonging to the family of Raclette cheeses, made with whole cow's milk and owes its family name (literally 'a scraper') to the traditional practice of setting it before a fire and eating it when melted. *Details on page 155.*

Sbrinz
A classic hard Swiss cow's milk cheese, for which the curd is cooked and then pressed. It is aromatic, extremely flavoursome and grates well, but is also served on occasion as a dessert cheese. *Details on page 147.*

Gruyère
In terms of production, this is the second most important Swiss cheese after Emmental, and it is made with whole cow's milk in the Cantons of Fribourg, Neufchâtel and Vaud. The flavour is both delicate and exquisitely tasty, slightly sweeter than Emmental but with a similarly nutty aroma. It is a wonderful cooking cheese (both in the famous *Fondue* and in a wide range of sauces) and Gruyère is equally good for eating. *Details on page 121.*

Tête-de-Moine
The uncooked pressed curd from cow's milk produced in the Bernese Jura ripens into a firm cheese which owes its name ('Monk's Head') to the yearly payment local farmers had to make of one cheese for each monk at Bellelay Abbey, where the cheese was invented.
Details on page 151.

Schabzieger (Sapsago)
This cheese has been made for centuries in Glarus, Switzerland, from skimmed cow's milk or whey, flavoured with chopped blue melilot. **Kräuterkäse.** It is very hard and dry and is used for grating.
Details on page 148.

Vacherin Mont-d'Or
A rich, creamy full-fat cheese which is made in both France and Switzerland from cow's milk. The flavour is deliciously sweet, the paste soft, and the aroma delicately resinous.
Details on page 154.

Vacherin Fribourgeois
Made in the Swiss canton of Fribourg with cow's milk. Not at all like its namesake from Mont-d'Or, this cheese has a firmish texture, though not as firm as Gruyère, and a more pronounced taste. During the making, the curd is cooked and lightly pressed.
Details on page 117.

Saanenkäse
A highly-prized and much sought-after Swiss cheese which is aged for a very long time and produced in very small quantities. The cow's milk curd is cooked and pressed and eventually the cheese matures into a very hard, fragrant delicacy which can be grated or cut off in shavings as a dessert cheese.
Details on page 145.

Val di Muggio
An uncooked Swiss cheese made from cow's milk.
Details on page 154.

Bruscion
A goat's milk cheese manufactured in Switzerland. Its taste is easily recognisable – strong, acidulated and slightly piquant.
Details on page 103.

Tomme Vaudoise
A small, soft cheese made in the Swiss canton of Vaud with whole or partially skimmed cow's milk. The texture is uniform and quite dense with a thin rind covered with white mould.
Details on page 152.

Formaggella della Val Bavona
These little uncooked Swiss cheeses made with cow's milk have a softish consistency and a delicate taste.
Details on page 116.

Chabichou
A goat's milk cheese from Switzerland which resembles the French cheese of the same name in taste and texture but has a snowy bloom on its rind.
Details on page 108.

Piora
This cheese comes from the Ticino, the Italian-speaking region of Switzerland, and is made with whole cow's milk, sometimes mixed with a little goat's milk. The curd is pressed and the cheeses are matured for 3 to 6 months.
Details on page 138.

Klosterkäse
Partially skimmed cow's milk is used to make this soft, closely-textured German cheese. Either round or oblong in shape, the surface is coated with dark wax. This cheese was originally a monastery cheese and it has a mildish, sweet flavour.
Details on page 124.

Rham Brie
The German version of the original French Brie cheese, but with a higher fat content than the genuine article.
Details on page 141.

Rham Camembert
This German version of Camembert is made from milk with a higher fat content than the original, classic French cheese.
Details on page 141.
(For Camembert see pages 44 and 105.)

Weichkäse
This is the generic name for German surface-ripened soft cheeses which develop a snow white bloom or a dark, blueish-black mould on their crust depending on the variety. The example shown has a delicate, very palatable taste.
Details on page 156.

Bavarian Emmental
This German version of the famous Swiss cheese is produced by following the original processes as closely as possible and similarity in organic composition and texture has been achieved without presenting a serious challenge to classic Emmental in taste.
Details of Emmental on page 113.

Bergader
An uncooked blue cheese for which the German producers use cow's milk. The blue-green veining produced by the action of the mould adds a spicy element to its strong taste.
Details on page 98.

Alpsbergkäse
Also known under the names of **Bergkäse** and **Alpenkäse,** this is a German cooked-curd hard-pressed cheese made with whole cow's milk. It has a well-defined but subtle flavour and is not at all sharp.
Details on page 94.

Edelpilzkäse
A blue cheese produced in
Germany and Austria with
cow's milk. The paste has
blueish-green veining of
mould in small fissures.
Details on page 112.

Doppelrhamstufe
A soft German cheese with
a very high fat content,
made with cow's milk. The
name actually means
double-cream cheese.
Details on page 111.

Echtermainzerkäse
A soft German cheese
made with skimmed cow's
milk. When unmatured it is
mild but grows considerably
stronger in aroma and taste
as it ripens.
Details on page 112.

Limburger
A soft washed-rind cheese
which originally came from
Belgium, made with
pasteurized cow's milk, but
production has now spread
to other European countries
(Germany and Austria
being the largest
producers) and to the USA.
The paste is homogenous
with a decided, rich flavour.
*Details on page 125
(Limbourg, Limburger).*

Geheimratskäse
Semi-hard cheese from
Germany and Austria which
has a delicate flavour, the
texture being dense and
smooth with small,
scattered holes.
Details on page 118.

**Weichkäse mit
Champignons**
This soft German surface-
ripened cheese gains
flavour and texture from the
addition of mushrooms. It
has a high moisture content
and a mild taste.
Details on page 156.

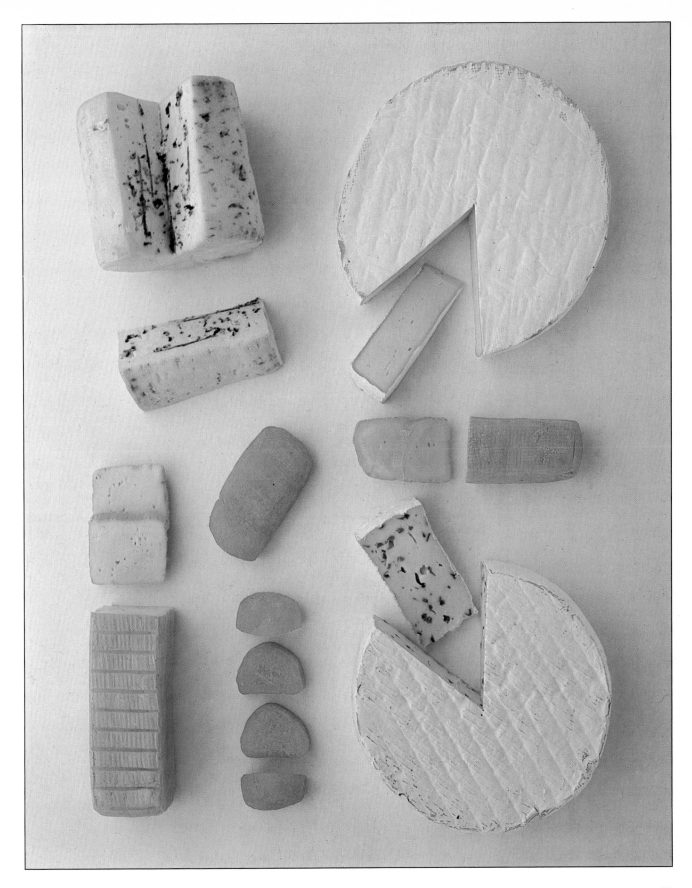

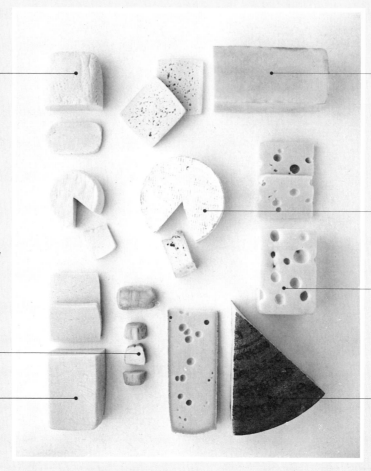

Butterkäse
Both Germany and Austria manufacture this cow's milk cheese, the paste of which is soft, dense and supple. Two shapes are illustrated, one (top, left) being oblong and the one below it disc-shaped.
Details on page 103.

Romadur
A Bavarian cow's milk cheese; besides being produced in south Germany it is also made over the border in Austria and in other central European countries such as Czechoslovakia. The texture of the cheese is soft and it has a full, strong taste.
Details on page 144.

Edamer
A German version of the well-known Dutch Edam cheese, made by following the original cheese's manufacturing technique, but marketed in rindless forms and sometimes packaged in coloured wrappings.
Details of Edam on page 112.

Tilsit, Tilsiter
Both oblong and cylindrical shaped cheeses of this type are produced in Germany and several central European countries. It is made with raw or pasteurized cow's milk; the unmatured cheeses have a mildly acidulated taste which becomes sharper as the cheese ages.
Details on page 151.

Edelblankkäse
A soft German cheese which is mild when young but grows sharper and stronger when matured for any length of time.
Details on page 112.

Austrian Emmental
An Austrian version of the famous Swiss cheese; produced on a highly-industrialized scale, the cheese is vacuum packed in plastic film before maturing.
Details of classic Swiss Emmental on page 113.

Bergkäse
A cooked, pressed cheese with an aromatic flavour typical of those cheeses produced in Austrian mountain regions.
Details on page 98.

Bou de Fagne
Belgian cow's milk cheese.
The interior of the cheese
has infrequently spaced
small holes and a pleasant
aroma, and it is covered by
a thin, slightly bloomy rind.
Details on page 100.

Bouquet des Moines
A firm, homogenously
textured Belgian cow's milk
cheese with a subtle,
delicate flavour.
Details on page 100.

Trou de Sottai
Belgian cow's milk cheese,
with a soft buttery texture.
Details on page 153.

Prince-Jean
A small soft Belgian cheese
made with cow's milk. The
paste is homogenous with
very few holes and a
pleasant aroma; the rind
has patches of white bloom.
Details on page 139.

Passendale
An easily recognisable soft,
uncooked Belgian cheese
with small irregular holes.
Made with cow's milk.
Details on page 136.

Folies de Béguines
Belgian cow's milk cheese
with an unusual shape, like
a cake or bun with pinched,
irregular edges. The texture
is soft and the taste
appealingly pronounced.
Details on page 115.

Frisia
A Dutch uncooked pressed cheese made with whole or partially skimmed cow's milk. Spiced with cloves and cumin.
Details on page 117.

Baby Edam
A smaller version of the classic Dutch cheese left uncoated with paraffin wax, and with a hint of sharpness in its taste.
Details of Edam on page 112.

Leyden
A hard Dutch cheese made with partially skimmed cow's milk. It has a full, well-defined taste, and is spiced with cumin or caraway.
Details on page 125.

Maasdam
A recent introduction to mass-produced Dutch cheeses marketed on a large scale under various trade marks. The paste has large holes produced by gas given off by bacteria trapped in the paste while the cheese is ripening. It has a slightly nutty aftertaste, though the flavour is otherwise mild.
Details on page 126.

Edam
The most famous Dutch cheese after Gouda. Made with partially skimmed cow's milk, the taste changes depending on the length of maturation. The cheeses which are exported are covered by a protective coating of red paraffin wax over a yellow rind.
Details on page 112.

Kernhem
A very soft cheese (the paste clings to the knife when cut) made in the Netherlands with whole cow's milk. The mild and delicate taste becomes fuller and stronger as the cheese ripens.
Details on page 124.

Gouda
This world-famous Dutch cheese owes its renown to its consistently high quality. It is a semi-hard cow's milk cheese which is mild when young but acquires strength and sharpness if allowed to mature. Excellent for cooking.
Details on page 119.

Tybo
A Danish cheese made with cow's milk, supple in texture, with a few scattered holes and a delicate, slightly acidulated taste.
Details on page 153.

Samsø
Called after the Danish island of the same name, this is a pressed whole cow's milk cheese with a firm texture and sparsely scattered round holes; the flavour is mild and sweet, yet decided.
Details on page 146.

Danablu
Whole raw cow's milk is used to make this Danish blue cheese. The taste is strong, spicy and sharp, and is a perfect substitute for Roquefort in culinary use.
Details on page 110.

Danbo (Dessert quality)
When matured for a short time, this Danish cheese is traditionally served in slices to round off a meal. Made with whole or partially skimmed cow's milk; the supple paste has a lightly acidulated flavour.
Details on page 111.

Elbo
This hard Danish cheese is made with cow's milk. The paste is broken by round, regular holes and the flavour is mild and delicate.
Details on page 113.

Havarti
Usally made in rectanguar shapes; the taste of this partially skimmed Danish cow's milk cheese is aromatic and mildly acidulated. The paste is scattered with irregular holes and the surface of the cheese is sometimes coated with wax.
Details on page 122.

Molbo
The region of Mols, in Denmark, is the home of this cheese made with pasteurized cow's milk. The texture is firm with sparse round holes. The taste is mild with a hint of acidulation. The cheese's surface is usually coated with a layer of paraffin wax.
Details on page 129.

Fynbo
Bland in flavour, like so many other Danish cheeses, Fynbo is made with pasteurized cow's milk and has very few holes. The rind is usually coated in wax.
Details on page 117.

Esrom
Danish cow's milk cheese with a firm yet supple paste; it has a full, fruity flavour with a pleasing hint of sharpness.
Details on page 113.

Maribo
A semi-hard Danish cheese made with pasteurized cow's milk. The flavour is aromatic and quite strong. The paste is liberally sprinkled with irregular holes, and the rind is usually encased in yellow wax.
Details on page 127.

Sveciaost
A hard cow's milk cheese
made in Sweden; the taste
varies from mild to sharp.
Herbs are often added to
the cheese and this variety
is called *Kryddost*.
Details on page 150.

Graddost
A scalded-curd whole cow's
milk cheese from Sweden.
Details on page 120.

Västerbottenost
Swedish scalded-curd
cow's milk cheese, the
texture of which is dense
and hard with tiny holes.
The taste is strong and
assertive. The dry rind is
protected by a layer of
paraffin wax.
Details on page 155.

Port Salutost
A Swedish version of the
French Saint-Paulin
cheese.
*Details of Saint-Paulin on
page 146.*

Ridder
A semi-hard cow's milk
cheese made in Sweden
and Norway. The curd is
uncooked and pressed.
Details on page 143.

Prästost
Semi-hard Swedish cheese
made with cow's milk, with
a few very irregular holes.
Details on page 139.

Drabant
A bland Swedish cow's milk
cheese often served for
breakfast.
Details on page 112.

Hushållsost
A scalded-curd Swedish
cow's milk cheese with a
delicate taste.
Details on page 123.

Herrgårdsost
Partially skimmed cow's
milk is used for this mild,
slightly nutty quality
Swedish cheese.
Details on page 122.

Edamerost
The Swedes' version of the
classic Dutch Edam
cheese, which it resembles
quite closely in flavour,
shape, and consistency of
paste. The rind is also
coated with red paraffin
wax.
*Details of Edam on page
112.*

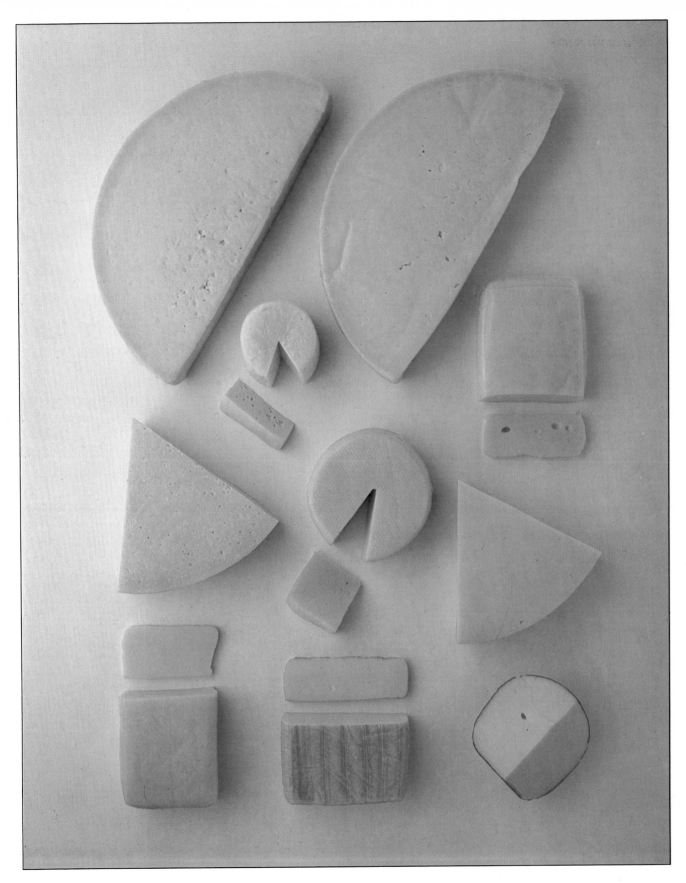

Leicester
A hard English cheese made with whole cow's milk and coloured with annatto: this gives the cheese its glowing orange colour.
Details on page 125.

Lancashire
An English cheese made with whole cow's milk. It has a sharp slightly sour flavour and crumbly texture; excellent for rarebits and other culinary uses.
Details on page 124.

Double Gloucester
A dense, English cheese made with cow's milk. The flavour is rich and mellow. The near-extinct Single Gloucester is made with some skimmed milk.
Details on page 111.

Derby
An uncooked, hard cow's milk cheese. Similar to Cheddar. Sage Derby is most popular.
Details on page 111.

Caerphilly
Originally a Welsh cheese, now mainly produced in the west of England with cow's milk. The paste has a crumbly, moist texture and the cheese, like many other English varieties, is wheel-shaped. Slightly acidic but rich farmyardy flavour. Goes 'off' very quickly.
Details on page 104.

Cheshire
A typical hard English cheese. Its fragrance and unmistakable flavour derived originally from the milk of cows grazed on the salty pastures of the Cheshire plain. White Cheshire is also available and Blue Cheshire is thought by many to be one of the finest cheeses: nutty and fragrant.
Details on page 109.

Dunlop
A Scottish cheese which is rather like Cheddar, though with a softer paste and less 'bite' to its taste.
Details on page 112.

Stilton
A highly-prized semi-hard English blue cheese, the flavour evolving from mild with a slight tang when the cheese is relatively young, to rich and spicy when mature.
Details on page 149.

Cheddar
Originally an English cheese, its production has now spread to many other countries, especially to Ireland, Australasia and the USA. It is a scalded-curd cheese, made with whole cow's milk, either pasteurized or raw. The texture is dense and the cheese has an agreeably nutty flavour. Farmhouse Cheddar must be at least 6 months old before being sold, and some are kept as long as 2 years.
Details on page 108.

Aragón
A distinctively shaped
Spanish cheese for which a
mixture of ewe's and goat's
milk is used.
Details on page 95.

Villalón
A fresh, mild Spanish
cheese made from ewe's
milk, which also goes by
the name of 'Pata de Mulo'
(Mule's Hoof), suggested
by its original shape, and
still occasionally adopted in
the case of farmhouse
production when the curd is
rolled up in a cheesecloth.
Details on page 155.

Roncal
A strong-tasting ewe's milk
cheese made in Navarra
(Spain): it has many
similarities with Manchego.
Details on page 144.

Cabrales
Also known by the name of
Picón, this Spanish blue
cheese has a strong, sharp
taste and a very decided,
distinctive aroma. The
cheese is wrapped in
sycamore leaves when it is
cured; the paste gradually
becomes streaked with
greenish-blue veins.
Details on page 103.

Mahón
A semi-hard Spanish
cheese made mainly in the
Balearic Islands
(particularly Minorca) with
cow's and ewe's milk. The
uncooked, pressed cheese
has a slightly acid, salty
flavour.
Details on page 126.

Castellano
An uncooked hard ewe's milk cheese from Spain. The taste is strong.
Details on page 107.

San Simón
A Spanish cow's milk cheese which is pear-shaped and smoked. The paste is dense and homogenous.
Details on page 147.

Burgos
A ewe's milk cheese from Spain which is traditionally cylindrical; nowadays it is also produced in block form as shown in this illustration. The close-textured paste is sometimes cracked and fissured and has no rind.
Details on page 103.

Torta del Casar
A pressed Spanish cheese made with ewe's milk: it is crumbly in consistency.
Details on page 152.

Selva
Pasteurized cow's milk is used for this Spanish pressed-curd cheese. The paste is supple and slightly salty in flavour.
Details on page 148.

Tupi
This is not actually a cheese but a Spanish mixture of grated well-aged ewe's milk cheeses mixed and blended with oil and alcohol. The result is very strong and savoury. Sold in glass jars.
Details on page 153.

Idiazabal
Spanish ewe's milk cheese. Smoked and hard with a waxy texture.
Details on page 123.

Tetilla
A Spanish cow's milk cheese made in a distinctive pear shape. The savoury, flavoursome paste is slightly acidulated.
Details on page 151.

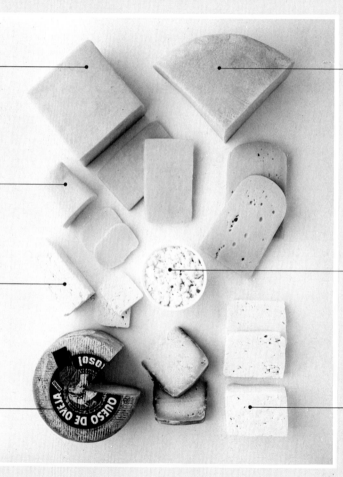

American Cheddar
Manufactured on a very large industrial scale in the United States using cow's milk, American Cheddar resembles the original English version at a technical level rather than in genuine flavour.
Details of Cheddar on page 108.

Pizza Cheese
A spun or plastic curd cheese produced in the United States as a cooking cheese for the preparation of pizzas. It is not unlike Italian Mozzarella cheese but has a firmer consistency.
Details on page 138.

Feta
A rindless Greek cheese cured in brine, now made in many other countries, including Scotland, France, Denmark and Bulgaria. It is mainly eaten as a slicing cheese but also used in cooking and salads. The flavour is sharp and salty.
Details on page 114.

Manchego
A famous ewe's milk cheese which comes from the plain of La Mancha in Spain (Don Quixote's countryside). It is a hard, pressed cheese which is aged for varying lengths of time and has a strong, unmistakable and oustandingly sapid flavour. During the ripening process the rind is covered with a blue-black mould.
Details on page 127.

Irish Gloucester
The Irish product emulates the original English Double Gloucester; it is also made with cow's milk.
Details of Double Gloucester on page 111.

Cottage Cheese
Enormous quantities of this soft, white unripened cheese are produced throughout the world. It is very popular due to its low fat and sugar content. The size of the bland curds varies, and they go well with a wide selection of flavourings.
Details on page 109.

Telemea
A Rumanian cheese usually made with pasteurized ewe's milk. Ripened in a brine of soured whey and salt in barrels, it somewhat resembles Feta and also has no rind.
Details on page 151.

ACKNOWLEDGEMENTS

The publishers wish to acknowledge the assistance of the following organizations:

Consorzio del Formaggio Parmigiano Reggiano, Reggio Emilia; Consorzio per la Tutela del Formaggio Grana Padano, Milan; Confédération Générale del Producteurs de Lait de Brebis et des Industriels de Roquefort, Millau (Aveyron), France; Lallemand Publicité, Paris; Istituto di Microbiologia della Facoltà di Agraria dell'Università Cattolica, Piacenza; Sopexa, Milan; Centro Marketing delle Industrie Casearie Danesi, Como; Het Nederlands Zuivelbureau, Rijswijk, Holland; I.D. Studio – Drs W.A. van Meeuwen, Milan; Buhllmann & Co. s.r.l., Milan; Centro Commerciale di Svezia, Milan; Ufficio Irlandese per il Commercio Estero, Milan; Sig. Luciano Nelli, Milan; CMA Italia, Milan; Bayernland-Vipiteno, s.r.l., Vipiteno (Bolzano); Interform, Milan; Peri G.m.b.H., Bolzano; Franco Parolari, Agente Primolait, Offanengo/Crema; Publidan Wirz, Milan; La Tavola Tedesca, Milan.

Acknowledgements for quoted matter:
p. 12 *Decameron*, Boccaccio, translated by Richard Aldington, Granada Publishing Ltd, London.

Picture credits

t(op)
b(ottom)
l(eft)
r(ight)

The photographs on pages 42–91 were specially taken for this book by Marzia Malli and Paolo Belloni, Milan. *Cover photograph* by Giuseppe Zarini, Milan.
Other photographs: pp. 10 b, 14, Giorgio Lotti (Mondadori Archives, Milan); 10–11, 13, 15, 19, Mondadori Archives, Milan, 17, Michel-Charles Gaffier, by courtesy of Lallemand Publicité, Paris, and the Confédération Générale des Producteurs de Lait de Brebis et des Industriels de Roquefort; 23 t, 31 b, Marcella Pedone, Milan; 23 b, Claudio Patriarca, Rome: 25 l, Fotocolor Fiore, Turin; 25 r, Claudio Patriarca, Rome; 26 t, M.-C. Gaffier, by courtesy of Lallemand Publicité, Paris, and the Confédération Générale des Producteurs de Lait de Brebis et des Industriels de Roquefort; 26 b, by courtesy of the Consorzio per la Tutela del Formaggio Grana Padano, Milan; 27, Photo Gian Paolo Cavallero, Savona; 28–29, Claudio Patriarca, Rome; 30, by courtesy of the Consorzio per la Tutela del Formaggio Grana Padano, Milan; 31 t, G. Lotti (Mondadori Archives, Milan); 33, Gilles Walusinski, by courtesy of Lallemand Publicité, Paris and the Confédération Générale des Producteurs de Lait de Brebis et des Industriels de Roquefort; 36 l, by courtesy of the Istituto di Microbiologia della Facoltà di Agraria dell'Università Cattolica, Piacenza; 36 r, Marzia Malli and Paolo Belloni, Milan; 37, Teubner Studio, Füssen, 38, by courtesy of the Consorzio del Formaggio Parmigiano Reggiano, Reggio Emilia; 39, Agence Nature, Chamalières; 164, by courtesy of the Instituto di Microbiologia della Facoltà di Agraria dell'Università Cattolica, Piacenza.

Dictionary of world cheeses

Aarey

This is a semi-hard, rindless cheese made near Bombay, India, from whole buffalo milk. It is somewhat similar in flavour to Gouda but has small, round holes which are evenly distributed.

Abgesottener

An Austrian cheese for which skimmed cow's milk is used; the earlier stages of production follow the same procedure as for making Quark.

Once the curd has formed, using the Quark technique, it is broken up and kept at a temperature of 20°C (68°F), being turned daily until it acquires a uniform texture; salt is added and the curd is then heated in a vat by direct steam or by hot air in double-bottomed vats.

Abgesottener is then cooked in moulds or *becker* to produce cheeses weighing 200 g (7 oz), 400 g (14 oz) or 1 kg (2.2 lb). The cheese is golden-yellow with 70% water, 10% fat and 16% protein.

Ädelost

This cheese is made in Sweden and Finland with whole cow's milk. It is a blue cheese, with greeny-blue veining on the inside and exterior of the paste; the consistency is homogenous and soft to semi-hard, the rind soft and thin. It is ripened for two months.

Ädelost is wheel-shaped, 8–9 in (20–22 cm) in diameter and 5½–6½ in (14–16 cm) high. It contains 44% water, 28% fat and 25% protein.

Agrafa

A Greek hard cheese similar in certain aspects to Gruyère. It is made from ewe's milk and has few holes and a dry rind.

Agrini

A soft Swiss cheese made with cow's or goat's milk; the cheeses are small

and cylindrical, weighing 1½–2 oz (40–60g), just over 1 inch (3 cm) in diameter and 1 inch (3 cm) high. The making of the cheese entails the use of lactic acid as a curdling agent and the curd is drained without being broken up or cut. The flavour is fresh and pleasantly acidulated.

Alcobaça

Semi-hard Portuguese variety made from ewe's milk. The wheel-shaped cheeses, weighing about 7oz (220 g), measure 3 in (8 cm) in diameter and are 1½ in (4 cm) high. The consistency is smooth and even with a thin, dry rind with patches of bloom. Very white in colour, it contains 45% water, 30% fat and 20% protein.

Alicante

Made in the province of the same name in Spain, from goat's milk. This is a fresh, rindless cheese; the paste is smooth and white.

Coagulation is usually achieved using rennet; the whey is drained from the curd in a vat and the curd is then placed in moulds to drain further for a few hours. It is either eaten fresh, or stored (very briefly) in a weak brine of water with 10% salt. The cheese contains 58–60% water, 15% fat and 20% protein.

Alpin

A soft, dense French cow's milk cheese rather like Vacherin Mont-d'Or but lacking a rind. The milk is coagulated at 79–83°F (26–28°C) with rennet; the curd is placed in circular moulds 3–4½ in (8–10 cm) wide and 1–2 in (3–5 cm) deep. After draining and turning, the cheese is dry-salted and ripened for 7–8 days.

Contains 55% water, 21% fat and 21% protein.

Alpbergkäse

A cooked German whole cow's milk cheese with a dense, dry rind; the paste has sparse, medium-sized holes and the taste is well-defined. The wheel-shaped cheeses weigh between 42–64 lb (20–30 kg). Composition: 40% water, 27% fat and 24–25% protein.

Altay

Russian hard cow's milk cheese with medium-sized holes; the rind is hard and dry. The cheeses vary in weight from approximately 25 lb (12 kg) to 42 lb (20 kg).

Water content is 42%, fat 28–30% and protein 22–24%.

Altenburger

Produced in the Altenburg region of East Germany from goat's milk, sometimes mixed with cow's milk.

A round, flat cheese 4½ in (11.5 cm) in diameter and 1–1¼ in (2.8–3 cm) thick. Production techniques are along the general lines of those used for most soft cheeses with a thin rind producing white flora (such as Camembert).

Four types are made in which the fat content varies and the cheeses are graded accordingly: the 'half fat' (*Halbfettstufe*) cheeses contain 66% water, 7% fat and 25% protein; the 'three-quarter fat' cheeses (*Dreiviertelfettstufe*) contain 62% water, 10.5% fat and 21% protein; and the 'fat' cheeses contain 58% water, 17% fat and 21% protein. 'Full fat' cheeses contain 56% water, 20% fat and 20% protein.

The rind is covered with a white bloom and the paste of the cheese is white, smooth and creamy without any holes; the flavour is strong.

Also known as **Altenburger Ziegenkäse** (Altenburg Goat's Milk Cheese).

Alvorca

A hard Portuguese ewe's milk cheese, the rounds of cheese weighing 7–10 oz (200–300 g) with a dry, russet rind covering a dense paste; used for grating.

Composition is: 25% water, 37% fat and 33% protein.

Ancien Impérial

This can be classified under the general heading of the French *carré* cheeses and as this name would suggest, Ancien Impérial is square; it can be eaten fresh or ripened. Whole cow's milk is used and the resulting cheese is soft and mild.

Appenzell (Appenzeller)

Named after the Swiss canton of Appenzell, this whole cow's milk cheese was originally made in the Abbey of St. Gallen in north-eastern Switzerland; it is also produced in the Canton of Turgovia.

The wheel-shaped cheeses measure 12 in (30 cm) in diameter and 3½ in (9 cm) in height, weighing from 12¾ lb (6 kg) to 17 lb (8 kg). The paste is fat and pale straw in colour, with sparse holes measuring up to ¼ in (3–5 mm) in diameter; the rind is dense with a yellowish-brown mould. Production techniques follow the classic method for semi-cooked cheeses like Fontina and Tilsit. The cheese is cured for 4–6 months in cool conditions with 85–90% humidity, and the cheeses are turned regularly in a brine of water, white wine, salt, pepper and spices. This treatment confers the characteristically pronounced aroma which makes these cheeses so delicious.

Appenzell contains 43% water, 28% fat and 26% protein.

The arms of the Appenzell canton show a bear rampant and this is the sign to look for on the label of a genuine cheese: the reputation of Appenzell is officially protected by a special authority with its headquarters at St. Gallen. It is said that this cheese, which was once only made in the high Alpine pastures, was particularly prized by the Emperor Charlemagne for its intense, slightly bitter but delectable flavour.

Aragackij

A round, sliceable cheese from Armenia, made with a mixture of ewe's and goat's milk.

The raw milk is left to curdle for 30 minutes at a temperature of 86–95°F (30–35°C) and then the whey is drawn off and drained from the curd at 104–107°F (40–42°C). This curd is placed in moulds, pressed, and salted by immersion in brine. The cheese is matured for 2 months, initially at a temperature of 59–60°F (15–16°C) with 90% humidity and then at a temperature of 50–53°F (10–12°C) with reduced humidity. Aragackij has a thin dark, greenish-blue rind.

The cheese contains 40% water, 30% fat and 25% protein.

Aragón
also known as Tronchón

This is a semi-hard Spanish cheese made with ewe's or goat's milk or a mixture of the two. The cheese is made by curdling the milk with animal rennet or extract of thistle flowers at a temperature of 95°F (35°C) over 40 minutes. The curd is then cut into small pieces, drained, placed in special conical moulds and hand pressed. It is then dry salted and

allowed to ripen for a week in a humid atmosphere. The paste of the cheese is firm with a few small holes or no holes at all, covered by a supple rind.

Armada
also known as Calostro

A Spanish uncooked cheese made from milk of the first milking after the cow has calved (beestings or colostrum, hence the alternative name), and matured in cool conditions for two months. It has a sharp taste.

Asiago d'Allevo

A semi-fat, scalded-curd cheese which takes its name from the mountain plateau of Asiago in the Italian province of Vicenza. Skimmed evening milk is mixed with whole morning milk, or sometimes partially skimmed milk from just one milking is used. The name and origin of the cheese are regulated by law, limiting approved production zones to the provinces of Vicenza, Trento and certain areas in the provinces of Padua and Treviso.

The cheeses are wheel-shaped, 3½–5 in (9–12 cm) thick, 12–14 in (30–34 cm) in diameter and vary from 17–25½ lb (8–12 kg) in weight, depending on production methods and ageing. This can last as long as two years, and the cheeses are graded *mezzano*, *vecchio* and *stravecchio*.

The evening milk is poured into special bowls and left to stand for 10–12 hours at a temperature of 60–64°F (16–18°C), so that the fat content can separate and the milk

ripen, resulting in higher acidity.

The evening milk is then separated from the cream and transferred to a vat, together with the morning's milk, and heated to 89–93°F (32–34°C). A starter of lactic acid-producing bacteria culture is introduced to the heated milk. A curd is produced by coagulating the milk with liquid or powdered rennet; for a firm curd, cutting continues until the pieces are about the size of sweet corn grains. This curd is then cooked at 104–113°F (40–45°C) for 20–40 minutes; subsequently it undergoes a second cooking process, this time at 114–118°F (46–48°C). The curd is then gathered up into cheesecloths, placed in moulds and pressed for 24 hours. After 3 or 4 days the emergent Asiago is dry-salted and it is then time for the ageing process to begin under cool conditions (at a temperature of 59–60°F/15–16°C).

Asiago d'Allevo has a thin, smooth, glossy rind without any marks and yellowish-buff in colour; as the cheese matures this turns reddish-brown. The paste is very firm and granular in texture with a few evenly-distributed small or medium-sized holes; it is a pale straw colour and has a subtle fragrance. As the cheese is aged it becomes sharper. Both the unaged and matured Asiagos make very good table cheeses and when well-matured grate well for use in cooking.

The minimum fat content in dry matter is 24%, but the fat content is normally much higher than this.

Asiago Grasso Monte

A semi-soft cooked-curd cheese made during the summer months on the Asiago plateau in the foothills of the Dolomites. The raw whole cow's milk is coagulated at a temperature of 95–98°F (35–37°C) over a period of 30–40 minutes and the curd is then broken up into pieces approximately ½ in (1 cm) square; it is then cooked at 118–123°F (48–52°C), placed in moulds and dry-salted and matured for 30–50 days. The paste of the cheese is pale straw in colour with numerous holes, and has a delicate taste.

Asiago Pressato

This is a scalded-curd cow's milk cheese, wheel-shaped (12–13½ in – 30–40 cm in diameter and 4½–6 in – 11–15 cm thick), and weighing on average 23½–32 lb (11–15 kg).

The milk is coagulated in the same way as for Asiago d'Allevo; its preparation differs in that the curd is drained of its whey and then dry salted before being placed in the moulds, when it is pressed. The cheeses ripen in a cool atmosphere (60–64°F : 16–18°C) for anything from 20 to 40 days.

Asiago Pressato has a thin, elastic rind and the paste is white or a very pale straw colour with abundant irregular holes; the taste is pleasantly mild and delicate.

The fat content averages 23%, water 37% and protein 33%.

Aura

A Finnish semi-soft whole cow's milk cheese with greenish-blue veining throughout; the average weight of this cheese is slightly in excess of 5½ lb (2.5 kg).

Composition of the cheese is 44–45% water, 27–28% fat and 23–24% protein.

Azul

The name for this popular cheese made in Latin America and Denmark simply means 'Blue', and it is similar to commercially produced Danish Blue. It is made from pasteurized, homogenized cow's milk. The paste is dense with greenish-blue veining and the taste is rather strong.

The water content is usually 40–42% (rising as high as 50% in Denmark); fat content is 30–31% and protein 20–22%.

Babybel, Mini Babybel

These well-known soft, whole cow's milk cheeses are really French versions of the Dutch Edam cheese, having the same smooth, homogenous paste and red wax covering.

Bagozzo

A cooked-curd semi-fat cow's milk cheese made in much the same way as the Grana family of cheeses and resembling them in texture. The paste is yellow and very hard with a strong sharp flavour; the rind is usually coloured red.

Bagozzo is the Italianized form of the dialect word *bagoss* meaning 'from Bagolino', the mountain village in the high valley of Caffaro where most of this cheese is produced. The local people claim the cheese has aphrodisiac properties and call it 'the cheese of love'.

A traditional method of preparing the cheese to bring out its full flavour and aroma is slicing and grilling it.

Bakers'

Produced in the USA and widely used in the bakery trade – hence its name. It is rather like cottage cheese but is smoother and softer with a sourer taste; made from pasteurized, skimmed cow's milk.

A starter culture is added to the milk at a temperature of 86–89°F (30–32°C), sometimes with a little rennet. The curd is often salted and is separated from the whey by draining in cheesecloths or by centrifuge.

The cheese is stored in polythene-lined tins and chilled to 35–37°F (2–3°C) until needed for commercial use.

Bakers' cheese contains 74% water, 0.2% fat and 19% protein.

Balaton

A semi-hard cow's milk cheese from Hungary. The paste is buttery and melting with a pleasantly aromatic flavour. The moisture content is 42%, fat 26% and protein 25%.

Barberey

This soft French cheese is made from partially skimmed cow's milk. It is disc-shaped, 4½ in (11 cm) in diameter, 1 in (2.5 cm) thick and weighs around 9 oz (250 g). The cheese is cured with a covering of wood ash, and ripens for a month in a moist atmosphere.

Battelmatt

Although this cheese originated in the Swiss Canton of Ticino, nowadays its production has spread to northern regions of Italy and to Austria. It is a full-fat or semi-fat cooked cow's milk cheese with a springy texture, soft yet firm. The cheeses vary in weight from 32–74 lb (15–35 kg), 16–20 in (40–50 cm) in diameter and 3–5 in (8–12 cm) in height, looking rather like small Gruyères.

Production methods are along the same lines as for other cooked whole or partially skimmed cow's milk cheeses, the milk being curdled with liquid rennet at a temperature of 91–104°F (33–40°C) for 20–30 minutes. The curd is then cut until the pieces are the size of sweet corn grains and stirred until the lumps of curd become glossy and elastic. The curd is then cooked at 118–129°F (48–54°C), stirring continuing for a further 30 minutes. The next step involves placing the curd in moulds and pressing it. The cheese forms are either salted in brine for 10-15 days or dry-salted. Ripening lasts for 3–4 months at a temperature of 59–68°F (15–20°C).

Battelmatt is white to pale straw-yellow in colour, the texture tender and melting with numerous tiny holes, and delicate to taste.

Beaufort

This is a cooked cheese, produced in the neighbourhood of Beaufort in the Haute Savoie region of France, using whole milk from a local breed of cows.

Production methods follow those used for Gruyère. Fresh milk straight from the cow is curdled with natural rennet (made locally by soaking the lining of a calf's fourth stomach in acid whey) together with lactic acid-producing bacteria to act as a starter. The curd is produced in 30–40 minutes at 68–77°F (20–25°C) and then cut and allowed to release the whey for 10–15 minutes; it is then heated to 104–113°F (40–45°C) and subsequently stirred at a higher temperature of 129–131°F (53–55°C). After this the curd is transferred to moulds and pressed for 24 hours.

The resulting cheese forms are kept in a cool atmosphere for 24 hours and then dry salted for 10 days, or soaked in brine for 24 hours. Curing takes 3 months at a temperature of 54–59°F (12–15°C) by which time the cheese has a smooth, thin rind.

Beaumont

A semi-hard cheese which takes its name from a town in the Haute Savoie region of France and which is made with cow's milk. Beaumont is disc shaped, about 8 in (20 cm) in diameter and 1½–2 in (4–5 cm) thick.

The manufacturing technique involves the same processes as for Toma (see p. 152). Beaumont is springy in texture, without any holes; the rind is soft and thin and retains the marks made by the cheesecloth with which it is wrapped.

Beda

Produced in Egypt from buffalo or cow's milk, either whole or partially skimmed. It can be oblong or cylindrical in shape and measures 3 in (8 cm) in length or diameter according to which form is chosen, and 2½ in (6 cm) thick.

The milk is curdled at 100–109°F (38–43°C) and salt is added. The unbroken curd is placed in cheesecloths to drain for 2–3 days.

Beda is often eaten fresh but is also matured for a few months at whatever the prevailing temperature happens to be; it has no rind, and the white paste is without any holes.

Belfermière

Luxembourg produces this semi-hard cow's milk cheese which is like a squat cylinder in shape and weighs nearly 4 lb (1.8 kg). Organic composition and production techniques for making Belfermière resemble those of Port-Salut.

Bellos
Also known as Bellusco

This *Queso* (cheese) *de Los Bellos* (a region of the Asturias mountains in Spain) can be made of ewe's or goat's milk or a mixture of both. The form is cylindrical and weighs 1–1½ lb (500–700 g). The hard, closely-textured paste, white in colour, has no holes and a dry rind; the taste is strong and pungent. These cheeses are often smoked and contain 27% water, 36% fat and 27% protein.

Bellusco see Bellos, above.

Bel Paese

A soft, uncooked Italian cheese made from whole cow's milk on an industrial scale by the Galbani dairy factories: the name is their registered trade mark for this particular version of Italico cheese (semi-soft table cheese) and is often used by purchasers abroad as a generic term for this type of quick-ripening product.

The name was inspired by Father Antonio Stoppani's book *Il bel paese* (*Beautiful Country*), originally published in 1873. The cheese was perfected for industrial production in 1906, and the author's portrait forms

part of the label, superimposed on a map of Italy (in the United States the map shows the western hemisphere).

Bergader

Germany produces this soft, uncooked cow's milk cheese which has pronounced blueish-green veining. The texture is smooth, without holes, but with cracks and a strong flavour. The rind is wrinkled and light brown in colour.

Bergkäse (Mountain Cheese)

Under this generic name are classified many different types of cooked, pressed Alpine cheeses, such as Battelmatt, Gruyère, Fontina, Montasio, Walliser, etc., most of which have rinds with traces of dark, dry mould or a moist bloom. The pastes are springy in texture with occasional, widely-scattered holes.

Bergues

This cheese resembles Saint-Paulin and takes its name from a small French town near Dunkirk which is the centre of the production zone. The soft, disc-shaped whole cow's milk cheeses weigh about 4½ lb (2 kg), and the white paste is dense and supple with a few small holes. The thin washed rind is covered with a blueish-black mould.

Beyaz Peynir

A soft Turkish cheese (its name means 'white cheese') made from ewe's milk, sometimes mixed with goat's milk. It is eaten fresh, or sometimes ripened in brine.

Bijeni Sir

Sir is the generic word for 'cheese' in Balkan and some Slavic countries, and this cheese comes from Greek and Yugoslavian Macedonia. Made with ewe's or ewe's and cow's milk.

Bitto

Production of this cheese is confined almost exclusively to the Italian province of Sondrio and it takes its name from a tributary of the River Adda.

Cylindrical in shape, measuring 12–14 in (30–50 cm) in diameter and 3–5 in (8–12 cm) high, Bitto cheeses weigh between 33–55 lb (15–25 kg). The curd is formed by adding rennet at a temperature of 95–104°F (35–40°C). After 30–40 minutes the process of cutting the curd begins, resulting in pieces only ⅛ in (2–3 mm) square; these are then scalded at 122–125°F (50–52°C), causing the particles of curd to release whey and, as they shrink, take on a wrinkled, firm and dry appearance. The curd is then transferred to moulds and pressed.

Two to three days after the cheeses have been moulded, they are dry-salted in cool surroundings; this is repeated every 2–3 days for two or three weeks. The cheeses are cured at 57–60°F (14–16°C) with 80–90% humidity for 2–6 months for table cheese, and from 2–3 years for grating cheese.

The rind of unaged, sliceable Bitto is thin, yellow and smooth; with maturity it becomes darker and thicker. The paste of the younger cheeses is buttery in texture, white to pale straw-yellow in colour, with a few small holes and a sweet, delicate taste; with age the cheese becomes more dense and crumbly, melting in the mouth.

Bitto has gained much of its native Italian popularity through being an essential ingredient in the Valtelline dish *Polenta taragna* – a cornmeal porridge liberally sprinkled with grated Bitto and butter. Another specialty called *Sciatt* also calls for Bitto – in this case melted with grape marc or *grappa* and served piping hot as a stuffing for pancakes.

Bjalo Sirene

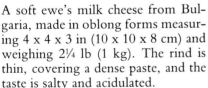

A soft ewe's milk cheese from Bulgaria, made in oblong forms measuring 4 x 4 x 3 in (10 x 10 x 8 cm) and weighing 2¼ lb (1 kg). The rind is thin, covering a dense paste, and the taste is salty and acidulated.

Analysis of this cheese reveals 50% water, 25% fat and 20% protein.

Blarney

Produced in Ireland from cow's milk. Blarney resembles Danish Samsø cheese and is a semi-hard, waxy, dry rind cheese with small scattered holes in a yellow paste, encased by red rind.

Water content is 38–40%; fat 28–29% and protein 24–25%.

Bleu d'Auvergne

Made from whole cow's milk in several regions of France (Puy-de-Dôme, Cantal, Loire, Aveyron, Corrèze, Lot, Lozère), Bleu d'Auvergne is a soft, unpressed blue cheese. The fat content in dry matter is at least 50%, the water content averaging 48%. Shaped like a squat cylinder and normally made in two sizes, the larger being 8 in (20 cm) in diameter and weighing 4½–6½ lb (2–3 kg) while the small size measures 4 in (10.5 cm) in diameter and varies in weight from 5 oz – 2¼ lb (150 g – 1 kg). Dairy cheeses are also produced for export in oblong shapes 11½ in (29 cm) long; 4½ in (11 cm) thick and 3½ in (8.5 cm) wide, weighing 5½ lb (2.5 kg).

Production follows the traditional blue cheese formula. The curd takes 1 hour to form at 86–91°F (30–33°C) once the starter (penicillin spores) and rennet have been added. The curd acquires a very distinctive lactic flavour and is then drained for 48–72 hours, after which it becomes firm enough to be placed into moulds but is not pressed, thus encouraging fissures to form along which the *penicillium glaucum* will develop. The newly moulded cheeses are then dry salted for 5–6 days at a temperature of 46–50°F (8–10°C) and ripened in the same temperature with 90–95% humidity for 2–4 weeks.

The cheeses are regular in shape with smooth surfaces, the paste being even, white and creamy without holes; the blue veining should be well defined and evenly distributed throughout the cheese and the natural rind, while not being hard, should be dry and not at all sticky. The taste is very distinctive with no sharpness or saltiness. A classic dessert cheese.

A genuine Bleu d'Auvergne will be labelled *Syndicat du Véritable Bleu d'Auvergne.*

Bleu de Corse

A soft Corsican ewe's milk cheese, made in a thick disc shape 8 in (20 cm) in diameter and 4 in (10 cm) high, weighing on average 5 lb (2.5 kg). The paste has a few cracks with mould blueing the cheese, the texture is firm and buttery and the taste is strong and very savoury.

The best white Corsican ewe's milk cheeses are sent to the Roquefort caves near Millau to ripen.

Bleu de Gex

This French cheese takes its name from a town in the Ain region where it originated; it is a blue cheese made with cow's milk, the drum-shaped forms varying in weight between 15½–17½ lb (7–8 kg). The cheeses ripen for 3–4 months before they are ready for consumption.

The curd takes 1½ hours to form at 68°F (20°C). It is then drained and often mixed with the previous batch of curd, by layering the curds alternately in the cheese mould. It is then pressed for 10–20 hours before dry salting. Curing takes place in damp, cool conditions.

The cheeses contain 31% water, 33% fat and 30% protein.

Bleu de Laqueuille

Similar to Bleu d'Auvergne but with a milder and less salty taste, and a dryer, harder rind.

Bleu de Sassenage

Named after a neighbourhood in the vicinity of Grenoble (France) where it is produced. A blue cheese made from cow's milk in thick disc shapes, weighing 13¼–15½ lb (6–7 kg), for which production is governed by the same principles as for Bleu de Gex. Water content is 33%; fat 31–33% and protein 30–32%.

Bleu des Causses

The high, rugged limestone pastures of this region in southern France provide the whole cow's milk used for this soft blue cheese which is protected by law – as shown on the label of genuine cheeses. When the delicate rind of the squat cylindrical-shaped cheese is cut, it should reveal an even veining in the firm rich paste.

Bleu du Haut-Jura

Also known as Septmoncel, Gex.

This is the official name covering blue cheeses made in the Gex (Ain)

region and in the Septmoncel area of the Jura mountains, both being blued, uncooked cow's milk cheeses with a high fat content.

For a description of the taste and texture, see the details given for Bleu de Gex: Septmoncel differs only in having a slightly smoother rind.

Bleu de Quercy

Another French blue cheese made from cow's milk which is protected by an official label of origin; the thick disc-shaped cheeses are 7–8 in (18–20 cm) in diameter and 3½–4 in (9–10 cm) high and are produced in the dairying region of Aquitaine. The blue-veined cheese has a strong, full flavour and is encased in a greyish-green natural rind.

Blue Vinny see Dorset Blue

Bondon

A soft French uncooked cow's milk cheese which comes from Normandy. The word *bondé* means 'bung' and is descriptive of its shape. The rind is covered with bloom.

Bou de Fagne

An oblong Belgian cheese weighing abut 14 oz (400 g); the paste has small fissures and occasional holes, with a pleasant flavour and fragrance. The orangey-yellow rind is covered with bloom.

Boulette d'Avesnes

Made from buttermilk in the Avesnes region of Flanders in northern France. This is an acid-curd cheese and when the casein (cheese protein) has coagulated the curd is kneaded by hand, before being seasoned with pepper, allspice, salt and other flavourings, such as herbs.

The cheeses then mature for three months at 53°F (12°C).

Bouquet des Moines

A Belgian cheese, cylindrical in shape, with a smooth, even texture and a delicate taste. The rind is golden-brown with patches of white flora, and the cheeses usually weigh about 14 oz (400 g).

Bra

This cheese has taken the name of the small rural Piedmontese town in the province of Cuneo where it originated. Both a soft and a hard version are produced from partially skimmed cow's milk which is curdled by the addition of rennet.

Preparation entails heating the milk to a temperature of 80–89°F (27–32°C); liquid rennet is then added and 30–40 minutes elapse during which time the curd is formed. This is then shredded into tiny pieces, moulded and pressed before being salted and dry-cured for 45 days (for a soft cheese) or for 6 months for the hard version. Bra is disc-shaped with a smooth rind, 12–13½ in (30–40 cm) in diameter, 3–3½ in (7–9 cm) thick and weighs 13¼–17½ lb (6–8 kg). The paste of the softer, younger cheeses is a pale ivory colour and this deepens to a dull yellow ochre in the aged cheeses whose texture is very dense, with minute holes.

Branzi

Called after a town which lies at the heart of the production zone in the province of Bergamo. Branzi is a scalded-curd cheese usually made during the summer months from whole cow's milk into wheel-shaped cheeses weighing 30–33 lb (14–15 kg), 16–20 in (40–50 cm) in diameter and 3–4 in (8–10 cm) high.

Milk is brought fresh from the cows into the dairy and immediately curdled at 89–93°F (32–34°C) for 25–30 minutes. The curd is turned and sliced before being cut into small pieces the size of wheat grains. The next step involves scalding the curd at 111–114°F (44–46°C) for 30 minutes, while stirring gently. The curd is allowed to release more whey, and is then placed in moulds and pressed for half an hour.

The cheese forms are given 2–3 days at room temperature before they are salted in brine and then transferred to the curing rooms for three to five months where they will ripen at a temperature of 55–59°F (13–15°C) in 80–85% humidity.

Branzi has a hard, smooth, close-textured rind and a soft, supple texture inside with very small, evenly distributed 'eyes'; it is a sliceable cheese which, when aged, can also be used as a grating cheese.

Composition is usually similar to Fontina and other scalded-curd whole cow's milk cheeses.

Brick

This scalded-curd whole cow's milk cheese was first created in Wisconsin (USA) and probably owes its name quite simply to its shape, or to an old practice of pressing the curd with brick-shaped weights.

Brick's taste and texture have been likened to Munster, Tilsit, Bel Paese and Port-Salut and, like all these, it is a surface-ripened cheese. The rind is smeared with a culture of *Bacterium linens* and wiped with a brine-dipped cloth at regular intervals during the ripening process. The rind is reddish and soft while the paste of the cheese is firm yet supple. The flavour is sweet, spicy and clean with a slight touch of nuttiness.

Manufacture starts with the milk being pasteurized at 89.6°F (32°C); lactic bacteria are added as a starter, then rennet, and a curd is formed. This is then cut and scalded at 98°F or 113°F (37°C or 45°C). Water is sometimes added at this stage to dilute the lactose or milk sugar in the cheese; the curd is removed from the whey and

drained for 24 hours at room temperature, being turned frequently. Once the cheese forms have taken on shape and firmness, they are salted in brine for 1–2 days.

The cheese begins its ripening process at 59°F (15°C) in 90–95% humidity. Within a few days the newly formed cheeses are covered by rind flora, and these flourishing surface micro-organisms (which include enzymes, yeasts and *Bacterium linens*) turn the skin a reddish orange-yellow.

After 15 days the cheeses are transferred to a cooler atmosphere (41°F – 5°C) to continue ripening; the rind is washed to keep the flavour relatively mild, and then wiped dry and wrapped in paper.

Brie

This famous soft uncooked French cheese is made from whole cow's milk and originated in the Brie region of the Seine-et-Marne department, to the east of Paris. The cheese is made by much the same technique as Camembert and is also a surface-ripened cheese.

Ripening progresses quickly, and these cheeses must therefore be eaten as soon as they are 'à point', or the flavour, texture and aroma will quickly deteriorate.

A perfect Brie tastes somewhat aromatic and acidulated, with a hint of tanginess and a faint mushroomy flavour and smell. The presence of ammonia indicates over-ripeness, unless unpasteurized milk has been used.

The moisture content amounts to 46%; fat 30% and protein 21.5%.

Brie owes its renown principally to its exquisite taste, though it became particularly highly-prized as a result of an amusing historical event.

While the representatives of thirty countries were attending the Congress of Vienna which lasted from 1814–1815 (to re-draw the map of Europe after the Napoleonic wars), they found time to relax and enjoy some gastronomic delights together, yet even in their leisure hours national pride and a wish to uphold their countries' prestige remained uppermost in their minds. Metternich was guest of honour at a dinner given by Talleyrand (representing the defeated French) and the subject of cheeses and their merits led to a lively discussion between the assembled guests. Talleyrand put forward the claims of Brie to be the world's greatest cheese – hotly refuted by the English delegate, Lord Castlereagh who extolled the qualities of Stilton; Baron Falk naturally put his case for the Netherlands' Limburger cheese, and each of the other statesmen present joined in, putting forward his own country's best cheese as a contender for the title of 'King of Cheeses'.

When the argument seemed to have reached stalemate, Talleyrand suggested that each man should send for a sample of his own nation's product, and he sent to Normandy for some Brie. The cheese which had the honour to represent France came from Villeroy and was made by a cheesemaker called Baulny – the equivalent today in quality and region of production would be sold under the name of Brie de Meaux. Gathered round the table once more, when all the cheeses had arrived in Vienna and been sampled and compared, the company were unanimous in proclaiming Brie as the king of all the cheeses – and the only king, as one of the judges declared, who would never disappoint his subjects.

Brie de Meaux

A soft, uncooked French farmhouse cheese made with unpasteurized cow's milk. Disc-shaped, it weighs about 5¾ lb (2.6 kg) and measures 14–15 in (35–37 cm) in diameter and is 1 in (2.5 cm) thick.

The texture is creamy, without any holes and the colour is a pale straw yellow, the surface of the rind being covered in white flora with reddish patches. The flavour is fruitier than ordinary Brie with a delicate tang.

Brie de Melun

The department of Seine-et-Marne in the Île-de-France region gave birth to what can be considered the grandfather of all Brie cheeses. This is still made by farmhouse producers with unpasteurized milk by traditional methods; the character of the cheese changes slightly according to the season as the quality of the pasture and milk varies.

A soft, uncooked-curd cheese which is round and flat, 10½ in (27 cm) in diameter, 1¼ in (3 cm) thick and weighs 3¾ lb (1.7 kg). The rind is covered with white flora with patches of brownish-orange mould and the paste is a soft pale yellow, smooth, homogeneous and creamy in texture. Sold on straw mats.

Brinza

A soft, rindless Israeli cheese made from ewe's milk, with irregular holes. It contains 60% water, 18–20% fat and 20% protein.

Brînză

Produced in Romania with ewe's milk taken from two successive milkings. May be hard or soft.

The curd is drained of whey, pressed and allowed to ripen for 4–5 days at 59°F (15°C). It is then mixed with salt and wrapped in greaseproof paper, ready to be placed in wooden containers or barrels to mature.

Broccio

Soured ewe's or goat's milk can be heated and used to make this Corsican cheese or the whey drained from the curds of such cheeses as Venaco are used as the basic material.

Broccio is an unsalted fresh cheese which must be eaten soon after it has been made; the flavour is delicate.

Brucialepre

Piedmont, in Italy, is the home of this soft goat's milk cheese; it is shaped like a thin cake and weighs about 10 oz (300 g). The rind is soft and thin, covered with surface mould and a white bloom.

Inside, the paste is white and creamy with a mild taste when the cheese is young.

Bruscion

Fresh goat's milk cheese made in Switzerland and eaten after a short ripening period.

Bûche de Chèvre

A soft French goat's milk cheese, rather like Sainte-Maure in character and shape – resembling a log – but usually larger and heavier, weighing about 2 lb (900–950 g).

Burgos

This cheese comes from the province of the same name in Spain and is a fresh, scalded-curd ewe's milk cheese, disc-shaped and weighing 2 ¼–4½ lb (1–2 kg).

The milk is curdled by the addition of rennet at 89°F (32°C) and the curd is scalded at 100–104°F (38–40°C); it is then placed in moulds to drain at room temperature before being salted in brine. It has a typical ewe's milk flavour and no rind, the paste being even textured and without holes.

Moisture content is 64–66%, fat 20–22% of dry matter, and the cheeses contain 12–13% protein.

Burrino see Manteca

Butirro see Manteca

Butterkäse

Both Germany and Austria produce this cheese which is reminiscent of the Italico type of fast-ripening cheeses. Like them, it is a close-textured, soft, cow's milk product with a certain amount of elasticity but without holes. The cheeses weigh about 4½ lb (2 kg) and have a thin rind lightly covered with mould.

Water content is 60%, fat 18% and protein 17%, although the German version can have more fat.

Cabrales
Also known as Picón

A hard Spanish cheese made with cow's milk, the curd being formed by the addition of rennet.

Once the cheeses have been dry-salted they are wrapped in foil and matured for 5–6 months in natural limestone caverns in the Asturias at a temperature of 41–50°F (5–10°C).

The rind is rough, enclosing a white, blue-veined paste without holes.

Cabrales contains 30–35% water, 31% fat and 28–30% protein.

Caciocavallo

The origin of this cheese's name is uncertain: it is sometimes said that it derives from the method of spinning the curd over or astride (*a cavallo*) a wooden pole, and similarly that the custom of hanging the cheeses, strung together in pairs over poles, could also have given rise to the name. The cheese has its counterparts in other countries, in each case the name showing striking similarities to the original, although the cheeses may have only some methods of preparation in common. The Bulgarian *Kaschkaval* is one, as are *Kascaval, Katschkawaly* and *Kaschkawall* which come from Hungary, Romania, Russia and Turkey.

The most traditional shape looks rather like a spindle with one end rounded and slightly bulbous while the apex is elongated, ending with a ball just above the string tie. This is a spun-curd cheese, also known as plastic or kneaded curd, prepared in the same way as Provolone cheese when it is to be cured for a short time, the main distinction between the two cheeses being the shape. Whole cow's milk goes into the making of Caciocavallo and it is a typically southern Italian cheese: ripened for 2–3 months to produce a sliceable cheese and for 6–12 months for a grating cheese. The rind is thin, smooth and a pale straw colour, even-textured or with a tendency to flake or scale; the paste is homogenous, white to pale straw-yellow. The table cheese has a sweet and delicate flavour while the grating variety is sharper and more flavoursome. The composition of Caciocavallo is the same as Provolone cheese.

Caciocavallo is known to date well back into the early Middle Ages and has even inspired some idioms of everyday speech: in Naples 'to end up like Caciocavallo' means to be hanged.

Caciofiore

This is an uncooked ewe's milk cheese which is made in central Italy in round shapes weighing 2¼–4½ lb (1–2 kg) and measuring 8–10 in (20–25 cm) in diameter. Milk is curdled at a temperature of 86–95°F (30–35°C) by the addition of vegetable rennet extracted from cardoons or thistle flowers, or liquid animal rennet may be used. The soft curd takes 30 minutes to form and is then cut up into walnut-sized pieces. It is then drained and placed in moulds before being dry-salted on both sides.

A high fat content table cheese, which can also be used for cooking, Caciofiore is tender and rindless.

Cacioricotta

A high fat content uncooked cheese made from ewe's milk, the name indicating the fact that the cheese is made in much the same way as Ricotta. This is traditionally a cheese of central and southern Italy, but is now produced in Sardinia where two varieties are made: soft and hard.

When soft Cacioricotta is wanted, whey is added to the milk as a starter and when the lactic acid content is high enough, the milk is heated to 176–194°F (80–90°C). The surface is soon covered by a layer of soft white curd which becomes progressively firmer until it is ready to be skimmed off and placed in wicker moulds to drain and shape. The cheese is ready to eat only 24 hours after it has been made, but can be salted and then cured for 2–3 months, and at this age it is suitable for grating as well as for consumption as a dessert cheese. The fresh Cacioricotta is white, rindless and has a delicate lactic flavour, whereas the mature product is denser, rougher in texture, salty and slightly sharp.

To make hard Cacioricotta, the milk is heated to 194–203°F (90–95°C)

and then cold water is added to cool it to 104–113°F (40–45°C); liquid rennet or fig juice is next added to coagulate the milk. The curd is cut, placed in moulds and subsequently dry-salted before it is cured for 3–4 months.

Caciotta

A sliceable, soft cheese made with whole cow's milk or a mixture of any types of milk. The main producing region is in central Italy but it is also made elsewhere. The cheese is disc-shaped, 4–8 in (10–20 cm) in diameter and 2–3 in (5–8 cm) thick, while the weight varies from about 1–2¼ lb (500 g – 1 kg).

The milk is pasteurized at 158–161°F (70–72°C); lactic ferments are used as starter cultures and the milk is coagulated at 95–104°F (35–40°C) using kid's rennet or liquid calf's rennet. The curd is cut as soon as it is firm enough, placed in moulds and cooked in a jacketed vat heated by steam. The cheeses are then salted in brine and ripened at 39–42°F (4–6°C) in an atmosphere of 80% humidity for 10–40 days.

The cheese is encased in a thin, smooth, pale straw-coloured rind and the paste is firm with no holes. The cow's milk Caciottas are usually snowy white and mild but when made with a mixture of cow's and ewe's or goat's milk they are much more fragrant and flavoursome.

Caciotta usually contains 50% water, 32% fat and 22% protein.

Caciotta di Pecora

A soft cheese made with whole ewe's milk in Sardinia and central Italy, and shaped like a small drum, 5½ in (14 cm) in diameter and 2¾ in (7 cm) high. Milk is curdled at 96–100°F, and the curd takes 30 minutes to form; it is then cut into small pieces measuring ¼–¾ in (1–2 cm), stirred gently and placed in moulds where it is allowed to drain for 4 hours at room temperature before being salted in brine. It takes a month to ripen at a temperature of 44–50°F (7–10°C). The taste is mild and the dense, homogenous paste of the cheese is covered by a smooth, thin, soft rind.

Water content is 50%, fat 26% and protein 23%.

Cádiz

Goat's milk is used for this fresh Spanish cheese which is disc-shaped and weighs about 3¼ lb (1.5 kg).

The cheeses are ready for consumption after a few days' ripening in a cool place.

Caerphilly

A Welsh semi-hard cheese shaped like a millstone or squat cylinder and measuring about 9 in (22 cm) in diameter, 3 in (7 cm) in height and weighing 8–8½ lb (3.6–3.8 kg).

Immediately after the cows have been milked the milk is innoculated with a starter of moisture-loving lactic bacteria; sometimes a starter is not used and the milk is then allowed to stand and ripen at 84–89°F (29–32°C) for 20–40 minutes before being curdled with liquid rennet. The curd is cut into small cubes, stirred gently for 20 minutes and then gathered into cheesecloths and hung up to drain for 1–2 hours. It is then broken up, salted and pressed for 3 days before being cured. Caerphilly has a tender, slightly crumbly, moist white paste. Farmhouse varieties are now being made, usually with raw milk.

Calcagno

Calcagno is always made with fresh, whole ewe's milk, curdled with kid's rennet or a mixture of lamb's and kid's rennet in solid form. It is a hard uncooked cheese which undergoes ageing for at least 6 months and can be used for grating or as a table cheese. The marks of the wicker moulds used to drain and shape the cheese forms can be seen on the cured Calcagno. The uneven rind is white or very pale straw-yellow in colour.

Calostro see Armada

Camembert

The most widely marketed of all French cheeses. Named after the town of Camembert in the Orne department of Normandy, its traditional centre of production. It is a soft, uncooked cow's milk cheese, typical of lactic-curd cheeses. At the beginning of its ripening cycle it is crumbly and granular, becoming creamier as it matures, due to the casein or cheese protein being hydrolized by the action of enzymes released by the surface moulds which flourish on the crust of the cheese.

Production commences by heating the milk to 86–104°F (30–40°C) when rennet is added. Coagulation starts after 10–15 minutes have elapsed but the curd is only firm enough to be placed in perforated moulds after 60–90 minutes. The curd is then drained at a temperature of 82–86°F (28–30°C) for 15–20 hours. Once the cheeses have been removed from the moulds they are sprinkled with spores of the mould *Penicillium candidum* and they are dry-salted to a 3% salt content. Camemberts are then ripened at 55–59°F (13–15°C) in an atmosphere of 90% humidity.

When 10–14 days have gone by the cheeses are covered with an even coating of white rind flora and they are placed on tables and turned several times so that their surfaces can dry evenly. They are then wrapped in vegetable parchment and placed in chipwood boxes. After a further 8–10 days' ripening at a temperature of 50–53°F (10–12°C) the cheeses are ready to be marketed.

The method described above is traditional but since this cheese is widely manufactured in industrial dairies on a very large scale, production has been streamlined to ensure consistent quality (if not such an interesting flavour and aroma).

Camembert cheeses are shaped in round, shallow moulds 4–4½ in (10–11 cm) in diameter and 1¼ in (3 cm) deep; the cheeses weigh just over ½ lb (250 g). Fat contents of the genuine French cheeses average 21%, moisture contents 57% and protein accounts for 20%, 50% of that having been hydrolized by the time the cheese is mature and ready for eating.

Tradition has it that Camembert was created in 1791 by a certain Marie Harel who had been given the recipe by a friar to whom she had given shelter. She is known to have perfected the cheese and a statue was erected in 1928 at Vimoutiers, the centre of the original Camembert region, in her memory.

Camembert production is not restricted to France alone by certification and today it is produced all over the world by slightly varying techniques with a greater or lesser degree of success. But authentic Camembert bears the seal of the *Union des Producteurs Normands* who monitor quality, and it is still produced on a farmhouse scale as well in much larger factories, under minute supervision. The initials V.C.N. – *Véritable Camembert de Normandie* – should appear on the label of a farmhouse cheese, and if it states that it has been made from unpasteurized milk, so much the better for the taste, aroma and texture.

Camerano

Made in the Sierra de Cameros region of Spain from goat's milk. Camerano has an easily recognizable shape and markings, being moulded in basketwork moulds.

Camerano is a fresh, rennet-curd cheese which is ready to eat within 24 hours of draining and salting.

Canestrato

This cheese originates in southern Italy and is traditionally made with ewe's milk, though sometimes with mixed milk and occasionally with cow's milk. It has other names (In-canestrato, Rigato, Rigatello) which are descriptive of its ridged surface.

Production follows the traditional procedures used for making scalded-curd cheeses; the milk is curdled at 89–95°F (32–35°C) and paste rennet is often used. The curd is cut once it is firm enough, heated to 107–114°F (42–46°C), drained and placed in moulds. When the curd has been pressed, the newly-formed cheeses are dry-salted and placed in brine. Peppercorns are sometimes added to the curd when it is put in the moulds.

The composition and taste of Canestrato may vary considerably, depending on the variety of milk used, the type of rennet or curdling agent and the duration of the ripening period.

Cantal
Also known as Fourme du Cantal, Salers, Fourme de Salers.

A famous semi-hard French cow's milk cheese protected by law. This uncooked, pressed cheese is shaped like a squat cylinder, measuring 14–16 in (35–40 cm) in diameter and 12–14 in (30–35 cm) in height, the weight being 77–99 lb (35–45 kg). Produced in the Auvergne, both farmhouse cheeses (*Cantal fermier*) and commercial creamery versions (*Cantal laitier*) are available.

For the farmhouse cheeses raw milk straight from the cow is used; pasteurized milk is used for the industrialized dairy production, heated to 89–91°F (32–33°C), and curdled with liquid rennet. After 30–40 minutes the curd is cut into walnut-sized pieces and allowed to precipitate

and fall to the bottom of the vat. When the whey has been drawn off, the curd is pressed, sliced and placed in moulds where it is pressed again before being dry-salted. Cantal is then cured for 3 months at 46–50°F (8–12°C). Its rind has red streaks amidst the predominantly grey colour; the taste of Cantal is agreeably full, nutty with a hint of bite.

Composition of the cheese is 43–45% water, 25–27% fat and 22–24% protein.

Cantal is probably the oldest of all French cheeses and the elder Pliny makes mention of it in his *Naturalis Historia*, written nearly two thousand years ago, saying how these cheeses from Gaul found favour in Rome.

Cantal is a light, digestible cheese which used to be shaped in moulds lined with beech leaves.

Caprice des Dieux

Cow's milk enriched with added cream is used for the production of this oval, straight-sided soft French cheese; it measures 5½ in (14 cm) in length, 2½ in (6 cm) wide and 1½ in (4 cm) high. The rind is white, covered with a pure white bloom and the texture of the cheese is smooth.

Caprino a Pasta Cruda

An uncooked Italian cheese made with whole, raw goat's milk. Most of these cheeses come from Sardinia.

Preparation entails home production of the rennet with which to curdle the milk; this is done by soaking vells (the lining of the fourth digestive stomach of a calf) in brine heated

to 95–98°F (35–37°C) to extract the ferment. The curd is cut, stirred, pressed by hand to expel the whey and then placed in cheese forms to drain further for 6 hours. The cheeses are then salted in brine and cured at the prevailing temperature for at least 3 months.

Caprino Semicotto

Sardinia is the main source of this Italian scalded-curd goat's milk cheese, which is drum-shaped, 7 in (18 cm) in diameter, and 5 in (13 cm) thick, varying in weight from 4–7¾ lb (1.8–3.5 kg). The cheese is made by coagulating the milk at 98–102°F (37–39°C) with liquid rennet, following which the curd forms in 30 minutes; it is then cut, stirred, pressed and cooked at 107–113°F (42–45°C), then placed in moulds to drain for 6 hours. The cheeses are salted in brine, or dry-salted, and matured for at least 3 months at 53–59°F (12–15°C).

Carnia

A scalded-curd cow's milk cheese produced in the neighbourhood from which it takes its name, in Friuli, Italy. Made by the same process as Montasio.

Carré de l'Est

In the Champagne, Lorraine and some other eastern regions of France this cow's milk cheese is made on a large scale. As its name indicates, it is square, the sides measuring 3–4 in (8–10 cm) and 1–1¼ in (2.5–3 cm) thick. It is a Brie or Coulommiers-style cheese, being covered by a thick, even coating of white rind flora; inside the paste is dense and without holes. This is a soft cheese and contains 52% water, 25–26% fat and 18–22% protein.

Casanova

A soft German cow's milk cheese which is creamy and delicate to taste, becoming sharper with age; the surface is covered with a white bloom.

Casanova contains 54–55% water; 21–22% fat and 18–20% protein.

Casatella

This fresh, rindless cheese is produced in Lombardy, northern Italy, with whole cow's milk, usually from two milkings.

The milk is heated to 100°F (38°C) and rennet added, the curd taking 30 minutes to form. The curd is cut into ¾–1¼ in (2–3 cm) squares, left to rest for half an hour and then placed in cheese forms. The curd drains and the cheese is then salted.

Castelmagno

Takes its name from an Alpine village in the Italian province of Cuneo, situ-

ated at an altitude of 3,608 ft. (1,100 m). The gradual population shift away from such isolated mountain communities has meant that less milk is produced and consequently only relatively few of these cheeses are made nowadays.

Castelmagno is disc-shaped, soft and made with cow's milk, measuring 8 in (20 cm) in diameter, 4–4½ in (10–11 cm) high and weighing 13¼–15½ lb (6–7 kg): it belongs to the family of blue cheeses.

Milk from two successive milkings is heated to 121–124°F (37–38°C) and curdled. The curd is cut, given a preliminary draining in the vat, and then drained in cheesecloths for 24 hours before being placed in tubs or vats for 2–3 days. It is stirred and turned, and then placed in moulds for 5–6 days; when it has attained the correct consistency it is unmoulded and dry salted at intervals. Castelmagno is cured in cellars or caves at a temperature of 32–39°F (10–12°C) with 80–90% humidity for 4–6 months. Under these conditions, where the surroundings are only ventilated at night, the cheeses ripen in almost total darkness; the floors of beaten earth help to provide the ideal fresh, cool and damp conditions which the cheeses must have to age properly.

Castelmagno has a mild taste when young which becomes stronger and more savoury as it matures; the paste is yellowish-white with blueish-green veining. This cheese can best be described as a milder, more delicate version of Gorgonzola.

Castelo Branco

A Portuguese cheese named after the middle of the region where it is made; a mixture of cow's and ewe's milk or cow's and goat's milk is used. It is an

uncooked, semi-hard cheese, disc-shaped and weighing 1¾–2¼ lb (800 g – 1 kg). It has no holes and is rindless.

Castigliano

This Spanish ewe's milk cheese is shaped like a thin disc or cake. The rind is greyish-brown, enclosing hard, uncooked, pale ivory-coloured paste with a strong, full flavour.

Cebrero
Also known as Piedrafita

Another Spanish cheese, this variety has a strange shape – almost like a mushroom with a very thick stalk and a cap just overlapping it. It is made with cow's milk and the consistency of the cooked paste is hard.

Cécil

A spun curd cheese from Armenia for which cow's or ewe's milk is used. Weight is 6½–8¾ lb (3–4 kg). When the curd is spun it is twisted round into a spiral shape. These cheeses are eaten fresh and have no rind.

Chabi

Produced in Brazil with pasteurized goat's milk, Chabi is disc-shaped, measuring 4¼ in (11 cm) in diameter and weighing 9 oz (250 g). A soft, uncooked-curd cheese.

The pasteurized milk is heated to 95°F (35°C) and rennet in solid form is added. The curd is then cut, drained of whey and placed in cheese moulds. The newly-formed cheeses are then dry-salted, and given 15 days to ripen at a temperature of 39°F (12°C). The rind is dry with green mould on its surface and the paste is smooth.

Chabichou

The province of Poitou, in France, is the source of many good goat's milk cheeses. This particular cheese is also known as *Chabi,* and it is ripened for 15–20 days in cool, dry cellars, resulting in a soft cheese, shaped like a foreshortened cylinder or truncated cone. This form measures nearly 2½ in (6 cm) in diameter across the base and 2 in (5 cm) across the top, it is just under 2½ in (6 cm) high.

Chamois d'Or

A French cheese made with cow's milk enriched with cream. Shaped like Brie, in a large flat cake, but somewhat thicker. The rind is covered with white flora, enclosing an even-textured, creamy paste.

Chaource

This soft French whole cow's milk cheese looks like a small, thick cake, 4¾ in (12 cm) in diameter, 2½ in (6 cm) high and weighing 1¼ lb – 1 lb 10 oz (600–650 g). Chaource can be eaten fresh or when it has been cured for a month in a dry atmosphere. The rind is covered with mould and the consistency of the interior is creamy with tiny cracks; the flavour is subtle.

Moisture content is 63%, fat 19% and protein 15%.

Charolais

Goats grazing the Charolais hills in the Burgundy region of France provide the milk for this soft cheese, shaped like a small drum or fat cylinder, 2 in (5 cm) in diameter, 3¼ in (8 cm) high and weighing 7 oz (200 g). It is cured for 2–3 weeks and has a delicate texture with small cracks; the thin rind has no mould or bloom.

Contains 58% water, 24% fat and 21% protein.

Cheddar

Originally thought to be from the village of the same name in the southwest of England, this cheese is now the most widely manufactured and consumed product of its kind in the world and is made by varying methods, usually on a highly mechanized, industrial scale, although genuine farmhouse cheeses are still to be found.

It is a hard, scalded-curd cheese made with whole cow's milk which is usually pasteurized, though farmhouse cheeses often use unpasteurized milk. Genuine Cheddar is shaped like a drum, 15 in (38 cm) in diameter and about 15–17 in (38–42 cm) high, weighing 55–60 lb (25–28 kg). Smaller versions called Truckles weigh from 2 lb (1 kg) to 15 lb (6–7 kg). Milk is heated to 86°F (30°C) and innoculated with a lactic ferment starter culture. After 45–60 minutes have elapsed, the rennet is added and as soon as the curd has become firm it is milled into pieces about the size of a pea. These are heated to 102°F (39°C), the whey is drawn off and once the curd has formed into one cohesive mass, it is sliced into large blocks or thick slabs which are stacked on top of one another and turned so that more whey can drain out (the combination of milling and turning is known as *cheddaring*). The curd is then placed in chessits, pressed overnight and subsequently allowed to stand in a cool, dry place for 3–4 days.

Farmhouse Cheddar must be matured for at least 6 months at 32–41°F (0–5°C) and is traditionally cloth-bound, allowing the cheese to mature properly, for the cloth permits unwanted gas to escape slowly.

Most factory and farm production is block Cheddar which is vaccuum packed in plastic and allowed to age up to 2 months, but the air-tight wrapping and low storage temperature means ripening is minimal. Traditional Cheddar has a very appetising, nutty flavour and a firm, buttery texture; it is yellowish-white in colour with occasional tiny cracks. The rind is very thin and almost non-existent.

Average content of moisture is 35–37%; fat varies between 32–36% and protein between 25–33%.

Cheddar-style cheese is produced and sold on a far vaster scale worldwide than any other cheese.

Cheshire: Red, White and Blue

Red Cheshire is a hard, drum-shaped cow's milk cheese weighing about 40 lb (18 kg), and it is the oldest English variety. Some of the stages in its preparation are similar to those for Cheddar cheesemaking.

White Cheshire is simply Red Cheshire that has not been coloured with annatto.

The outer surface is smooth, soft and sometimes dipped in wax or bandaged with cheesecloths dipped in lard. The paste is more friable and moist than Cheddar and has a delicate, slightly salty taste, which originally resulted from grazing cows on the salty pastures of the Cheshire plain. The quality of this cheese has remained consistent for centuries.

Blue Cheshire is fast becoming thought of as at least as great as Stilton – and perhaps greater. It is a marigold colour with a tangy rich flavour and many blue veins. It is matured up to 6 months and made in 18 lb (8 kg) cylinders.

Chester

In spite of its English name, this is a purely French hard cheese, made with whole cow's milk, sometimes enriched with cream. Made in oblong or block form or tall cylinders, weighing 44–66 lb (20–30 kg).

The cheese is produced by highly automated methods in large vats. Pasteurized milk is used, innoculated with lactic ferment cultures and then curdled with rennet. The curd is cut, drained, left to stand free of its whey until the pieces combine to form one large mass of curd. This is then sliced, salted and placed in cheese forms before being cured at 35–37°F (2–3°C). The texture of Chester is smooth, with a fairly mild flavour. The rind is thin and the paste even with occasional small cracks.

Analysis reveals 38–40% water, 30–31% fat and 23–25% protein.

Chevrotin des Aravis

This goat's milk cheese comes from the province of Savoie in France; it is sometimes made with a mixture of goat's milk and cow's milk. Shaped like a flat disc, the cheese has a firm consistency, smooth surface and a pronounced taste typical of goat's milk cheeses.

Colby

A scalded-curd hard cheese created in the United States by a special process in which, after the whey is drained off, cold water is added until the temperature falls to 80°F (27°C); the remainder of the cheesemaking process then adheres to the Cheddar procedure, although the curd is not cheddared.

Comté, see Gruyère de Comté

Cottage Cheese

Cottage cheese originally came from Central Europe where each household used to make sufficient for family consumption. It is produced and consumed on a very large scale in the United States, Great Britain, Australasia, Israel and Denmark and is a fresh cheese made with skimmed pasteurized milk.

The pasteurized milk is coagulated at a temperature of 82–86°F (28–30°C). Four to five hours incubation time is allowed for the faster curds; in the case of slower coagulation as many as 16 hours may be necessary, particularly if rennet is not used. The curd is cut, water is added at 114°F (46°C) equal to the volume of the curd and whey, and the temperature is gradually increased to 123–125°F (51–52°C) with continuous gentle stirring. The required consistency is usually reached after about 2 hours. It is then time to remove the whey covering the curd and replace it with cold water, until the temperature has fallen to 84–86°F (29–30°C). The resulting mixture of water and whey is then replaced with fresh cold water, reducing the temperature still further; finally a last 'washing' of water at a temperature of 39°F (4°C) is added and this last rinsing water is drained off.

Cottage cheese has the appearance of snowy white moist granular curds and the flavour is very mild and fresh with a hint of acidulation.

The neutral taste of cottage cheese means that it lends itself particularly well to a wide variety of flavourings, and since it is a very good source of protein it can be served as part of a main dish. The analysis of cottage cheese varies, depending on exactly what has been added to it; the most widely-marketed type contains 75% water, 4% fat and 15.5% protein.

Coulommiers

A soft French cow's milk cheese similar to Brie but much smaller.

Whole raw or pasteurized milk is used and the technique resembles that of Brie cheesemaking. The surface of the cheese is smooth with white rind flora, the paste is velvety, white and creamy with an acidulated taste when young, becoming more savoury if the cheese is matured. Often sold on mats of straw.

Cream Cheese

The fat content of this soft cheese is very high and the consistency is smooth and homogeneous. It is an acid-curd cheese made with a mixture of homogenized milk and cream containing 16% butter fat.

Once the curd has formed it is placed in a centrifugal separator; it is then drained and blended, at which stage stabilizing agents can be added to prevent the remaining whey and small quantities of salt separating from the curd. Sold in tubs or cartons.

Crédioux aux Noix

A processed French cheese for which cow's milk cheese is used as the basic material; the surface is covered with walnuts pressed lightly in.

Crescenza

Originally raw cow's milk went into the making of this soft, uncooked Italian cheese but nowadays pasteurized milk is used.

It is made as follows: the milk is heated to 100–104°F (38–40°C) and innoculated with a culture of *Streptococcus thermophilus* or natural milk starter cultures: the curd is formed by the addition of liquid rennet. It is cut into 1-1/4–1-1/2 (3–4 cm) cubes, left to firm and then placed in square moulding frames measuring 7–8 in (18–20 cm). The curd is then 'cooked' at 75–82°F (24–28°C) for 6–10 hours, and when this scalding process is over the cheese forms are salted in brine and cured for 7–10 days at 46–50°F (8–10°C).

The paste of this rindless cheese is white and it has a buttery texture, melting in the mouth. Crescenza cheeses contain on average 56–58% water, 20–24% fat and 18–22% protein.

Crotonese

A hard cheese from Calabria in southern Italy. Whole ewe's milk is curdled with kid's rennet in solid form.

The finished cheese retains the markings left by the willow basket moulds in which the curd is placed to drain. The disc-shaped cheeses vary in weight from 4–4½ lb (1.8–2 kg). The rind is dry and rough, orange yellow in colour with brown patches. Inside, the paste is firm, white or pale straw yellow, its otherwise even texture broken here and there by small holes or scaling. Depending on the maturity of the cheese, it can be used as a slicing table cheese or for grating.

Crottin de Chavignol

An uncooked, hard French cheese made with whole raw goat's milk. The curd is formed over 24–36 hours at a temperature of 68–71°F (20–22°C) with liquid rennet; it is then cut, drained in cheesecloths and placed in moulds for 24 hours. Dry-salting follows and curing for 1–4 weeks at 50–53°F (10–12°C). The cheeses are very small, weighing only about 3 oz (80 g) and are cylindrical, 1½–2 in (4–5 cm) in diameter and 1–1½ in (2.5–4 cm) long.

Danablu

Uncooked Danish whole cow's milk blue cheese was invented early this century as an alternative to the exquisite but expensive Roquefort.

Milk for the cheese is pasteurized at 167°F (75°C), cooled to 100°F (38°C), innoculated with starter culture and curdled with liquid rennet. Once the curd is cut, spores of *Penicillium roqueforti* are added and the curd is placed in cheese forms to drain before being dry-salted. The cheeses are then matured for 3 months at 50°F (10°C) and kept in cold store for two months longer before they are ready to market.

Danablu has a firm, white paste with even blueing; the rind is thin and white to pale straw-yellow in colour and the taste is strong and savoury.

Danbo

Another Danish product, Danbo calls for whole or partially skimmed cow's milk. It is a hard dessert cheese which can also be grated.

Pasteurized milk is innoculated with moisture-loving lactic bacteria as a starter culture and coagulated with liquid rennet at 86°F (30°C); the temperature of the milk is then gradually raised to 100–102°F (38–39°C) to encourage the whey to separate. The curd is cut, and allowed to settle on the bottom of the vat to form a single, solid mass. It is then placed in moulds, pressed, and salted in brine.

Danbo's rind is dry and hard, golden-brown in colour and covered with a layer of paraffin wax; the body of the cheese is supple, white to dull yellow with medium-sized holes.

Moisture content varies from 45–50%; fat is 25% and protein 30%.

Dariworld

Semi-hard, cooked cow's milk dessert cheese made in the United States. The cheeses are salted in brine and have a delicate taste. Usually ripened when vacuum-packed in plastic. Moisture content is 45–46%; fat 27–28% and protein 23–24%.

Demi-Sel

A very small, soft, white, fresh cow's milk cheese weighing only 2½–2¾ oz (70–75 g). These very smooth-textured rindless cheeses are produced in industrial creameries.

Demi-Suisse, see Suisse

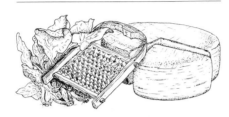

Derby

This is a hard, rindless, uncooked cow's milk cheese produced in a similar manner to Cheddar and resembles that cheese in some respects. Sage Derby has also been a favourite for many years and recently, immense public demand for authenticity has seen the reintroduction of cheeses containing real, rubbed sage.

Domiati
Also known as Beda

Made in Egypt with whole or partially skimmed buffalo milk. The cheeses are oblong or cylindrical and are soft without holes. If eaten shortly after making, the taste is subtle and savoury, becoming more acid with ripening. An unusual feature of the cheesemaking process is the addition of salt to the milk *before* it is curdled. The curd is then placed in metal moulds, turned frequently, and then sold; or it may be kept in brine or whey for 4–8 months before being marketed.

Domiati contains 52–54% water, 20–22% fat and 18–20% protein.

Doppelrahmstufe

This is the name of an official German category of cheeses: it literally means 'double cream', and denotes that the cheese concerned has a fat content of 60–85%.

Dorset Blue
Also known as Blue Vinny

True Blue Vinny has not been made for many years; happily there is now one farmhouse producer, and more may follow. The cheese used to be made during the summer months, and its close texture meant that Blue Vinny was not veined but clouded with mould.

Double Gloucester

This is a hard, cow's milk cheese which used to be farmhouse-made in summer, but is now made in large commercial creameries with the exception of one or two traditional cheesemakers. It is full in flavour and coloured a bright orange with annatto dye. The texture is satiny and almost waxy. The name comes from the old practice of using full-cream milk from two milkings and the Double Gloucesters were twice as large as Single Gloucester cheeses, made with skimmed evening milk and full-cream morning milk.

Drabant

A pressed, scalded-curd cheese made in Sweden with whole cow's milk. The shape is oblong and the consistency is supple and springy with occasional medium-sized holes; it has no rind and the taste is bland.

Dreux

Also known as Feuille de Dreux

A soft cheese made in Normandy, France, with partially skimmed cow's milk. It looks like a flat disc, 6–7 in (15–18 cm) across, ¾–1½ in (2–4 cm) thick and 10½ oz – 1 lb (300–500 g) in weight. The surface is covered with white rind flora.

The moisture content is 54–56%, fat content is 13–15% and protein 25–26%.

Dunlop

Hard Scottish cow's milk cheese which resembles Cheddar – not sur-

prisingly, since it is made in very much the same way. It is moister than Cheddar and has a thin, smooth rind, surrounding the dense paste which has no holes. The taste is mild – pleasant but unremarkable.

Contains 42–44% water; 27% fat and 23% protein.

Dunlop has been made in Scotland for centuries and can be considered as that country's national cheese. It is thought to have been invented in 1688 by Barbara Gilmour, a farmer's wife living in Dunlop, Ayrshire.

Echtermainzerkäse

An acid-curd soft German cheese made with skimmed cow's milk, and falling into the large category of Handkäse.

This cheese has a smooth, orange-yellow rind and an ivory white creamy paste. Can be mild or sharp, whether young or mature.

Edam

Dutch cheese made with partially-skimmed cow's milk and marketed when young, at which point the texture is supple; when the cheese is matured for longer it becomes drier and harder.

The cheesemaking procedure starts with the pasteurized milk being cooled to 86°F (30°C) before it is innoculated with lactic bacteria which raise the acidity level of the milk. Liquid rennet is added and the resulting curd is cut in small pieces measur-

ing about ⅛–³⁄₁₆ in (3–4 mm). The temperature is then increased to 104°F (40°C), the curd is drained and transferred to moulds and pressed, after which the cheeses are dry-salted or salted in brine. Edam then ripens at 50–68°F (10–20°C) for a few weeks. Export cheeses are covered in a layer of red paraffin wax. Edam has a delicate taste and the mellow straw-yellow paste is surrounded by a thin rind.

Edam contains 45% water, 25% fat and 28% protein.

Together with the equally famous Gouda, Edam epitomizes Dutch cheese production. It is also called Manbollen, Katzenkopt and Moor's Head because of its spherical shape.

Edelblankkäse

A soft German cheese; disc-shaped, its surface is covered with white rind flora; flavour varies from sweet and mild when young to sharper-tasting.

Edelpilzkäse

In Austria and Germany these semi-hard cheeses are made from cow's milk; the paste has cracks in it, and a blueish-green mould. Weight is usually between 3¼ and 11 lb (2.5–5 kg), and its rind can be soft or dry.

Average moisture content is 48–50%, fat 22–30% and protein 15–18%.

Elbo

This Danish cow's milk cheese is similar to Danbo and also belongs to the Samsø family of cheeses. It is oblong or loaf-shaped and weighs 6½–11 lb (3–5 kg), close-textured with small holes or no holes at all; the taste is mild and slightly acidulated. The production technique differs little from that of Danbo.

The rind is dry, smooth and golden-brown.

Emmental, Emmentaler

One of the most famous Swiss cheeses, outstanding for its size, delicate, aromatic flavour and for its unmistakable and characteristic holes. It was originally made in the Emmental area of the Bernese Oberland; it is now produced throughout the German speaking cantons of Switzerland – and in many other north European countries, where the Swiss technique is imitated as closely as possible. Whole cow's milk is used to make this exceptionally fine cooked, pressed cheese. Emmental is wheel shaped with slightly bulging sides and measures 32–36 in (80–90 cm) in diameter, 11½ in (29 cm) thick and weighs 110–176 lb (50–80 kg).

To make the cheese, milk is heated to 86–89°F (30–32°C) and small quantities of starter cultures which will produce lactic acid and propionic acid are added to the whey, as well as rennet. After 25–30 minutes the curd is ready to be cut to only ³⁄₁₆–¼ in (5–8 mm); the curd is then slowly heated to 116–118°F (47–48°C), and then the temperature is raised quickly to 125–127°F (52–53°C). The curd is gathered into cheese cloths and placed in moulds; after 24 hours it is pressed, then salted in brine for 2–3 days. Subsequently the cheeses are kept at 71°F (22°C) for 4–5 weeks, then transferred to curing rooms for maturing at 53–57°F (12–14°C) for 4–6 months; it can be marketed at that point, but is at its best when matured for 10 months.

Emmental has a hard, smooth golden-brown rind; the paste is glossy, pale gold and springy with holes ½–1¼ in (1–3 cm) across; the taste is mellow and sweet with a pleasing faintly nutty aftertaste.

Moisture content is 35%, fat 37% and protein 27%.

A genuine Swiss-made Emmental cheese will have 'Switzerland' stamped in red in radiating spokes all over the rind. At the Stresa Convention in 1951, it was agreed that cheese made to the Emmental recipe in other countries must be marked with the country of origin – such as French Emmental.

It is worth noting that although many people maintain that the correct way to spell the name Emmental is with an 'h' (Emmenthal), this is, in fact, incorrect. The Swiss Cheese Marketing Board states categorically that the name should be written without the 'h' – Emmental.

Epoisses

This French cheese has taken its name from the village in the heart of the region where it is made on the Côte d'Or in Burgundy. It is a soft cow's milk cheese, weighing 10½–14 oz (300–400 g). Shaped like a disc, its orange-red rind is washed in brine or locally-produced, unmatured *eau-de-vie-de-marc*. Sometimes flavoured with black pepper, cloves or fennel.

Ermite

Homogenized cow's milk cheese produced in the province of Quebec, Canada, by Benedictine monks. It is a blue cheese and has no holes. Made in much the same way as traditional veined cheeses.

Erimys Peynir

A spun-curd Turkish fresh cheese which is made with ewe's or goat's milk. To be eaten fresh.

Erkentaler

This name was decided on for marketing a German cheese which resembles Emmental in constituents and preparation technique.

Esrom

Danish semi-hard whole cow's milk cheese which is oblong and varies in weight from 1–2¼ lb (500–1 kg). The rind is thin and yellowish in colour, the paste firm with small holes and the taste is pleasantly spicy. It is ripened for 7–8 days at 59–64°F (15–18°C) and then for a further 12–15 days at 46–50°F (8–10°C).

Analysis shows 50% water, 22.5% fat and 22% protein.

Estonskij Syr

These Estonian (USSR) round cow's milk cheeses weigh 4½–6½ lb (2–3 kg). The milk ripens quickly after the addition of hydrolising agents (skimmed milk with microflora and pepsin); it is then coagulated at 86–89°F (30–32°C) with rennet. The curd is heated in its whey to 102–104°F (39–40°C), pressed in cheese moulds, salted, and cured at 55–59°F (13–15°C). The taste is mildly acid and aromatic.

Moisture content is 45%, fat 24.5% and protein 22–23%.

Euda

A semi-hard cow's milk cheese with a low fat content.

Creameries in the United States have perfected a technique for making this cheese, using mainly skimmed milk, together with 20% whole homogenized milk. The milk is kept at a temperature of 104°F (40°C) for 1 hour; lactic ferment starter cultures are added and the milk is left to ripen further and increase in acidity for another hour at a temperature of 87–89°F (31–32°C). It is then time to add the rennet. The curd is cut and scalded at 109°F (43°C), the whey is

drawn off and the curd washed with water at a temperature of 50–59°F (10–15°C), salted, placed in moulds and pressed then cured for 1–3 months.

Färsk Getost

A semi-hard Swedish cheese made with goat's milk. The rectangular forms measure 8 x 4¾ in (20 x 12 cm) and are 3½ in (9 cm) high. Weight varies from 1¾–2¾ lb (800 g – 1.2 kg).

To prepare the cheese, rennet is added to whole raw milk and the curd takes 1–2 hours to form at 77–86°F (25–30°C). It is not cut or stirred but simply placed straight into cheese moulds, pressed and drained for 2–8 hours, sometimes salted and kept at a temperature of 41°F (5°C) for 1–7 days.

Feta

The name of this cheese derives from the fact that it is cut into large blocks or slices (*fetes*) and stored in brine in large barrels. It is the most widely-produced and consumed of all Greek cheeses and in recent years other countries have taken to manufacturing their own versions. Bulgaria is one producer which keeps to the traditional practice of using ewe's milk or ewe's and goat's milk, but cow's milk is increasingly used nowadays, especially by such large producers as Denmark.

This is a table cheese which is also used for cooking, and the taste is sharp and salty. The weight varies

from 2–4½ lb (900 g – 2 kg).

The small curds, measuring about ¾–1¼ in (2–3 cm) are placed in moulds, just under 16 in (40 cm) in diameter and 8 in (20 cm) deep. Once the curd has drained the newly-formed cheese is cut in three and dry-salted, washed with water and placed in barrels or other containers. A 7–8% salt solution brine is added until the cheese is covered.

When the cheese is fresh – that is, ripened for only 15–30 days at 64–68°F (18–20°C) – it has no rind and the paste is quite soft with occasional holes. For a harder cheese, Feta has to be kept for 2–3 months.

The fat content is 27–28%, protein 21% and moisture 46%.

Feuille de Dreux see Dreux

Fior di Latte

Originating in the south of Italy but now internationally popular, Fior di Latte is a cow's milk, spun-curd cheese prepared in the same way as Mozzarella. It has a more acidulated taste than Buffalo Milk Mozzarella and is ivory coloured, without the pure white colour and the delicate texture and aroma of the buffalo cheese. Fior di Latte is made in oval, bun shapes or plaits, the weight varying from 2–10½ oz (50–300 g), and when cut it reveals the same layered effect as in the Buffalo Milk Mozzarellas.

Fior di Latte used to be produced by the same method as traditional Mozzarella, for which the curd is formed in wooden vats or tubs at 89–93°F (32–34°C) using raw milk and no starter culture; the rest of the cheesemaking was carried out by hand. Nowadays the bulk of Fior di Latte is produced in industrial creameries and the entire production line is fully mechanized. Lactic ferments which thrive in warm conditions are added to pasteurized milk which is curdled at 96–100°F (36–38°C) in enormous steel vats holding 1,250–2,500 gallons (5,000–10,000 litres). Stirring, cutting and emptying the curd and whey from the vat are all fully automated operations.

Recent improvements in the techniques of spinning or kneading the curd have also paved the way for measures intended to improve the keeping qualities of this cheese. To this end producers are tending to discontinue the practice of leaving the milk to ripen and produce its own lactic acid and are adding citric acid just before coagulation. The efficiency of citric acid in separating the cheese protein means the curd is easier to spin, and fewer enzymes and contaminants are present than if ordinary bacteriological means of producing lactic acid were adopted.

The cheeses last longer, making them a more attractive commercial proposition, due to pasteurization and the care taken to ensure very high standards of hygiene in the creameries. The packaging of the cheese in pasteurized whey as a keeping liquid inside sealed containers also helps to extend the cheese's life.

Fior di Latte contains 60–62% water, 18% fat and 17% protein. Besides being eaten as a table cheese, a great deal of Fior di Latte goes into the making of pizzas and other fresh or frozen traditional Italian dishes.

Fiore Sardo

The original Sardinian Pecorino cheese which used to be made on the island before the production of Pecorino Romano began. It is an uncooked ewe's milk cheese with an unmistakable shape, like two cones joined at the base, and it is said to resemble a mule's back. The cheese measures 5–6 in (13–15 cm) high and weighs 3½–9 lb (1.5–4 kg).

Whole raw milk is used, warmed to 95–98°F (35–37°C) to which solid rennet is added; the curd takes 20–30 minutes to form and is then cut, stirred in its whey, hand-pressed and then drained for about 6 hours before being salted in brine and dry-salted. The cheeses are matured for at least 3–4 months at a temperature of 54–61°F (12–16°C). The dry rind is golden-brown enclosing a blind, white or pale straw-yellow, sharp-tasting paste.

The cheese is officially classified and is produced throughout Sardinia. It makes a good table cheese when fairly young and is used as a grating cheese when mature.

Water content is 26%, fat 35% and protein 30%.

Fløtemysost

A Norwegian cheese made in the same way as Mysost but with a higher fat content due to the cow's milk whey being enriched by the addition of cream. It has no rind and a smooth regular texture and contains 20% water, 25–26% fat and 50% protein (albumen and casein).

Folies de Béguines

Belgian cow's milk cheese shaped like a bun or loaf with uneven edges. The rind is golden-brown and the cheese paste inside flecked with small holes; it has a decided but not overpowering taste.

Weight is 15½–17½ lb (7–8 kg).

Fontal

Uncooked-curd, whole cow's milk sliceable cheese, very like Fontina in taste and appearance. The wheel-shaped cheeses are 16 in (40 cm) in diameter; 3½ in (9 cm) thick and weigh anything from 13¼ (6 kg) to 44 lb (20 kg).

To make the cheese, pasteurized milk is innoculated with lactic ferment starter cultures which develop at warm temperatures; the milk is then coagulated with liquid rennet. The curd forms in 30–35 minutes and is cut, then 'washed' with water heated to 176°F (80°C) until the temperature of the curd has been raised to 86–104°F (30–41°C). (This process reduces the acid content as well as the lactose or milk-sugar content, eventually producing a mild, smooth paste rich in calcium.) The curd is then drained while being stirred for 45–60 minutes, before being placed in moulds, pressed, salted in brine and matured for 40–60 days at 46–53°F (8–12°C).

Fontal is usually made on a large industrial scale and several stages of manufacture are carried out in the same highly mechanized vats.

Fontal's consistency is tender and buttery, the dense, pale, straw-yellow paste being broken by an occasional hole; the rind is thin and supple with a little bloom and is waxed or sometimes wrapped in plastic. The taste is mild and almost bland.

Water content amounts to 43%; fat 27% and protein 27%.

Fontina

The origin of this name is unclear, although it may be a corruption of the name of one of the villages in the Aosta Valley, where Fontina has been made for hundreds of years by farmhouse cheese producers following traditional methods, and using milk fresh from the cow: the cheese was made in Alpine huts in summer and in dairies in the valley in winter. The character of Fontina depends on both the special milk used and on the skill of the cheesemakers, who even today follow traditional techniques very closely, and cure the cheeses properly in caves, or in cheese stores in which the carefully controlled atmosphere reproduces conditions which occur naturally in the caves. Fontina is protected by law and only cheeses made in the Aosta Valley may bear this name.

The cheese has to be made within two hours or less of milking. The milk is warmed to 96–98°F (36–37°C) and rennet is added (at one time this was made by the cheesemakers themselves); after 40–60 minutes the curd is turned with special skimmers and then cut with a special instrument called a 'harp' until the pieces are the size of wheat grains. The curd is then heated in its whey to a temperature of 116–118°F (47–48°C), stirring continuously with a sharp-edged utensil known as a 'thorn-bush'; stirring continues for 15 minutes longer once this temperature has been reached. The curd is lifted out of the vat in coarse cheesecloths and placed in wooden moulds which will shape the Fontina into its classic wheel shape, with slightly bulging sides 2¾–3⅛ in (7–8 cm) high, weighing 19¾–22 lb (9–10 kg). The next stage is the pressing of the cheese for 12 hours, with frequent turnings and changes of cheesecloth.

Next the cheeses are placed in caves where they undergo dry salting alternated with wiping with brine-soaked cloths. This stage lasts for about 2 months and wiping with the damp cloths will continue until the cheese is completely ripe. The temperature of the caves where the cheeses are cured never exceeds 53°F (12°C) and humidity is 90–95%.

The most highly-prized Fontina is the summer production made in the high Alpine huts; it has a more buttery consistency due to the higher fat content of the milk and, compared with winter cheeses of the same maturity, more fragrance and savour. The paste is a very pale straw-yellow, supple and almost spreadable; the few round holes are evenly distributed through the cheese.

Summer Fontina contains 37–38% water, 31–33% fat and 25–26% protein. The winter production shows a moisture content of 38–40%, 29–30% fat and 25–26% protein.

Cheeses of the Fontina type (apart from Fontal) are also made in Switzerland, the United States (Midget Fontina), Sweden and other countries.

Formaggella della Val Bavona

A Swiss cheese made with cow's milk; the paste is uncooked and even-textured, soft and delicate in taste. The rind is thin and smooth.

Formaggella Ticinese

A soft cow's milk cheese made in the Italian-speaking Swiss Canton of Ticino. Cylindrical in shape with a tender rind, enclosing a close-textured paste with a delicate taste. Weight 3½–4½ lb (1.5–2 kg).

Formaggio Bianco

This is the Italian generic term for soft cow's milk cheeses which are ripened for only a very short time or not at all, and which have no rind or bloom – the equivalent of the French Fromage Blanc. These cheeses are only very lightly salted.

Fourme d'Ambert
Also known as F. de Montbrison, F. de Pierre-sur-Haute

This French cheese comes from the Auvergne and is a semi-hard cow's milk cheese, shaped like a large cylinder or drum. It is traditionally made by the following method: the partially skimmed raw milk is curdled with liquid rennet, and the curd is placed in cheese forms but is not pressed, so that small spaces and air pockets will remain in which the blue-green mould can develop. Fourme d'Ambert is ripened in a very damp atmosphere for 2–3 months at a temperature of 46–50°F (8–10°C). The rind is dry and wrinkled with patches of mould, and the paste is creamy yellow with blue veining and a subtle and aromatic taste.

Fourme de Cantal see Cantal

Fourme de Montbrison see Fourme d'Ambert

Fourme de Pierre-sur-Haute see Fourme d'Ambert

Fourme de Salers see Cantal, Salers

Freiburger Vacherin, Vacherin Fribourgeois

Produced in the Swiss canton of Fribourg, a soft cow's milk cheese weighing 17½–26½ lb (8–12 kg) and measuring 14 in (35 cm) in height. Preparation entails inoculation of the pasteurized milk with specific acid-producing milk bacteria; coagulation is brought about at a temperature of 96–100°F (36–38°C) by the addition of liquid rennet. The curd is cut into large pieces and heated to 104–107°F (40–42°C). Once in the cheese moulds, the curd is pressed and is then salted in brine after which the cheese forms are cured at 53–57°F (12–14°C) in very damp conditions to encourage the growth of surface flora.

Friese

Produced in the Netherlands with whole or partially skimmed cow's

milk; a very hard, uncooked cheese.

Friese is made by inoculating the milk with lactic ferment starter culture and then coagulating it with liquid or powdered rennet. The curd is then cut, removed from the vat, drained of whey and then mixed with cloves, cumin and salt before being placed in moulds and pressed. The resulting cheeses are cured for several months.

Friese has a smooth, pale straw-yellow rind, usually rubbed with vegetable oils. The texture of the cheese is very dense, and it has a strong taste.

Friulano

Scalded-curd cow's milk cheese from the Friuli region of North Italy. The paste is pressed and firm, with some small holes and yellow-brown rind. In shape and texture it recalls a slightly cured Montasio.

Fromage des Pyrénées

Also known as Fromage du Pays

This is a semi-hard ewe's milk cheese from France, cylindrical in shape and weighing 6½–15½ lb (3–7 kg). The taste is strong or sharp and the dull yellowish-white paste has no holes; the surface is dry and is sometimes coloured black.

Fromage du Pays see Fromage des Pyrénées

Fynbo

The Danish island of Fyn has given yet another member of the Samsø family of cheeses its name. Fynbo is shaped like a squat cylinder and varies in weight from 1–5 lb (500 g – 7 kg).

It is produced with pasteurized cow's milk, inoculated with a culture of lactic ferments which develop in warmth, the milk being heated to 86–89°F (30–32°C), and then curdled with liquid rennet. The dry rind is a golden-brown colour, usually coated with paraffin wax and the paste is creamy white with very large holes.

Gammelost

A Norwegian cheese which is thought to date back to Viking times. It is a skimmed cow's milk product and has internal and external moulds.

The skimmed milk is soured and curdled naturally by the action of *Streptococcus lactis*, a bacterium which occurs in milk. The acid curd is then heated, using one of two techniques: the first entails heating the curd to 145°F (63°C), draining off the whey, and placing the curd in perforated moulds which are placed for several hours in boiling whey. The other method is to bring the whey to boiling point, drain off the whey, cool the curd and then inoculate it with spores of *Penicillium roqueforti* before placing it in moulds.

Gammelost is cured at 50–53°F (10–12°C) in a very damp atmosphere for 4 weeks; colonies of bacteria develop all over the outer surface of the cheese and inside the mould develops along the small fissures in the paste. The rind is soft with a slightly sticky sheen to it and the paste is soft with plentiful blueing from the action of the *Penicillium*.

Geheimratskäse

Germany and Austria both produce this cow's milk cheese. Semi-hard and close-textured with small holes, it has a tender rind and a delicate taste.

Moisture content amounts to 50%, fat 25–30% and protein 20–21%.

Gervais

As well as being the trade mark of the manufacturer who produces these soft, usually acid-curd cheeses on a very large scale, the name Gervais is also used in France and other countries to denote more generally a type of fresh cow's milk cheese packaged in very small tubs.

Getmesost, Gjetost

A Scandinavian speciality which is not strictly speaking a cheese. Made from pure goat's milk whey, it is rectangular, brick-shaped and varies in size and weight from 1–6½ lb (500g – 3 kg) and can be hard or soft depending on the moisture content.

The whey remaining when an ordinary white cheese is made is boiled until it has reduced and thickened and the milk sugar or lactose has caramelized – a process which can take up to 12 hours. The whey can be drained off or not, according to the desired consistency for the end product. The softest Getmesost can be spread on bread; the harder type is served in a block and shaved off in thin flakes with a special knife.

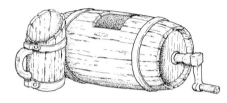

Getost

A hard Swedish goat's milk cheese. It is rectangular and measures 8 x 4¾ in (20 x 12 cm) and is 3½ in (9 cm) high, weighing 3½–6½ lb (1.5 – 3 kg).

The addition of liquid rennet to raw goat's milk produces a curd in 30 minutes at a temperature of 86–89°F (30–32°C). The curd is cut, placed in moulds, pressed and drained for 24 hours. The cheeses are dry-salted and ripened for 2–4 months at 53–59°F (12–15°C).

The rind is dry, sometimes with mould on the surface.

Giuncata

This is a curd cheese not entirely separated from the whey, and it is made from cow's or ewe's milk. The name refers to the rush container in which the curds are separated from most of the whey.

Gjetost see Getmesost

Gloucester, Single Gloucester

A hard, English cheese made with cow's milk and rather like Cheddar. Shaped like a squat cylinder, white in colour with a mild taste.

Only a very small number of these cheeses are made now on a farmhouse basis. Made with one skimmed-milk and one whole milk milking.

Gorgonzola

This famous Italian cheese takes its name from the village of Gorgonzola, near Milan, where the cheese was already being made in the eleventh century. It belongs to the family of soft, uncooked whole cow's milk, blue cheeses. Farmhouse production has now been replaced by industrial creamery manufacture, using pasteurized milk, lactic bacteria starter cultures and moulds selected and nurtured in laboratories – *Penicillium glaucum* – to produce the blueish-green internal veining. Ripening of some of the cheeses still takes place in natural caves, but the majority of Gorgonzola is cured in cheese stores or warehouses where the temperature and humidity are very strictly monitored. Note that this is a different mould from that found in Roquefort and most other blue cheeses.

Gorgonzola is protected by official certification and to qualify for this, the cheese must be produced and cured in one of the following provinces: Bergamo, Brescia, Como, Cremona, Cuneo, Milan, Novara, Pavia or Vercelli.

The technique of making Gorgonzola is as follows: lactic bacteria is added to the raw or pasteurized milk, which is then heated to 89–93°F (32–34°C) and curdled with liquid rennet. Once the curd has reached the required consistency it is cut into thick slices and then into ½–¾ in (1–2 cm) cubes. These are gathered into cheesecloths, placed in moulds and drained for 24 hours, being turned frequently. Heating the curd is the next step, at a temperature of 71–75°F (22–24°C), followed by dry-salting. After 3–4 days, when draining is complete, the cheeses are cured at 39–41°F (4–8°C) in 90% humidity by being subjected to further saltings, brushings, wipings and turnings; finally they are pierced with special steel needles on both sides to enable the air to penetrate the cheese and encourage blueing. After 23–30 days the blue-green moulds develop along the tiny cracks inside the cheese.

Gorgonzola is ready for consumption after 50–60 days, and before it is marketed it is wrapped in foil. The drum-shaped cheeses' average weight varies between 25¼–27½ lb (11.5–12.5 kg), and they measure 10–12 in (25–30 cm) in diameter and are 6¼–8 in (16–20 cm) high. The rind is wrinkly, rough and reddish in colour; inside the cheese is white or pale straw-yellow with the characteristic streaking of blue veins.

It seems that Gorgonzola became famous quite by chance; an innkeeper in Gorgonzola had built up a large stock of Stracchino cheeses in his cellars and when he examined the older ones, he found they had developed mould, and believed them spoiled. In an attempt to cut his losses he served them to his customers, albeit with some trepidation, saying that they were a great delicacy. To his surprise and joy, the guests found this strange blue-green streaked cheese absolutely delicious and kept asking for it – with the result that the local cheesemakers had to increase their output, and

revise their production methods, to keep up with the growing demand.

Another explanation for the origin of Gorgonzola's popularity is more credible. Gorgonzola was a staging post for herdsmen bringing their cows down from the mountain pastures in autumn. The milch cows used to arrive in Gorgonzola in great numbers towards evening, tired after their long journey, and needing to be milked. With such an abundant quantity of milk available the logical step was to make a soft cheese, and since this was made from 'tired' cows, and the Lombard dialect word for tired is *straccho*, the resulting cheese was called *stracchino*. The curds which formed from the evening's milk were mixed with curds from the following morning's milk. So **Stracchino di Gorgonzola**, which came to be called simply Gorgonzola owed its creation to the mixing of the curds from two milkings. The evening curd (having grown cold during the night) and the warm morning curd did not blend together perfectly, leaving spaces and fissures in the new cheese forms, along which the mould could flourish and spread.

Either story may be historically correct, but the very fact that a variety of legends exists concerning Gorgonzola's origins, shows the passionate curiosity that this cheese excites amongst its devotees. Today it is copied in many countries including the United States.

Gorgonzola a Due Paste

An uncooked curd, cylindrical shaped cheese, 10 in (25 cm) in diameter, 7–8 in (18–20 cm) tall and 17½–33 lb (8–10 kg) in weight, made with whole milk fresh from the cow.

Evening milk is curdled with liquid rennet for 30–35 minutes at 82–89°F

(28–32°C) and is cut into pieces the size of hazelnuts; once these have released their whey, they are removed from the vat and hung up to drain in cheesecloths for 12 hours at 68°F (20°C) in a very damp atmosphere full of mould spores. The next morning, straight after milking, the process is repeated with milk still warm from the cow, but draining only lasts 30 minutes. The two curds (*due paste*) are placed in moulds together, the evening's curd being placed in a cone shape in the centre of the cheese form and the warm morning's curd being arranged round it to enclose and hold the curd together. The cold evening's curd leaves air spaces, along which the mould can grow.

After a month the cheeses are pierced with special needles to admit air and encourage even development of the veining.

When the Gorgonzola is ripe it should have a close-textured paste with small holes or patches of slight crumbliness, dark blueish-green veining, a pronounced taste and a sharp, almost spicy flavour.

Gorgonzola Bianco see
Pannerone

Gouda

The old town of Gouda near Rotterdam is the home of one of Holland's most famous cheeses, though now it is made all over the world. It is marketed as a table cheese, or used as the raw material for processed cheeses.

Gouda is a semi-hard cow's milk cheese, and production techniques are similar to those used in making Edam. The rind is hard and dry, the cheese paste mild. Mature or Very Old Gouda has a richer colour and a firm to hard paste. The taste is strong and piquant, with a sharp edge.

Gournay

A soft fresh cheese from Normandy, France, made with whole cow's milk, shaped like a flat cylinder and measuring 2¾–3¼ in (7–8 cm) in diameter; ¾ in (2 cm) thick, and weighing 4 oz (120 g). The paste is close-textured and slightly salty without any covering rind.

Gournay Affiné

This is the ripened version of fresh Gournay; these soft cow's milk cheeses are cured for 7–8 days in damp cellars until the surface is covered with a white bloom. The paste is smooth and has a fairly mild flavour. The cheese is the same shape as fresh Gournay, measuring 3¼ in (8 cm) in diameter and is ¾ in (2 cm) thick.

Graddost

Whole cow's milk is used for this scalded-curd Swedish cheese, which varies in shape (being cylindrical or oblong) and in weight (2¼–33 lb (1–15 kg). The paste is pale yellow in colour, close-textured and easy to slice, with numerous small, irregular holes.

Grana (Padano)

The name of this cheese is descriptive of its texture which is grainy or granular. Grana-type cheeses are cooked, hard and semi-fat and need long, slow ageing. Grana was already being made in the fourteenth century and production spread throughout the dairying provinces of northern Italy; today about one quarter of Italian cow's milk production is taken up in the manufacture of Grana cheeses.

Depending on where the cheese is made, how it is made and the end product's taste and appearance, Grana cheese is classified under several names indicating the various qualities available and the cheese's origin: Grana Parmigiano (see under Parmigiano Reggiano heading), Grana Padano (see below), Grana Lodigiano, and Bagozzo which comes from the wide valleys of the province of Brescia.

Fresh raw cow's milk is taken straight from milking to small rural dairies without delay. Two successive milkings are used for each batch of cheese; the evening's milk having rested in the dairy overnight and the following morning's milk for an hour or so. Some of the cream is skimmed off the top of the milk. These farmhouse producers still work with enormous 2,000 gallon bell-shaped copper kettles – that being enough milk for two cheeses. Natural lactic ferment, whey, starter-culture and powdered calf's rennet are added. The main steps are then as follows:

a) ripening the partially skimmed milk (2% fat content);
b) heating to correct temperature for coagulation: 87–91°F (31–33°C);
c) addition of fermenting whey, full of lactic flora, which will raise the acidity level of the milk naturally;
d) adding the rennet;
e) cutting the curd into pieces the size of rice grains;
f) once the curd has separated from the whey, it is heated to a temperature of 127–131°F (53–55°C);
g) the curd will have sunk to the bottom of the vat and formed a solid mass: this is lifted out, divided in half and placed in cheesecloths in the cheese moulds;
h) when the newly-formed cheese is sufficiently firm, springy and has reached the correct level of acidity (after 48 hours) it is salted in brine; this stage lasts for 26–28 days;
i) ripening under carefully controlled conditions: the temperature must be 64–68°F (18–20°C) and humidity must be maintained at 85%. The cheeses mature for 14–18 months, with regular brushings.

These cheeses weigh about 66 lb (30 kg) each and look like squat cylinders or barrels 14–18 in (35–45 cm) in diameter with a smooth old-gold-coloured rind. The mellow, golden yellow paste has a granular texture with tiny holes evenly scattered throughout it, and the grain of the cheese is radial.

When the cheese has just taken shape in the mould a matrix is introduced and this imprints on the cheese the words 'Grana Padano', guaranteeing the integrity of the product and enabling purchasers to identify the cheesemaker. The words 'Grana Padano' are also imprinted on the rind of the cheese with a hot branding iron.

Mature Grana Padano melts in the mouth like butter, even though its texture is so hard, and it leaves no grainy or gritty aftertaste. The flavour is unmistakable, not sharp but pleasantly appetising and satisfying. The colour of the cheese is soft straw-yellow.

Grana Padano is most widely used as a grating cheese; it is also served as a dessert cheese.

Grana Lodigiano

Another member of the Grana family, nowadays produced in dwindling quantities in its native region, to the south of the province of Milan. The technique is much the same as for Parmigiano Reggiano but the milk is more thoroughly skimmed when it has been left to stand in shallow copper bowls.

Lodigiano cheeses have hard, smooth and shiny rinds. Inside the cheese has a coarse, granular texture with tiny scattered holes containing tears or tiny drops of colourless moisture and a full flavour; once the cheese has been cut, it tends to turn a greenish colour.

Grana Padano see Grana

Grazalema

A hard ewe's milk cheese from Spain which tastes rather similar to Manchego.

Grazalema usually contains 30–35% water, 33% fat and the protein content is 25%.

Grevéost

A Swedish scalded-curd cow's milk cheese produced on an industrial scale. The taste is mild and delicate and the paste has very large round holes.

Greyerzer see Gruyère

Gruyère, Greyerzer

Taking its name from the Swiss village of Gruyères in the French-speaking canton of Fribourg, this cooked whole cow's milk cheese is shaped like a wheel with slightly bulging sides; the diameter is 20–24 in (50–60 cm); height: 4¾ in (12 cm) and weight 77–88 lb (35–40 kg).

The manufacture of Gruyère starts with heating the raw milk to 89–93°F (32–34°C), followed by the addition of liquid rennet. When the curd has formed, it is cut into ⅛–⅜ in (4–10 mm) pieces and these become firmer as they release more whey while being gently stirred; the curd is then cooked, firstly at 109–113°F (43–45°C) and then the temperature is raised to 129–132°F (54–56°C). Gradually the pieces of curd become more dense and grow more shrivelled and shrunken in appearance. The curd is placed in cheese moulds and subjected to pressure by a hydraulic press.

Dry-salting or salting in brine ensues and lasts for 8 days; the cheeses are then ripened for 10 days at 50–55°F (10–13°C), or at 60–62°F (16–17°C) for 2–3 months followed by

further curing at 50–55°F (10–13°C).

Gruyère is ready to eat after 3 months and fully mature after 10 months. The rind is a yellowish dun colour with rind flora, and the paste is ivory with a yellow tinge and widely-scattered round holes ³⁄₁₆–⅜ in (5–10 mm) across. The taste is nutty and flavoursome, yet delicate.

Gruyère is a very famous cheese and the second most important Swiss cheese in terms of production, after Emmental. It is made with milk from two breeds of cow: Fribourg and Simmenthal, which graze the alpine pastures, with their sweet flowers and aromatic grasses. This gives the milk an inimitable fragrance and quality which helps to set genuine Swiss Gruyère apart from the many imitations.

Gruyère de Beaufort

Also known simply as Beaufort after its birthplace in the Haute Tarentaise region of France. Shaped like a flat cylinder, it is a hard cheese with small holes, (or sometimes without holes); the rind is dry and close textured, and the cheeses weigh 55–143 lb (25–65 kg).

Gruyère de Comté

A hard French cheese from the Franche-Comté which has many of the characteristics of the original Swiss Gruyère, being made along similar lines. The interior of the cheese is a soft yellowish-white with medium sized holes and the paste has an aromatic taste, which is also nutty and delicate.

Gudbrandsdalsost

Cow's milk whey enriched with cream and goat's milk are the ingredients for this Norwegian hard cheese.

Coagulation is brought about by heating the milk, cream and whey together.

Haloumi

A soft or semi-hard Cypriot cheese made with goat's milk; rectangular in shape and measuring 28 x 4¾ in (70 x 12 cm) and 1½ in (4 cm) thick.

Raw or pasteurized milk is curdled at 93°F (34°C) in 30–45 minutes, using powdered rennet. The curd is cut until the pieces measure only ⅜–⅝ in (10–15 mm) in diameter, stirred and cooked in whey until boiling point is reached. It is then salted and placed in a whey brine.

Haloumi can be eaten at this point but it can also be kept for up to 40 days in the whey brine. It is a soft, white cheese with no rind and has a lactic, salty flavour.

Handkäse

These are acid curd cheeses, coagulation being brought about by adding acid-producing natural milk bacteria and letting the sour milk curds form at room temperature. Made in central Europe (Germany and Austria) with skimmed milk, they take their name from the fact that they are pressed and moulded by hand.

Handkäse have a strong taste and *very* pronounced aroma when ripened; the texture is homogenous and supple and the rind is delicate, yellow to reddish-brown with patches of mould and white bloom. They are most often oblong or disc-shaped, weighing from 1 oz to 4 oz (25–125 g).

Handkäse are also made in the United States, German immigrants having taken the recipe with them, and the cheeses are now both farmhouse and factory produced.

Average moisture content is 50–55%, fat content is 2% and protein 27–35%.

Harzkäse see Handkäse

Havarti

A Danish semi-hard cow's milk cheese whose paste is liberally scattered with small holes. The cheeses are oblong or shaped in flat rounds, weighing 11 lb (5 kg) or more, and there are two types: one with a dry rind and one with a washed rind, the latter having a fuller flavour.

Herrgårdsost

Made in Sweden with partially skimmed cow's milk, a hard, close-textured cheese with occasional medium-sized holes. The rind can be dry but is usually soft or non-existent when covered in wax or vacuum packed in plastic; the flavour is mild and pleasantly nutty.

Pasteurized milk is used and lactic bacteria are added as a starter culture as well as acid-producing bacteria. The curd is cooked and then placed in moulds and pressed. The freshly-moulded forms are then salted in brine, covered with paraffin wax and cured for 3–4 months at 60°F (16°C), reduced to 53°F (12°C).

Herrgårdsost contains 40–42% water, 24–25% fat and 30–33% protein.

Herve

This is a Belgian cheese made in and around the town of Herve, to the east of Liège, which has been an important cheesemaking and marketing centre for hundreds of years. The cheese is shaped like a squat cube, usually only about 3 in (7.5 cm) thick. It is made with whole cow's milk and the consistency is supple and velvety; the washed rind develops a thin reddish-brown crust; weight varies from 2–14 oz (50–400 g).

Moisture content is 50–52%, fat 23–25% and protein 21–23%.

The pungency of these cheeses is suggested by the English writer Robert Senthy's description of a visit to Herve after the Battle of Waterloo, when he found the air was oppressive with the scent of these cheeses.

Hopfenkäse see Nieheimer

Hushållsost

Swedish scalded-curd cow's milk cheese which is drum or disc-shaped, varying in height from 2–6 in (5–15 cm) and weighing 2¼–4½ lb (1–2 kg). The surface is smooth, and covered in paraffin wax or vacuum-packed in plastic.

Idiazabal

This Spanish ewe's milk cheese comes from the Basque country in north eastern Spain. It is a hard, lightly smoked cheese.

Italico

The generic term 'Italico' was officially approved in 1941 to designate a wide variety of semi-soft, quick-ripening cheeses and to protect the 'Bel Paese' trade mark; the latter had become so popular.

Italico cheese is disc-shaped, 8 in (20 cm) in diameter, the sides being 2–2½ in (5–6 cm) high, and weighs 4–4½ lb (1.8–2 kg). Pasteurized milk is inoculated with starter cultures of *Streptococcus thermophilus* and liquid rennet is added, forming a curd in 15–20 minutes at 107–113°F (42–45°C). The curd is then cut until the pieces are the size of hazelnuts and placed in cylindrical moulds in which it is gently heated and maintained at a temperature of 77–82°F (25–28°C) for 10 hours with 90% humidity.

The cheese forms are salted in brine for 12 hours and then cured on dry wooden planks at 42–46°F (6–8°C) with humidity at 80–85%.

Twenty to thirty days after the cheese has been made, it is ready for consumption. The rind is then smooth and even-textured without cracks, white to pale straw-yellow in colour. The paste of the cheese is dense, supple and buttery with a mild, sweet taste.

Percentages of water, fat and protein are 50.5%, 25% and 21% respectively. An excellent table cheese.

Jack see Monterey

Jarlsberg

A comparatively recent revival of this hard cow's milk cheese has had great success, not only in its home country, Norway, but on the export market. Although softer and sweeter, it is an excellent substitute for Emmental.

Jerome

A semi-hard cheese from Austria and Germany which is made with cow's milk. The rind is a warm reddish-yellow with a dry sheen to it; the paste is mild or slightly sharp.

Kachkaval

Hard ewe's milk cheese from Hungary (but also produced in several other Balkan countries). It is a plastic curd cheese belonging to the same family as the Italian Caciocavallo.

The curd forms in 30–35 minutes at 86–89°F (30–32°C); it is then cut, stirred, and once separation of curd and whey has taken place, warmed at 104–107°F (40–42°C). The cheeses are pressed and drained in their moulds for 2–3 hours, dry-salted and salted in brine before curing starts at 50°F (10°C), lasting 2–3 months.

Kachkaval has a dry, supple rind and an aromatic, salty flavour.

Kaşar

Turkish hard ewe's milk cheese which varies greatly in weight from 2¼–22 lb (1–15 kg).

The cheesemaking process starts with the coagulation of the milk protein at 89–91°F (32–33°C) in 60–80 minutes. The curd is then cut into pieces the size of rice grains, gathered into cheesecloths and pressed for 24 hours until it has acquired a springy consistency. It is then placed in wicker basket moulds, and immersed in water at a temperature of 149–167°F (65–75°C) for a few minutes. Once the cheese has cooled it is ready to be dry-salted for 15 days and curing takes 2–3 months.

When the cheese is mature the rind is smooth and dry; the paste is very dense without any holes. Kaşar is particularly strong-tasting and quite pungent.

Kaseri

A plastic or spun-curd cheese made from ewe's milk in Greece, resembling Italian Provolone in consistency. The large flat wheels average 20 lb (9 kg) in weight.

Kefalotiri

A mixture of ewe's and goat's milk goes into the making of this hard cheese from Cyprus.

Whole milk, usually raw, is curdled at 93°F (34°C) in 30–45 minutes using powdered rennet. Cutting the curd into pieces measuring 3/16–1/4 in (5–7 mm) is followed by stirring for 30–40 minutes and pressing for 5–10 hours. The cheese forms are dry-salted and ripened for 2–3 months at 64°F (18°C). Kefalotiri has a dry, yellowish rind and close-textured, hard paste with a salty taste.

Kernhem

A very soft Dutch whole cow's milk cheese shaped like a squat cylinder and weighing 3¼–3¾ lb (1.5–1.7 kg). The surface is greyish-white and rindless, the paste close-textured, the taste mild. Ripened for 30 days in a cool, very damp atmosphere.

Klosterkäse

This soft, German surface-ripened cheese is very similar to Romadur. It is made with partially skimmed cow's milk and the paste is velvety and covered by a thin skin with a surface bloom. Like a flattened cube or block in shape, it is 1¼ in (3 cm) square and 3¼–3½ in (8–9 cm) high.

Water content is 50–55%, fat 18–20% and protein 22–25%.

Kopanisti

Greek ewe's milk cheese which has greenish-blue veining in the firm yet creamy paste.

After the curd has been drained of whey it is left in cheesecloths until covered in mould and then mixed with salt and placed in pots to ripen for 1–2 months.

Korbkäse

Soft, acid-curd cheese made in Germany from cow's milk. The texture is smooth and the thin crust has a white bloom on it; weight ranges from 1–4 oz (25–125 g).

Kümmelkäse

Another soft, German cow's milk cheese with a close-textured paste and mould-smeared surface; weighing 3½–5 oz (100–150 g). Resembles Cheddar in consistency but is flavoured with caraway seeds and other spices.

Kümmelkäse contains 55–60% water, 20–22% fat and 18–20% protein.

Kvarg see Quark

Laguiole
Also known as Laguiole-Aubrac

A cow's milk cheese which comes from Aquitaine in France and takes its name from the small town of Laguiole, high up (3,280 ft; 1,000 m) in the Aubrac mountains. A semi-hard, pressed, uncooked cheese with a supple homogeneous interior, the rind being soft and dry.

Whole or partially skimmed milk takes 30 minutes to coagulate and the curd is cut, drained and left to acquire the correct level of acidity before it is placed in moulds and pressed.

Moisture content is 35–40%, fat 27–28% and protein 23–28%.

Lancashire

Lancashire's white or pale cream paste is soft, crumbly and moist with superb melting qualities – indeed it is the proper cheese for a decent 'rarebit'. The rind is dry. The taste is mild and slightly salty when made in industrial creameries, farmhouse cheeses having a far fuller, superior flavour.

Langres

Produced in the Champagne region of France: a soft cow's milk cheese shaped like a truncated cone, measuring 4 in (10 cm) across the base and standing 1½–2 in (4–5 cm) high; weight is about 10½ oz (300 g). The texture is homogeneous and the soft delicate rind is covered with surface flora; the taste is savoury and tangy.

The milk is curdled slowly at 86–89°F (30–32°C) with a small quantity of rennet; the curd is then placed in cylindrical moulds and allowed to drain until it has become firm enough to be salted. After salting the cheeses are cured for 2–3 months in cool, damp conditions and the rind is washed at intervals.

Latteria

A widely-used generic term for cheese produced in dairies throughout the Friuli Plain in Italy using the same technique as that used for Montasio. 'Latteria Fresco' – fresh dairy cheese – is marketed 1–3 months after it has been made; semi-mature after 5 months and the mature cheese is aged for 11–12 months.

Leicester

Whole cow's milk is used for this English cheese made in a large cylindrical shape and varying in weight from 9–45 lb (4–20 kg), but

averaging 20 lbs. It is a hard cheese with a grainy yet moist texture, covered with a hard, natural dry rind.

The technique of Leicester cheese-making shows a certain similarity to that of Cheddar.

Interest in Farmhouse Leicester is reviving – fortunately, for it is infinitely better than the factory product, having a fuller, richer flavour.

León

A hard, uncooked Spanish cow's milk cheese, drum-shaped and weighing between 1 and 1¾ lb (500–800 g). The cheese is dry-salted and ripened at 53–57°F (12–14°C) for 20 days, by which time the white, bland, close-textured paste is covered with a hard, rough, yellowish rind.

Levroux

Soft goat's milk cheese made in the town of the same name in the French province of Berry. It is exactly the same as Valençay, and is shaped like a squat, truncated pyramid.

Leyden

The city of Leiden in the Netherlands gave this cheese its name; it is a hard, close-textured product made from partially skimmed cow's milk and the curd is flavoured with cumin, caraway seeds and spices. The natural

rind is hard.

The cheesemaking process entails curdling the milk at 82–86°F (28–30°C); the curd is then cut and heated to 95–98°F (35–37°C) and placed in moulds, flavourings being sprinkled between layers of curd. The cheeses are allowed to drain and are then pressed. Curing takes place in damp, cool cellars or curing rooms.

Liederkranz

This cheese was invented by a German immigrant in the United States towards the end of the last century. It is made with pasteurized cow's milk and has its own distinctive mild flavour and bouquet.

Limbourg, Limburger

This cheese was first made in Belgium in the province of Limburg but was adopted by Allgäuer cheesemakers in the nineteenth century and is now generally considered a German cheese. It is surface-ripened, depending on the growth of moulds to bring the cheese to maturity.

Pasteurized milk is used nowadays, replacing raw milk which was traditional, and the cheesemaking technique follows the procedure adopted for other soft, surface-ripened cheeses with flourishing surface yeasts and bacteria, such as Romadur and Maroilles. Once the milk has been pasteurized at 161°F (72°C) it is cooled to 86°F (30°C), inoculated with *Streptococcus lactis* and *Streptococcus thermophilus*; when the correct acidity has developed, the milk is coagulated with liquid rennet. The curd is then cut and heated in the whey to 95°F (35°C), and placed in rectangular moulds measuring 4 x 2¾ in (10 x 7 cm) and 2½–2¾ in (6–7 cm) deep. The cheese forms are then dry salted and ripened at 59°F (15°C) in an atmosphere of 95% humidity until the surface is covered with a characteristic reddish sheen, proof that the mould is developing which will ripen the cheese. After 10–12 days, the temperature is lowered to 50°F (10°C) and the cheese continues to ripen until it is mature.

Limburger is fairly close-textured, a creamy pale straw-yellow in colour, and with a strong aroma – the result of the action of the surface flora whose enzymes break down the casein (cheese protein). It is a washed rind cheese.

Liptauer

The German name for a cheese now produced in Hungary. It is a soft, dense ewe's milk cheese with no rind and a strong taste.

To make it, milk is coagulated at 75–77°F (24–25°C). The curd is drained, pressed and shaped into small blocks, then ripened for 8–10 days. The skin is then cut off and the cheese is blended with salt and shaped into small blocks to ripen further for a few more days at 46–50°F (8–10°C).

Liptauer contains 50% water, 22–23% fat and 20–22% protein.

Livarot

A soft French cheese made with whole cow's milk. The flat discs measure 4¾–5 in (12–12.5 cm) in diameter and are 1½–2 in (4–5 cm) thick, weighing about 1 lb – 1 lb 2 oz (450–500 g).

Milk is left to ripen for 15–24 hours at room temperature and then curdled at 82–89°F (28–32°C). The curd is placed in cheesecloths and given 24 hours to drain before it is placed in moulds. The resulting cheese forms are dry-salted and cured at 59–60°F (15–16°C) for 3–4 weeks; during this time the surface of the cheese is wiped with a cloth dipped in brine.

The rind is tough, smooth and glossy with surface mould, and inside the yellow paste is even-textured and springy with a tangy and well-defined flavour and smell. Water content is 50–52%, fat 20% and protein 23–25%.

Livarot is one of the oldest, finest and most famous Normandy cheeses. It takes its name from the town of Livarot in the Calvados country, situated in the middle of the region where the best Livarot is made.

Livarot is protected by an *appellation d'origine* and the label should show the words *Pays d'Auge* for the genuine article.

Lou Palou

In the south-west of France this hard, pressed scalded-curd cheese is made from ewe's milk and sometimes from cow's milk too. It is wheel-shaped and weighs 8¾–13¼ lb (4–6 kg); the

rind is dry and black, enclosing the dense yet supple interior.

The taste is typical of many ewe's milk cheeses – pleasantly tangy, strong and aromatic. When made with cow's milk the flavour is delicate and nutty.

Maasdam

This is a recently developed factory-produced hard cow's milk cheese which can best be described as a Dutch version of Emmental. The taste is pleasantly mild with a slightly nutty flavour.

Mahón

Made in Spain and in the Balearic Islands with cow's and ewe's milk.

The milk is coagulated at a temperature of 86°F (30°C) and the curd is then cut and pressed, moulded in cloths into oblongs and salted in brine before being cured at 64°F (18°C) for 20–30 days. The pale yellow, dense, oily rind encloses a paste which becomes harder and darker with age.

Mainauer käse

A semi-hard cow's milk cheese which is called after the island of Mainau on Lake Constance (bordered by Germany and Switzerland). The cheeses are shaped like flat cylinders.

Pasteurized milk is used, being curdled for 25 minutes at 100°F (38°C); the curd is then cut into ¹⁄₁₆–⅛ in (2–3 mm) pieces and heated to 109–113°F (43–45°C) and stirred; after that it is put into moulds. The cheeses are salted in brine and matured at 50–53°F (10–12°C) with 90% humidity. Mainauer's texture is smooth, and the cheese is aromatic and pleasantly acidulated, the thin skin being covered with mould.

Mainauer contains 43% water, 25–26% fat and 23–25% protein.

Málaga

Fresh goat's milk cheese made in the southern Spanish province of Málaga, Andalusia. The taste is delicate, recognisable as a goat's cheese, slightly aromatic but not sharp.

Usually eaten within a few days of being made.

Mamirolle

A semi-hard French cow's milk cheese which is brick-shaped and weighs usually/approximately 1–1½ lb (500–600 g).

Made by following virtually the same technique as for Limburger, but Mamirolle is a recently-invented cheese and not quite so savoury and pungent. It is a lightly pressed, washed-rind cheese with a reddish skin; smooth textured and delicately flavoursome.

Manchego

A famous Spanish cheese made with ewe's milk and called after the region of Spain where it is made, La Mancha, homeland of the immortal Don Quixote.

Nowadays pasteurized milk is used, with a starter of lactic bacteria, and curdled at 86–89°F (30–32°C). Once the curd is cut it is heated in the whey to 102–104°F (39–40°C), and the curd is then allowed to precipitate to the bottom of the vat and form a single solid mass, being gently pressed to bind it together and make it more homogeneous. This curd is then cut into pieces, placed in moulds and firmly pressed. Salting in brine is succeeded by curing. Also eaten fresh.

The rind is dry and covered with a greenish-black mould; sometimes this is brushed off before the cheese is marketed and the surface may be smeared with olive oil. The light-gold paste is compact, hard and has a decided flavour which becomes more pronounced as the cheese ages.

Manchego contains 35–40% water, 21–23% fat and 20–21% protein.

Manteca
Also known as Burrino, Butirro

In the south of Italy, the Spanish word for butter – *mantequilla* – has been modified and used to describe this cheese. Layers of spun curd cheese are wrapped around a pat of butter, forming a cheese shaped like a loaf, pear or ball; this custom probably dates back before the days of refrigeration, and was one solution to the problem of keeping butter fresh in a hot climate.

The cheeses are small, 5–9 oz (150–250 g) in weight, and the name varies from locality to locality: **Butirri, Burri** or **Burrini.** They are similar in shape to other soft spun-curd cheeses (such as Provolette) but once cut, the butter hidden in the middle of the cheese is exposed.

Preparation follows the method used for soft spun-curd cheeses until the spinning stage. A small bag is shaped by hand with a cylindrical hole about ½ in (1 cm) wide in the middle. Butter is placed in this hole and sometimes cream, then sealed in while the spun curd cheese is still warm. Salting follows, and sometimes smoking.

Margotin

Fresh cheese from the Périgord region in France. This is the trade name for a rich type of cheese flavoured with pepper or herbs.

Maribo

A semi-hard cow's milk cheese from the Danish island of Lolland. The cheeses can be oblong or wheel-shaped and weigh 11–30¾ lb (5–14 kg). Pasteurized milk is used, and liquid rennet is added to form a curd in 30–40 minutes. The curd is cut, and heated to 100–104°F (38–40°C); the whey is then drawn off and the curd is salted. The curd is pressed in moulds and may be salted in brine; the cheese forms are cured for 3–5 weeks at 59–60°F (15–16°C).

Maribo has a dry, yellowy-brown rind and is usually coated with paraffin wax; the paste is white with small holes, and the flavour varies from mild to quite strong and aromatic, depending on the age of the cheese.

Marmora

A soft uncooked Danish cheese made with cow's milk with blue veining. The cheese is wheel-shaped.

Maroilles
Also known as Marolles

This soft French uncooked cow's milk cheese is protected by law: only cheeses made within the approved region may bear the name of Maroilles. Production is therefore limited to the Departments of the Aisne and Nord, embracing four versions which vary in weight from 6 oz – 1½ lb (180–720 g), known as *Quart, Mignon, Sorbais,* and full-size *Maroilles.* Minimum fat content in dry matter is 45% and maximum moisture content is 50%. The cheese is square with a fairly dry reddish rind, smooth and shiny in appearance, and the interior is a pale straw colour, smooth, rich and creamy.

Whole milk from two successive milkings is used to make Maroilles; the milk is cooled to 39°F (4°C) in the milking parlour and kept at 44°F (7°C) in the cheesemaker's dairy. Just before the cheese is to be made, the milk is pasteurized at a relatively low temperature (154–161°F; 68–72°C) for 15 seconds, and inoculated with *Streptococcus cremoris, Streptococcus lactis, Streptococcus diacetilactis* and *Leuconostoc citrovorum*; it is then curdled at 82°F (28°C) with liquid rennet. When a thin layer of whey is observed to have collected on top of the curd, the curd is cut into walnut-sized pieces or a little smaller, depending on the type of Maroilles to be produced. The curd is allowed to drain and then placed in moulds, turned several times and salted in brine. The cheese forms are then kept at a temperature of 53–57°F (12–14°C) with 70–80% humidity to allow the surface of the cheese to develop a covering of moulds and yeast: these lower the acidity level of the rind and create ideal conditions for the red mould microflora to grow, once it has been brushed onto the rind after the surface has been washed with salted water. The curing stage proper then commences at a temperature of 51–53°F (11–12°C) with 90–95% humidity. During this phase the surface of the cheese turns the distinctive reddish colour and a rough crust.

Ripening continues for up to 6 months with regular washings of the rind in salted water. The tender rind's red colour betrays the presence of specific microflora which must produce the enzymes needed to ripen the cheese from the outside inwards towards the middle of the cheese: brushing and bathing the rind encourages this process.

The moisture content of Maroilles is about 50%, fat accounts for 25.5% and the protein content is 23%.

Maroilles is the oldest and most famous of Flanders cheeses and was invented in 960 by the monks of the Abbey of Maroilles where the remains of St. Hubert are enshrined. As the years passed the quality of the cheese was perfected and it is said to have been the favourite of Charles V, Philip Augustus, Louis XI, Charles VI, Francis I, Henry IV, the Abbé Fénélon, the great soldier Turenne and many other celebrities.

On 28 May 1961, the Abbot of the Abbey of Saint-Paul-de-Wisques delivered a sermon during a mass celebrated in the church of Maroilles to mark the 1,000th birthday of this local delicacy, and he described the cheese as being blonde, encased in a reddish skin, and with a strong, full attractive aroma: this last being the particular glory of Maroilles.

Mascarpone
Also known as Mascherpone

Mascarpone first came from the southern region of the province of Milan and production was almost exclusively confined to the winter months. Nowadays efficient refrigerated transport means that this cheese can be marketed all the year round.

Mascarpone is rather like clotted cream in appearance: velvety, thick and rich, with a sweet, delicate flavour. It is made with cream skimmed off the top of milk, or, better still, separated by centrifuge, the fat content of the cream being 25–35%. It is heated, over water, to 185–194°F (85–90°C) and stirred continuously. Citric or tartaric acid is then added and the mixture is stirred gently until the small lumps of curd grow larger. The curd is then turned into finely-woven hemp cloths or muslin cheesecloth, and drained for 24 hours at a temperature of 46–50°F (8–10°C). When this stage is completed the Mascarpone is beaten or whipped and then packed into small tubs, or occasionally special muslin bags. It is not only used a great deal in the same way as cream, with fruit and cakes, but also plays an important part in many local Italian specialities.

The moisture content is 45–50%, fat content is 45–55%, protein 7–8% and lactose (milk sugar) 2–3%.

Mascherpone see Mascarpone

Masnor

Made in Yugoslavia, Greece and neighbouring countries from goat's milk whey. Shaped like an elongated pear with a thin smooth skin and dense paste without any holes. The method of making the cheese resembles that of Ricotta, but Masnor is dry-salted and ripened for 1–2 months at 50–59°F (10–15°C).

Meshanger

A soft Dutch cheese made with cow's milk: the paste is even-textured and creamy with a delicate taste, covered by a thin yellow natural crust.

Meshanger contains 52–54% water, 23–24% fat and 20–21% protein.

Mesost

Made in Sweden from cow's milk whey. Usually firm and close textured but a soft and spreadable version is also sold.

Mimolette

A semi-hard cow's milk cheese made in France and the Netherlands. Look-

ing like a rather squashed ball, it weighs 5½–6½ lb (2.5–3 kg); the rind is dry and hard with brownish-grey mould, enclosing the ochre or orange-coloured paste (dyed with annatto) which contains the occasional small hole. It has a pleasantly nutty and rather salty savour.

Its manufacture entails curdling the pasteurized milk at 86–89°F (30–32°C) by adding starter cultures of lactic bacteria and rennet. Once the curd has been cut and has released some of the whey, hot water is added to raise the temperature to 89–93°F (32–34°C). When all the whey has been released, the curd is placed in moulds and pressed. The cheese forms are then salted in brine and kept at a temperature of 53–59°F (12–15°C) with 90% humidity for 6–8 weeks.

Minas
Also known as Minas Curado

A semi-hard aged cow's milk cheese from Minas Gerais in Brazil; the dry rind is thin and the interior of the cheese is scattered unevenly with holes. Weight varies from 1¾–2¾ lb (800 g – 1.2 kg). Analysis shows an average water content of 45%, 20% fat and 28% protein.

Minas Frescal
Also known as Mineiro Frescal

A fresh cheese from Minas Gerais (Brazil) made with cow's milk.

After the curd is cut it is salted and placed in moulds; in 2–3 days time the round cheese, weighing 1–2¾ lb (500 g – 1.2 kg) is ready for consumption. The skin is thin, smooth and white

and the paste is soft, white and without holes. The taste is pleasantly acidulated.

Minas Frescal can contain as much as 60% water; its average fat content is 15–16% and protein content is 17–19%.

Mīsh

Buffalo milk cheese from Egypt which is stored for a year in a brine of buttermilk and salt, sometimes seasoned with paprika.

Mischling

An Austrian hard cheese shaped like a wheel, 16 in (40 cm) in diameter, 3–4 in (8–10 cm) thick and weighing 17½–44 lb (8–20 kg). Cow's milk is coagulated at 86°F (30°C) using a starter of milk bacteria which develop in warmth and moisture. The curd is cut into 3/16–¼ in (5–7 mm) granules and re-heated to 96–100°F (36–38°C).

Mischling has a golden-brown rind, dry, close-textured, and without cracks; inside, the paste is creamy-white with holes formed by gas during the ripening process, as well as irregular fissures.

Molbo

Made in the region of Mols in the Danish province of Randers from pasteurized cow's milk. The round cheese looks very like Dutch Edam

and weighs 2¼–6½ lb (1–3 kg); it is a table cheese with a firm, close-textured bright yellow paste and few holes. The dry rind is golden-brown and usually coated with red paraffin wax. The flavour is delicate and slightly acidulated.

Moldavian

The USSR produces this smoked ewe's milk cheese which is shaped like a squat cylinder and weighs 4½–5½ lb (2–2.5 kg).

Milk is coagulated at 86–93°F (30–34°C), and the curd is cut as soon as it is firm enough, then heated in the whey to 107–111°F (42–44°C). The cheese forms are salted in brine and at one point during the curing process are immersed in hot water – 167–176°F (75–80°C) – until they have formed an outer skin. They are then smoked. This cheese contains 42% water, 30–31% fat and 23–25% protein.

Montecenisio

A soft blue cheese called after the region where it is made, which straddles the borders of France and Italy, west of Turin. Cow's milk is normally used, sometimes with an admixture of goat's milk to make these drum-shaped cheeses. Milk from two successive milkings is used (the first having been left to stand and some of the cream skimmed off the top); it is curdled at 77–86°F (25–30°C). The curd is drained for 24 hours, at which point a smaller quantity of fresh curd is added, and these two curds are placed in moulds and pressed. After

3–4 days the newly-formed cheeses are placed in the cheese-ripening store and dry-salted.

Mondseer

A semi-hard Austrian table cheese made with cow's milk in small wheel-shapes, 6 in (15 cm) in diameter and weighing about 2¼ lb (1 kg). Most of the coagulation is brought about by rennet, but the milk will have previously been inoculated with a starter culture of lactic bacteria which thrive in warm conditions. Once the curd has formed at 102–104°F (39–40°C) it is cut into ½–¾ in (1–2 cm) cubes, drained and salted in brine, then ripened for 6–7 weeks.

The cheese's interior is supple, pale yellowish in colour, dotted with small, irregular shaped holes. The rind is dry and thin. Taste evolves from mild in a young cheese to full and piquant in taste and smell.

Montasio

Produced in the region of Carnia in northern Italy and traditionally made with whole cow's milk in the provinces of Udine and Gorizia. A rich, hard, cooked cheese which is wheel-shaped with straight or slightly bulging sides. Diameter varies from 12–16 in (30–40 cm), depending on where it is made, and it is 3–4 in (8–10 cm) thick.

Manufacture includes the following stages: very fresh, unripened raw milk is heated to 87–95°F (31–35°C), and whey which has been left over from the previous batch of cheese will

sometimes be used as a starter. The milk is coagulated with powdered rennet, taking 30–40 minutes to form a curd, which is then gradually cut into smaller and smaller pieces until the curd is the size of maize grains. The temperature is then slowly increased to 118–122°F (48–50°C). Once the curd has been 'cooked' it is turned over and broken up with a special sharp-edged tool known as a 'thorn-bush'; it is then stirred for 15–35 minutes to promote the release of whey from the curd. By the end of this period, the pieces of curd are wrinkled and shrunken, ready to be placed in moulds and put under a torque press for 24 hours. The cheese forms are dry-salted for 10–12 days or salted in brine for 4–7 days; they are then aged at 59–63°F (15–18°C) with 80% humidity for 6–12 months.

If Montasio is only matured for a short period, it has a smooth, supple and even-textured rind, and a firm, homogeneous pale straw-yellow paste with a few scattered holes; at this stage it makes a good dessert cheese. When aged the rind becomes hard, dry and brown and the paste is friable and granular with tiny holes – it can then be used for grating.

Monterey
Also known as Jack

A semi-hard cheese made in the United States and Canada with cow's milk by much the same method as Colby. Monterey can be disc-shaped, weighing 6½–9 lb (3–4 kg), or oblong, weighing ½–1 lb (220–450 g); the rind is thin and the creamy-yellow paste is bland and buttery.

If skimmed milk is used, the cheese is hard; if a table cheese is wanted it is matured for 3–6 weeks in an atmosphere of 70% humidity at a temperature of 51–53°F (11–12°C); while a grating cheese will need at least 6 months' curing. Sometimes the surface of these cheeses is smeared with oil and black pepper.

The dessert quality of Monterey Jack contains 42–44% water, 23–25% fat and 25–28% protein; the grating type Monterey or Dry Jack, only has 34% water, 20–21% fat and 40–41% protein.

Morbier

A hard, uncooked cow's milk cheese which comes from the Franche-Comté in France. The thick discs measure 14–16 in (35–40 cm) in diameter, are 3–3½ in (7–9 cm) thick and weigh 13¼–17½ lb (6–8 kg).

Coagulation of the milk is effected at 89–93°F (32–34°C) after the milk has been inoculated with a starter culture of lactic bacteria, using liquid rennet. The curd is then heated to 96–100°F (36–38°C) by the addition of hot water; it is then drained, pressed and salted in brine. The cheeses are ripened for 2–3 months.

The paste has no holes and is delicate in flavour, covered by a thin yellowish skin. Moisture content is 44%, fat 28–29%, protein 23–24%.

Morbier looks rather strange when cut, revealing a thin horizontal black band or streak across the middle of its interior. This is caused by the cheese form being cut in half horizontally using a knife which has been dipped in the soot which collects underneath the vats used to heat the milk. The custom provides a link with the past, for Morbier cheeses used to be made with two curds, one made several hours after the other and a layer of soot was sprinkled over the earlier curd to protect it until the next curd was ready.

Morlacco

An Italian cow's milk cheese which resembles Montasio. Shaped like a squat cylinder, the cheeses weigh 15½–19¾ lb (7–9 kg). The rind is smooth and reddish-yellow, while the paste is firm, close-textured and has very few holes.

Mozzarella di Bufala

An unmistakable snow-white spun-curd soft cheese which originally came from the south of Italy, where only buffalo milk was used to make it; the forerunner of such cow's milk products as Fior di Latte and Pizza Cheese which are nowadays manufactured all over the world. In 1979 it was given official protection and makers of genuine Buffalo Milk Mozzarella have to comply with certain standards and methods of production to merit the right to call their cheese genuine Mozzarella. The cheese ripens very rapidly indeed and is past its best within a matter of days, so distribution and marketing must be efficient.

Farmhouse production in the provinces of Caserta and Salerno follows the traditional method of coagulating the milk at 89–93°F (32–34°C), using liquid rennet. The curd takes 35–40 minutes to form and is then cut, first coarsely and then into smaller pieces, until the curds measure ¾–1¼ in (2–3 cm). The curd is allowed to precipitate to the bottom of the vat and stand, covered by the whey, for 3–4 hours. This settling process gives the lactic acid a chance to work on the

curd and makes it easier to knead and spin. The curd is lifted out of the whey, broken up, and hot water is then added at a temperature of 194–203°F (90–95°C); the curd is kneaded until it forms a smooth, shiny mass of spun curd, from which small pieces are cut off (the term for this in Italian is *mozzare* – hence Mozzarella) and shaped into individual cheeses. These are placed in cold water to cool, then salted in brine for 10–20 minutes. The cheeses are now ready to be sold in their keeping fluid which can be either lightly acidulated water, some of the cooled water in which they were kneaded, or water and milk.

In pursuit of the highest standards of hygiene, the milk is increasingly being pasteurized, making necessary the use of specially prepared starter cultures of lactic bacteria which will develop in a warm, moist environment and raise the acidity level of the milk.

Mozzarella has the thinnest of soft skins, smooth, shiny and porcelain white. For a short while after the cheeses have been made the consistency is somewhat supple and springy but the texture gradually changes to a soft, almost melting consistency; when cut it can be seen that the cheese is composed of thin layers or leaves (not unlike a cut section of raw puff pastry) which tend to merge together towards the heart of the paste. As the cheese is cut, it releases drops of cloudy liquid which have a pleasant, fresh taste with a hint of acidulation.

Mozzarella has no holes and an even texture, slightly acidulated and very fresh-tasting with a pleasing fragrance. It usually contains 55–60% water (65% at the most), 16–21% protein and 18–22% fat, and is sometimes smoked.

Mozzarella is mainly made in winter and spring, when the buffalo milk is at its most plentiful since the calves are born in the autumn.

Munster

A whole cow's milk soft cheese whose character and ripening qualities are dependant to a great extent on the growth of microflora on its surface. Usually made in large disc shapes, varying in weight from 10½ oz – 3½ lb (300 g – 1.5 kg).

As is the case with so many cheeses, Munster owes its existence to the skill and inventiveness of monks. It was first made by Irish or Italian members of the Benedictine order who settled in the Munster valley in the Vosges region in France during the course of the 8th century.

The cheese is now safeguarded by an *appellation d'origine* and bears a label to show that it in the genuine article. It is made with pasteurized milk, cooled to 89°F (32°C), inoculated with lactic ferment cultures and curdled with liquid rennet in abut 20 minutes. The curd is cut until the pieces are only just over ¼ in (5–8 mm) in diameter and then heated in the whey to approximately 98°F (37°C) over a period of 30 minutes before being stirred to promote further release of whey for another 30 minutes. The curd is then placed is square or rectangular moulds and drained for 4–5 hours, with frequent turning.

Munster has a very distinctive orange-yellow rind, the paste is open-textured with cracks and the flavour is delicate but with a hint of saltiness.

Murazzano

Murazzano is called after the town of the same name in the Italian province of Cuneo. It is a soft, uncooked cheese with a high fat content, generally made from a mixture of milk types: ewe's milk must account for at least 60%, and cow's milk for not more than 40%, taken from two successive milkings. The cheeses are cylindrical, 4–4¾ in (10–12 cm) in diameter, 1¼–1½ in (3–4 cm) high and weighing 10½–14 oz (300–400 g).

The milk is heated to 98°F (37°C) and the curd forms within an hour following the addition of liquid rennet; it is then cut and placed in moulds which have perforated bases. After 24 hours the cheeses are sufficiently firm and well-shaped to be removed from the moulds, dry-salted and then stored for 7–10 days in a cool atmosphere, being washed each day.

The cheese has no rind and the texture is dense; when fresh, the colour is milky white, turning to pale straw-yellow in ripened cheeses which also have a very light glaze or sheen.

Murbodner

Wheel-shaped Austrian cooked-curd cheese made with cow's milk which weighs 26½–33 lb (12–15 kg). In taste, appearance and texture it is much like Emmental, but the rind is thin, tender and hardly discernible. Curing takes 2 months at 71–75°F (22–24°C).

Moisture content is 38–40%, fat 28% and protein 25–26%.

Murol

The Auvergne, in France, is the region which produces this semi-

hard uncooked pressed cheese made with cow's milk. It is disc-shaped, 4¾–5 in (12–13 cm) in diameter, 1¼–1½ in (3–4 cm) thick and weighs from 14 oz to just over 1 lb (400–500 g). The washed rind is reddish-pink in colour and the cheese has a hole in the centre 1¼–1½ in (3–4 cm) in diameter. The flavour progresses from being mild when young to having a strong aromatic savour when older. Ripening takes 6–7 weeks in damp, cool conditions.

Mycella

A semi-hard Danish cow's milk blue cheese which is drum-shaped; it is 10½ in (27 cm) in diameter, 8 in (20 cm) high and weighs 11–19¾ lb (5–9 kg). The paste is creamy yellow with greenish-blue veins and shows cracks where the cheese has been pierced to introduce the mycelium mould.

Nantais

Nantais, or *véritable Nantais* as it is known, is a semi-hard French cow's milk cheese which has a smooth-textured paste without any holes and a light brown washed rind with surface flora. The aroma is full and strong.

Neufchâtel

This cheese is called after the town which lies at the heart of the finest cheesemaking area in Normandy (the Pays de Bray). Neufchâtel is an uncooked cheese which is soft and delicate, made with skimmed or whole cow's milk, sometimes enriched with cream. It has much in common with such cheeses as Petit-Suisse and Petit-Carré, the main divergence being a lower fat content and Neufchâtel's wide variety of shapes.

Pasteurized, homogenized milk is cooled to 82–86°F (28–30°C). Starter cultures of lactic bacteria are added and sufficient liquid rennet to produce a curd in 16–18 hours. The curd is drained, cooled in water, salted and mixed; at this point it is ready for consumption.

The flavour is pleasantly fragrant and fresh and particularly well-suited for baked dishes which call for a fresh soft cheese.

Nieheimer

Also known as Hopfenkäse

A German cheese made with skimmed milk; a curd is formed by lactic acid coagulation and the whey is drained off. The curd is then mixed with salt and caraway seeds, blended and moulded into small cheeses, each weighing 1–1½ oz (30–40 g). After a short ripening period the cheeses are wrapped in hop leaves and are then ready for consumption. The texture is smooth without holes, and there is no rind.

Niolo

A soft Corsican ewe's milk cheese, sometimes made with a mixture of ewe's and goat's milk. Oblong in

shape, measuring 4¾ x 4¾ – 6 x 6 in (12 x 12 cm – 15 x 15 cm), it is 2 in (5 cm) thick, and varies from 14 oz to 1¼ lb (400–600 g) in weight. Making this cheese entails pasteurization of the milk, followed by coagulation at 82–86°F (28–30°C) with liquid rennet. The curd is cut, stirred and then drained for 8–24 hours in moulds; the cheese forms are then dry-salted and ripened for 15 days at 50–53°F (10–12°C).

The rind is washed at intervals with a solution of salt and water.

Niva

The USSR and Czechoslovakia both produce this blue cheese from cow's or ewe's milk which is reminiscent of Roquefort in taste and consistency. The veined paste is enclosed by a soft rind with surface mould. Niva contains 47% water, 23% fat and 21–22% protein.

Njeguški

A hard Yugoslavian cheese made with ewe's milk, sometimes mixed with cow's milk. The cylindrical cheese is 8–12 in (20–30 cm) in diameter and weighs 4½–6½ lb (2–3 kg).

The milk is coagulated at 86°F (30°C) and the curd is then cut and heated to 104–113°F (40–45°C), pressed in moulds, dry-salted and cured for 3–4 months.

Contains 30–35% water, 32–35% fat and 30–32% protein.

Nøgelost see Nøkkelost

Nøkkel see Nøkkelost

Nøkkelost

Also known as Nøkkel, Nøgelost

A Norwegian cheese made with partially skimmed cow's milk and flavoured with cumin and caraway seeds. The wheel-shaped cheese usually weighs 15½–19¾ lb (7–9 kg) but can be as heavy as 33 lb (15 kg).

Normal moisture content is 40–45%, fat 19–20% and protein 30–35%.

Nøkkelost's label shows the crossed keys emblem of the City of Leiden (Netherlands) and this cheese is a milder version of the Dutch cheese. The Norwegian word *nøkkel* means keys, hence the cheese's name.

Normanna

Another Norwegian cow's milk cheese. Normanna is a semi-hard cylindrical cheese weighing 6½ lb (3 kg).

The milk is pasteurized and homogenized before being curdled at 86–89°F (30–32°C), having first been inoculated with lactic ferment cultures which thrive in warm, moist conditions. The curd is cut, drained, salted and placed in moulds. The new cheese forms are then cured for 2 months at 46–50°F (8–10°C).

The paste has a sharp flavour and is white with patches of greenish-blue.

Norvegia

Semi-hard, sliceable Norwegian dessert cheese made with cow's milk. The cheeses are oblong or cylindrical, 9¾–14½ in (25–27 cm) in diameter, 2½–4¾ in (6–12 cm) thick, and weigh 8¾–26½ lb (4–12 kg). The cheese-making technique and resulting texture resemble Dutch Gouda. The milk is coagulated at 86–89°F (30–32°C) and then heated in the whey to 100°F (38°C). The curd is placed in moulds, pressed and salted, before ripening.

Oaxaca

A Mexican fresh plastic or spun-curd cheese, made with whole cow's milk using methods similar to the Provolone technique.

Oka

The Trappist monks in a monastery near Montreal invented this semi-hard creamy cheese made from cow's milk; it can be considered as the Canadian equivalent of Port-du-Salut.

Olivet

A whole or partially skimmed cow's milk cheese which is prepared along

the general lines of Camembert; this soft cheese comes from the Loiret department of France.

It can be eaten fresh – only 48 hours after it has been made – or matured (Olivet Bleu): the ripened cheeses are cured for 30 days in cool, damp cellars during which time they develop a layer of blueish-green mould, and the action of this growth of micro-organisms adds to the cheese's aroma and flavour.

Olmützer Quargel

Tiny German low-fat cheeses made with cow's milk by the acid curd method. The homogeneous paste has no holes and the skin is thin and soft. Weight is between ½–¾ oz (15–20 g). The flavour is very full and robust.

Orduna

Uncooked Spanish ewe's milk cheese made in cylindrical shape with a close-textured rind, and weighing 2½–3¼ lb (1.2 – 1.5 kg). The even paste has few or no holes.

Cured for 30–40 days in a cool atmosphere.

Oropesa
Also known as Estrella

Made in Toledo, Spain, from ewe's milk, this is a hard cheese similar to Manchego. It weighs 4½ lb (2 kg) and is cylindrical with a hard, thick rind. The paste is darker than Manchego and has little holes scattered through it. Cured for 2–3 months at a temperature of 64–68°F (18–20°C).

Ovci Hrudkovy

A Czechoslovak semi-hard ewe's milk cheese. Whole raw milk is curdled at 84–86°F (29–30°C); the curd is then cut, stirred and transferred to moulds but not pressed. Draining continues for 3 days at room temperature; the cheese forms are then ready to be ripened in brine at 59–71°F (15–22°C) for 7 days. Their shape is either spherical or oblong and average weight is 22 lb (10 kg).

Pannarone, see Pannerone

Pannerone
Also known as Pannarone

Made in southern Lombardy, the chief source of production being the province of Lodi. Pannerone gets its name from its delicately creamy taste (the local dialect word for cream being *pànera*). It has sometimes been mistakenly called *Gorgonzola Bianco* (White Gorgonzola) but the two cheeses have only their shape and weight in common. Pannerone is an uncooked-curd cheese made from whole cow's milk which ripens quickly and is not usually salted.

Pannerone starts life when milk is coagulated at 86–89°F (30–32°C), the curd taking 30 minutes to form. It is then cut gently and carefully until the pieces of curd measure 1¼–1½ in (3–4 cm). The curds are given a slow and gentle stirring for 30–40 minutes so that the pieces of curd can shrink as they release more whey and grow firmer. The curd is gathered into cheesecloths and placed in moulds to drain for 12 hours, then heated at a temperature of 77–82°F (25–28°C) for 7–8 days. Another 8–10 days' ripening at 46–50°F (8–10°C) is all the cheese needs before it is ready for consumption.

Mature Pannerone has a thin, soft, dull yellow rind. The paste is white to pale creamy straw-yellow with lots of little eyes formed by the gases trapped inside the cheese during the ripening process.

The taste is mild with a hint of bitterness that lends the cheese character and bite.

Pannonia

Hungarian cheese which is similar to Gruyère. It is made with whole cow's milk and the cheeses are 20–24 in (50–60 cm) in diameter, 6–6¼ in (15–16 cm) high and weigh 88 lb (40 kg). The smooth dry rind is even textured and golden yellow in colour.

The paste is pale with a few evenly-distributed regular-sized holes averaging ⁵⁄₁₆ in (8 mm) in diameter. The flavour is pleasant, reminiscent of Emmental but less distinctive.

The moisture content is 38%, fat content is 31% and protein 30%.

Păpuşi de Caş

A scalded-curd Romanian ewe's milk cheese made in the same way as other plastic or spun-curd cheeses. The cheese is hard and smoked, weighing about 1 lb (500 g), cylindrical or oblong in shape, with geometrical patterns on its surface left by the impressions of the cheese moulds. The taste is strong, sharp and salty.

Parenyica

Kneaded or spun-curd cheese from the USSR, made with ewe's milk and usually smoked.

Parmesan, see Parmigiano

Parmesão

A cooked cheese like Italian Grana, made in Brazil with cow's milk – it is usually pasteurized and partially skimmed.

Parmigiano Reggiano

The most famous of the Grana type cheeses, and although its main use is for grating, it is also extremely good as a dessert cheese. Parmigiano Reggiano cheeses are shaped like squat barrels, 14–18 in (35–45 cm) in diameter, 7–9½ in (18–24 cm) in height, and their weight varies from 66–77 lb (30–35 kg). Partially skimmed cow's milk is used for this cooked, hard cheese. Parmigiano Reggiano enjoys the protection of a certification of origin – this name can only be used for cheeses made in certain well-defined areas of Italy (Parma, Reggio Emilia, Modena, Bologna, and Mantua) and the classical methods of making these cheeses must be faithfully observed.

The evening's yield is taken to the cheesemaker as soon after milking as possible, and there it is left to stand in special round, shallow flat-bottomed bowls, to allow the cream to rise to the surface. The following morning's milk is left to stand for only 1–2 hours and then mixed with the previous evening's milk, skimmed of its top layer of cream. Both batches of milk are poured into very large inverted bell-shaped copper kettles; each kettle holds 110–220 gallons which will yield one or two cheeses.

The starter or fermenting whey is added, and the milk is then heated to 86–89°F (30–32°C), when liquid or powdered rennet is added to produce the curd. After 12–13 minutes the curd is cut, beginning slowly and gradually increasing in speed until the pieces measure ¹⁄₁₆–⅛ in (2–3 mm). The temperature is slowly raised to 125–128°F (52–54°C) while continuous stirring encourages the curds to release more whey; as they do so they become firmer through shrinkage and lose their gloss, acquiring a shrivelled appearance. The temperature is then increased quickly to 129–131°F (54–55°C) to cook the curd, which is allowed to drop to the bottom of the vat or kettle (pitching). After 20–40 minutes it is slowly lifted out with a wooden paddle and wrapped in cheesecloth to drain; if double vats are used the curd is divided in half to form twin cheeses.

The curd is then placed inside wooden and metal hoop moulds, still in its cheesecloth, and pressed for 12–24 hours, while being turned frequently. After another 24 hours the forms are salted in brine for 22–28 days at a temperature of 68–71°F (20–22°C) and then matured for 18–24 months at 64°F (18°C) with 85% humidity. Throughout this time the cheeses are turned and brushed at frequent intervals. When the cheese is mature the rind is smooth, even and fairly thin, slightly oily and an old gold or pale straw colour. The paste of Parmigiano Reggiano is pale straw-yellow, dense, close-textured with a fine grainy consistency and tiny holes; it melts in the mouth. The internal structure of the cheese shows a radial convergence from the outside towards the inside of the cheese and when pieces are prized off the cheese they will break off along this radial grain.

The quality of each cheese is scrutinized and assessed by the cheese tester: he taps the outside of the cheese with a small hammer, listening to the sound it makes; by the reverberations produced the expert can tell whether the cheese is any one of five degrees of quality.

Another distinction used for Parmesan is related to the season when it was made: *maggengo* means that the cheese was made between April and November, and *invernengo* between December and March. (Still finer distinctions exist: *di testa* means that the cheese must have been made in April-May-June; *agostano* or *di centro* during July and August, and *tardivo* during September-October-November.) Parmesan which has matured for 1 year is called *Vecchio* (old) and when 2 years old is called *Stravecchio* (mature or very old).

When 18 months old, Parmesan

contains 26–27% water, 37% fat and 31% protein.

Parmigiano Reggiano is one of the most famous cheeses in the world, although the distinction (which Italians feel to be very important) between the various types of Grana cheese is not always fully appreciated outside Italy.

Parmesan has been a favourite cheese for many centuries. For example, on the occasion of Charles VIII's visit to Piacenza in the sixteenth century, the inhabitants thought the best way they could pay homage to him was to make him a gift of some Parmesan cheeses which were as big as cartwheels. Sixteenth century Italians knew how to enjoy themselves, giving Lucullan feasts and great banquets, and contemporary recipes showed that they served Parmesan with fresh eggs and with pears.

Pasiego Prensado

Spanish soft cow's milk cheese which is sold after ripening for 6–7 days in cool cellars.

The cheeses are cylindrical, weighing 2¼–3¼ lb (1–1.5 kg), and the body of Pasiego is white with small holes. This uncooked-curd cheese has quite a decided flavour.

Passé l'An

Languedoc is the home of this hard, close-textured cheese made from partially skimmed cow's milk. The cheeses are shaped like drums, and have hard rinds; they measure 12–16 in (30–40 cm) in diameter; are 14 in

(35 cm) high and weigh 77–88 lb (35–40 kg). They are reminiscent of Italian Grana cheeses and have a fine, mellow flavour.

Passendale

A Belgian cheese made with cow's milk, shaped rather like a square loaf with rounded edges and weighing 13¼–15½ lb (6–7 kg). These cheeses have a moist and supple texture.

Pata de Mulo, see Villalón

Patagrás

A cheese which is made in Argentina and Cuba and resembles Edam and Gouda in both production techniques and appearance.

Pavé d'Auge, see Pont l'Evêque

Pavé de Moyaux, see Pont l'Evêque

Pecorino Foggiano

Made in the south of Italy with ewe's milk which is coagulated at 98–100°F (37–38°C) in 28–30 minutes using

solid kid's or lamb's rennet.

The curd is cut but not cooked or scalded; it is then drained, placed in moulds for 6 hours at room temperature and dry-salted before being cured for 6–7 months.

The cheeses measure 9–12 in (23–30 cm) in diameter, 4–5½ in (10–14 cm) in height and weigh 11–15½ lb (5–7 kg). The rind is hard and rough and the flavour is sharp.

Pecorino Foggiano is composed of 40% water, 28–30% fat and 25% protein.

Pecorino Romano

Traditionally this hard, cooked-curd ewe's milk cheese was made in the countryside surrounding Rome but today Sardinia accounts for the bulk of production. The cheesemaking season extends from November to June, and the cheese is made by a special method, the salient point of which is the custom of 'rummaging' the curd as soon as it has been placed in the mould in order to expedite drainage of the whey. Pecorino Romano is shaped like a squat cylinder with smooth, straight sides 8–12 in (20–30 cm) in diameter, 5½–8¾ in (14–22 cm) tall and weighing 17½–44 lb (8–20 kg) (the variations are due to wide differences in local production customs).

Immediately after milking, the yield is heated to 145°F (63°C) and then cooled to 95–102°F (35–39°C); a curd is formed in 20–25 minutes after the addition of solid lamb's rennet. The curd is then cut, stirred to complete the process of releasing the whey, heated to 118–122°F (48–50°C) and subsequently pressed in moulds. The process of rummaging the curd at this stage promotes rapid drainage

of the remaining whey and takes the form of tapping or piercing the surfaces of the newly-shaped cheese forms. The cheese is dry-salted all over and this process is spread over the period of 90 days, during which time the cheese is stored in a cool atmosphere. The cheese is pierced to facilitate penetration of the salt with small tapping needles. The curing period lasts for at least 8 months at a temperature of 53–60°F (12–16°C), and during this time the cheeses are turned and the rind is oiled.

Pecorino Romano is white or very pale straw-yellow; it is dense and has a typical ewe's milk aftertaste with a decided sharpness. The rind is smooth, light to dark brown and oiled or smeared with dark olive lees or mutton fat.

The production zones are officially recognized in the following provinces: Cagliari, Frosinone, Grosseto, Latina, Nuoro, Rome, Sassari and Viterbo.

Pecorino Romano is a popular dessert cheese and is also widely employed in cooking.

It contains 30–31% water, 32–33% fat, 26–28% protein and 4–5% salt.

This type of Pecorino is probably Italy's oldest cheese, Pliny the Elder referred to it and in the first century A.D. Lucius Junius Columella devoted some space to it in his *De re rustica*, describing how it was made. Pecorino is known to have been exported from ancient Rome.

Pecorino Siciliano

A hard, uncooked cheese made with freshly milked whole ewe's milk, curdled with lamb's rennet, and made between October and June.

The cheesemaking process starts by heating the milk to 145°F (63°C) and then cooling it to 96–98°F (36–

37°C). Once the solid rennet has been added to the milk, the curd takes 30 minutes to form, and it is then cut, drained of whey while being stirred, and given a further draining in the moulds for 6–8 hours (the moulds are immersed in heated whey for the first 30 minutes of shaping). The cheese forms are dry-salted and matured for 7–8 months at a temperature of 53–60°F (12–16°C).

Pecorino Siciliano has a rough yellowish-white rind with the marks of its basket mould imprinted on the surface and is smeared with a protective film of oil; the interior of the cheese is close-textured, varying from white to pale straw-yellow and has few holes. The typically sharp ewe's milk taste is given additional bite with a scattering of peppercorns throughout the paste. (Pecorino Siciliano without peppercorns is known as *bianco* (white) or *calcagno*.)

Pedroches

A hard cheese made in the Valley of Los Pedroches in Spain, weighing 3¼–5½ lb (1.5–2.5 kg). The ewe's milk used for the cheese is usually curdled with vegetable rennet. The cheeses are then cured for 30–60 days at room temperature. Moisture content is 40%; fat: 30% and protein: 22–25%.

Perilla, see Tetilla

Petit-Suisse, see Suisse

Picón, see Cabrales

Piedrafita, see Cebrero

Pikantinij

Russian semi-hard cow's milk cheese with a tender rind ripened by mould, and regularly-scattered holes in the paste. It contains 45% water, 25% fat and 22–23% protein.

Piora

A hard cheese from the Italian-speaking Swiss canton of Ticino, made with cow's milk, sometimes with an admixture of goat's milk. It is shaped like a squat cylinder, 12–14 in (30–35 cm) in diameter, 2¾–3¼ in (7–8 cm) high and weighs 15½–26½ lb (7–12 kg).

The milk from two successive milkings is curdled at 89–91°F (32–33°C) with liquid rennet; the curd is cut and heated in its whey to 100–104°F (38–40°C). It is then placed in moulds and pressed for 12 hours. The cheese forms are then salted and cured for 3–6 months.

Pizza Cheese

Plastic or spun-curd cheese manufactured in the United States especially for making pizzas. It is very similar to Mozzarella but has a lower moisture content and is shaped into oblong blocks weighing 4½–11 lb (2–5 kg). Made with pasteurized milk, curdled with liquid rennet; the use of starter cultures raises the acidity level of the milk and gives the cheese its particular flavour (*Lactobacillus bulgaricus* and *Streptococcus thermophilus* are used). Today citric acid is often added rather than the lactic ferment cultures. The curd is then kneaded and spun, placed in moulds, cooled in water and salted.

Pizza Cheese contains, on average, 47% water, 23.5% fat and 25% protein.

Plateau

A soft Belgian cheese, disc-shaped, 6–8 in (15–20 cm) in diameter and 1½–2½ in (4–6 cm) thick.

Pasteurized milk is used, curdled at 86°F (30°C); the curd is then cut, placed in moulds and ripened at 53–60°F (12–16°C). The delicate yellowish crust encloses a smooth paste with a fairly pungent taste.

Ploderkäse

Also known as Toggenburger Ploderkäse

Cow's milk is coagulated by lactic fermentation and then scalded for this Swiss cheese which is dry salted and then ripened in blocks weighing 15½–22 lb (7–10 kg) in cool cellars. The crust consists of a thick bacterial layer, and inside the texture is smooth and regular with no holes and a slightly bitter taste.

Pont-l'Evêque

Also known as Pavé d'Auge or Moyaux

A soft cow's milk cheese produced in the neighbourhood of the market town of Pont-l'Evêque in Normandy.

Whole or partially skimmed milk is used and curdled at a temperature of 89–91°F (32–33°C) for 30–40 minutes. The curd is broken to release its whey, partially drained and divided, then transferred to square moulds and turned frequently. The cheese forms are dry-salted and left to dry off for a few days in a dry atmosphere; they are then cured.

Pont-l'Evêque has a soft, rich consistency and may have a few small round holes; the rind is dry, smooth and golden-brown, with very thin smears of mould. It contains 45–48% water, 25–28% fat and 18–22% protein.

Pont-Moutier

French uncooked-curd cow's milk cheese which is smooth in texture except for a few cracks and tiny eyes. It is square and weighs 4-1/2–5-1/2 lb (2–2.5 kg); the rind is golden-brown with patches of white bloom. A fragrant, aromatic cheese.

Port-Salut

A registered trade mark which was sold by the monks of the Abbey of Port-du-Salut at Entrammes to a large French cheese manufacturer, ceding the right to make and market what was originally their own cheese. Today the cheese resembles Saint-Paulin very closely.

Port-Salut should not be confused with Port-du-Salut, which was made on a farmhouse scale by Trappist monks who, in 1815, after the French Revolution and the Napoleonic Wars were over, settled in the ancient abbey of Notre-Dame-du-Port-du-Salut. Once their Port-du-Salut cheese reached Paris, it became very popular and was widely copied – often to the detriment of its good reputation. In 1938 an attempt was made by the authorities of the Seine department to clarify the status of the cheese and the abbreviated name Port-Salut was legally defined as the trade name of Port-du-Salut cheeses. After the war, however, the monks sold the name, and Port-Salut became a factory cheese. The monks still make a small quanitity of their own traditional farmhouse cheeses, but they are no longer called Port-du-Salut but **Entrammes**.

Poshekhonskij

A hard cow's milk cheese made in the USSR. The paste has small irregular holes and the rind is dry and hard. This cheese contains an average of 40–42% water, 25–26% fat and 25–26% protein.

Pouligny-Saint-Pierre

A French goat's milk cheese, whose production and provenance are con-

trolled by law. Named after a village in the province of Berry. The paste is soft and the cheese is dry-cured for 1 month; it is shaped like a pyramid, the base being 2¾–3¼ in (7–8 cm) square and about 3½ in (8–9 cm) high; weight is 7–9 oz (200–250 g).

Prästost

Semi-hard Swedish cow's milk cheese. The soft rind is sometimes coated with paraffin wax or the cheese can be rindless, and the paste has scattered holes. Analysis reveals a moisture content of 40%, 30% fat and 25% protein.

Prato

Brazilian semi-hard cheese with a tender rind; inside the paste is broken by small round holes; it weighs 3¼–4½ lb (1.5–2 kg). Made with whole or partially skimmed cow's milk, the ripened cheese contains 35–45% water, 12–24% fat and 20–33% protein.

Prince-Jean

Cylindrical soft Belgian cheese which weighs about 1 lb (350–450 g). It is

covered with white surface moulds which ripen the cheese from the outside inwards. The texture is even and the taste is aromatic.

Provola

Originally made with buffalo milk, this spun-curd cheese is now also made with cow's milk. The consistency is firmer than Mozzarella, and the bulbous-shaped cheeses have string or raffia tightly tied around them at their apex, leaving a small protruding head of cheese, rather like a pear with a protuberance on top; weight is 9 oz – 1 lb (250–500 g).

Production methods are much the same as for Mozzarella, using the spun-curd technique: coagulation, ripening of the curd in its whey, kneading and spinning the curd, shaping the cheeses, cooling them in cold water, then finally salting, sometimes followed by smoking.

Buffalo Milk Provola usually has a higher fat content than the cow's milk type, and the latter has a higher moisture content.

Provolone

A plastic or spun-curd cheese which comes from the south of Italy and which takes its name from a round local cheese which used to be called *Provva*.

Since the early years of this century manufacture of Provolone has spread to northern Italy and also to the United States and Latin America, taken there by successive waves of immigrants who came from southern Italy.

Many versions and types of Provolone are made, and the cheese may be cured for only a short time, matured fully, or well-aged; shapes and sizes vary enormously too since the plastic curd lends itself to improvization.

Provolone's rind is smooth, thin and shiny, golden-yellow in colour, and sometimes covered in wax; the paste has no holes (but small cracks in the paste are a good sign in the aged, sharper cheeses). The flavour is mild and delicate in cheeses cured for 2–3 months but becomes sharper after ageing.

Manufacture consists of the following procedures: the raw milk is heated to 95–100°F (35–38°C) and fermented whey is added as a starter (this whey is left over from the previous day's cheesemaking and has been left to stand in a warm atmosphere so that the action of lactic bacteria raises its acidity). Liquid or solid rennet is added to curdle the milk. The curd begins to form within about 9–12 minutes and becomes firm enough in 20–22 minutes. It is then cut until the pieces are the size of hazelnuts and stirred for a few minutes before they are allowed to pitch or fall to the bottom of the vat. Some of the whey is drawn off, heated to 145–149°F (63–65°C) and then poured onto the broken curd to heat it to 118–125°F (48–52°C).

After 10–15 minutes cooking and stirring the whey is again drawn off and cooler whey (sometimes diluted with water) is poured on to the curd to cool it to 107–113°F (42–45°C). The curd is left to stand for 30–40 minutes and then the whey is drained off. This washing reduces the calcium content and means that the cheese can be drawn out into strings. The curd is then cut into thick slices (rather like Cheddaring) and placed on drainage tables at a temperature of 68–77°F (20–25°C) for 4–6 hours. The curd ferments and the lactic acid content of

the curd rises; the demineralized curd will now be easy to knead and spin. It is cut into strips ⅜ in (1 cm) thick and placed in water which has been heated to 185–194°F (85–90°C). Kneading then begins. The kneaded curd is shaped, placed in moulds and cooled in running water.

The cheeses are salted in brine for varying lengths of time, depending on their shapes and weights. They are then ripened at 59–64°F (15–18°C) in 80–95% humidity, hung up in pairs. During the curing period the cheeses develop *Aspergillus* and *Penicillium* moulds over their surfaces and these release enzymes which further ripen the cheese. Before the cheeses are sold, they are brushed, washed and may be given a coating of wax.

When mature, Provolone has a moisture content of 33%; fat: 35%, protein 28% and 4% salt. It is mainly used as a dessert cheese and, when aged, as a grating cheese, but Provolone can be put to very good account as a cooking cheese in a wide variety of dishes at any stage.

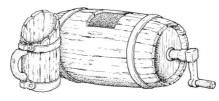

Pultost

A soft, rindless Norwegian cheese for which the curd forms naturally through the action of lactic acid-producing bacteria. The curd releases the whey when it is heated to 131–140°F (55–60°C) while being stirred; once the whey has drained away, the curd is salted and flavoured with caraway.

Pultost contains 60% water, 3% fat and 30% protein.

Puzol

Fresh ewe's milk cheese which is made in the neighbourhood of Puzol in Valencia, Spain. The milk is curdled with rennet, briefly drained and then salted, at which point it is ready for consumption.

Average water content is 60–62%, fat 20–21% and protein 16–18%.

Pyramide

A family of French goat's milk cheeses shaped like truncated pyramids. The surface may be covered with white rind flora or green mould; ashes are often rubbed over the surface to help dry out the cheese, and this covering speeds the process in which the enzymes destroy the lactic acid and sweeten the cheese while delaying ripening. The intensity of flavour of these cheeses depends on how long they are allowed to mature.

Quark

Also known as Quarg, Kvarg

A soft, acid-curd cheese which originally came from Central Europe, made from skimmed or partially-skimmed milk; the whey was drained off by filtration, though today it is more commonly done by centrifuge. Varying techniques and local preferences account for minor differences in this product from country to country.

On average Quark contains 70–80% water, 2–3% fat and 15–16%

protein, and it is most often eaten with fruit or vegetables and salads.

Quarg, see Quark

Quartirolo

A soft, uncooked Italian cheese which has a good deal in common with Taleggio, including its production technique. The paste of the cheese is smooth, and it is covered by a thin washed rind. It is still made on a small scale according to traditional methods by farmhouse producers using whole cow's milk; sometimes two milkings are used, the first milk being left to stand before it is partially skimmed. The name Quartirolo is explained by the fact that the cheese was originally made in the autumn with milk from cows fed on the fourth and last growth of pasture grass (*erba quartirolo*), in the vicinity of Milan.

Milk is heated to 86–95°F (30–35°C) and liquid rennet is added; sometimes the milk is inoculated with a starter of lactic ferment cultures. After 20–30 minutes the curd is ready to cut into ¾–1¼ in (2–3 cm) pieces; it is then gathered into cheesecloths and placed in moulds supported on slats to facilitate drainage, and warmed to a temperature of about 68°F (20°C) for 24–36 hours. This temperature brings about the right conditions for the formation of the homogeneous, smooth paste of these cheeses.

Salting – usually dry-salting – is the next step and then the cheese forms are ready to mature in special curing-rooms at 42–46°F (6–8°C) or in caves, from which the cheese acquires a distinctive mushroomy flavour.

Queso Blanco

Throughout Latin-America there is widespread production of this fresh, rindless even-textured cheese which is made with acid curd from cow's milk. When un-ripened it is served with fruit.

Whole or partially skimmed milk is heated to 179–181°F(82–83°C) and curdled with acetic acid. The curd is then removed from the whey, worked to make it smooth, and pressed and salted. This cheese can also be ripened for 2–3 months in cool conditions. It has a faintly acidic flavour.

Moisture content is 50%, fat 19% and protein 25%.

Queso de Cabra

A Chilean raw goat's milk cheese which is cylindrical in shape and weighs about 2¼ lb (1 kg). The flavour is strong with a definite goaty sharpness and the rind is dry without any mould or bloom. It is made by farmhouse cheesemakers.

Queso de Los Bellos, see Bellos

Raclette
see Valais Raclette, Walliser

Ragusano

A hard, spun-curd cheese made with whole cow's milk in southern Italy (Sicily), and sometimes smoked. Shaped like a rectangular block with rounded edges and faint marks and depressions left by the cords with which the cheeses are hung up to ripen. Weight varies from 13¼–26½ lb (6–12 kg).

The cheesemaking technique remains faithful to the traditional method for hard kneaded-curd cheeses. Ragusano is matured in cool curing rooms or cellars, hung up in pairs with cords slung over poles. Sliceable dessert cheeses are cured for 3 months and grating cheeses for 6–12.

Sliceable, dessert quality Ragusano has a smooth, thin, golden-brown or pale straw-yellow rind, while the aged grating cheese has a dark brown rind, and is smeared with oil. The interior is white or pale straw-coloured, dense and homogeneous when matured for a short time but developing cracks and scaling when aged for longer. The dessert cheese is mild and delicate in flavour, while the grating cheese is sharp and savoury.

Rahm Brie, Rahm Camembert

The word *Rahm*, meaning cream, is used to distinguish cheeses produced in Germany following the Camembert and Brie techniques, using milk with a higher fat content.

Rahmfrischkäse

A fresh German cow's milk cheese made by the acid-curd method. The texture is even and homogeneous and the rindless cheese has a quite a high fat content for a fresh cheese.

Moisture content is 70%, fat 18% and protein 9–10%.

Raschera

Also known as Raschiera

This whole cow's milk cheese comes from the province of Cuneo in Italy. Sometimes the cow's milk is mixed with ewe's or goat's milk. It is rather like Bra cheese and is square, measuring 12 x 12 – 14 x 14 in (30 x30 – 35 x 35 cm) and 2¾–4 in (7–10 cm) high. Weight is 15½–18½ lb (7–8 kg). The rind is thin and light brown in colour, enclosing the supple, very pale straw-yellow paste which is usually homogeneous but sometimes has a few scattered holes. The taste is delicate.

Rasskäse

Very much like Appenzell cheese but lower in fat content and stronger-tasting, with a hint of bitterness, and less supple in texture. The paste has more holes than traditional Appenzell.

Reblochon

Haute-Savoie in France is the home of this cheese, but it is also made over the border in Italy (in Piedmont and the Aosta Valley). Its name stems from the Savoyard word *reblocher* – to milk for a second time, and Reblochon was traditionally made from the milk which the herdsmen reserved for their own use, when enough milk had been yielded to satisfy the owner. This milk is very rich in butterfat. The cheese is soft and disc-shaped: 4¾–6 in (12–15 cm) in diameter, 1¼–2 in (3–5 cm) thick and weighing 10½ oz – 2¼ lb (300 g – 1 kg).

The cow's milk produces a curd in 25–30 minutes after liquid rennet is added at a temperature of 86–95°F (30–35°C). Once the curd is firm enough it is cut into hazelnut-sized pieces and then gathered into cheese-cloths and hung up to drain before being placed in moulds. To ensure satisfactory drainage the curd is pressed by hand as well as using weights. After 6–12 hours the cheese forms are dry-salted and then left to dry at 53–64°F (7–8°C). While in the curing rooms the cheeses will be turned and their rind bathed with a brine solution.

Reblochon has a thin smooth skin of reddish-brown hue; the interior is close-textured with very few small holes and the flavour is buttery with a subtle fruity finish.

The cowherds would make a point of not milking the cows dry on the occasion of the steward's visit of inspection to check the yield and collect the milk; and they were consequently very secretive about the magnificent cheeses which they made with the extra milk.

To protect their secret the cheeses were made with the milk still warm from the cow, an unusual technique which resulted in the specially rich flavour. Both creamery and farmhouse versions are made and both are expensive.

Requeijão

The Brazilian producers of this soft cheese use the acid-curd method, in which the milk coagulates as a result of the activity of lactic bacteria.

The hot, washed, salted curd is placed in cylindrical or oblong moulds and the resulting cheeses weigh 9 oz – 1 lb (250 – 500 g). The texture is homogeneous with a smooth surface and the taste is pleasantly acidulated.

Ricotta

This is not a cheese in the strict sense of the word; it is made with whey, often enriched with milk or cream. Cow's milk whey is used, left over from soft or even cooked-curd cheesemaking, but ewe's milk whey is the traditional basic material. Fresh whey is heated to 158–167°F (70–75°C) and if a thicker or creamier Ricotta is required, skimmed milk or cream is added.

To encourage the destabilising

effect of heat on the whey protein or albumen, citric acid or tartaric acid may be added. The temperature is raised to 176–185°F (80–85°C) and the flakes of lactalbumen increase in size and rise to the top of the whey, forming a cloudy layer rather like white of egg, which is skimmed off and placed in small wicker or perforated plastic moulds to drain. These are left for 20–22 hours at 46–50°F (8–10°C). The resulting Ricotta has a high moisture content (50–60%), contains 3% lactose or milk sugar, 23–26% protein (mainly albumen) and 15% fat. This analysis can, of course, vary depending on the whey used and how rich it is, and on whether milk or cream had been added.

Ricotta is a popular food eaten just as it comes, being both delicious and very nutritious (due to the high protein content in the particularly beneficial form of albumen), but it is also ideally suited to use in cooking for stuffings, fillings and baking, and it is therefore widely used in Italian dishes. The texture of Ricotta is crumbly, the colour snow-white, and it has no skin. Ricotta does not keep well, although its life may be prolonged a little by adding salt in the proportion of ½–1%; it can then even ripen a little.

There are several distinct types of Ricotta: *Moliterna* (see below); *Ricotta Piemontese*, made from cow's milk whey to which 10–20% milk may be added; and *Ricotta Romana*, made with whey left over from making Pecorino Romano.

Ricotta Salata Moliterna

Made from ewe's milk whey heated to 194°F (90°C) to release the whey protein. The layer of albumen is

skimmed off the surface, gathered into cheesecloths, salted and cured.

The resulting product is cylindrical in shape and can be eaten young as a sliceable dessert cheese or matured as a good grating cheese.

Ridder

This semi-hard cow's milk cheese is widely-produced in Sweden and Norway. The uncooked, pressed curd makes a rich, supple paste with a thin rind.

Rigatello

Several countries make their own versions of this whole or partially skimmed cow's milk cheese. The interior of the cheese is hard and dense with a few cracks, while the hard, dry rind is grooved with the imprint of the mould in which the cheese was shaped and drained. Rigatello has a strong taste and is cylindrical, 6–8 in (15–20 cm) in diameter, 2½–2¾ in (6–7 cm) high and weighs 4¼–6½ lb (2–3 kg). Besides being eaten as a dessert cheese, it is also used for grating and contains 36–37% water, 24–30% fat and 25–35% protein.

Rigato, see Canestrato

Rigottes

A French goat's milk cheese which is soft and velvety, with a delicate crust

usually covered in white rind flora. Weight is about 2 oz (50–60 g) and moisture content 45%; fat: 20–23% and protein 23–25%.

Robiola

A soft, uncooked-curd cheese from Italy which takes its name from its reddish skin. Originating in the foothills of the Alps in Lombardy, production has now spread throughout Lombardy and Piedmont and is carried on in both large and small creameries.

The cheese is square 3 x 3 – 4 x 4 in (8 x 8 – 10 x 10 cm), or rectangular: 2¾ x 4 in (7 x 10 cm), while in Piedmont it is disc-shaped. All the shapes are about 1½–2½ in (4–6 cm) thick, and their weight ranges from 9 oz (250 g) to 1¼ lb (600 g). Cow's milk is used in Lombardy, whereas in Piedmont ewe's or goat's milk is preferred, either alone or mixed with cow's milk. The paste has no holes and a thin bloomy skin.

Modern methods of production differ only slightly from the techniques followed for Taleggio but this cheese relies even more heavily on surface-ripening to attain its correct consistency and flavour. Rennet is used for curdling the milk, but once the curd has formed it develops in acidity due to the action of natural airborne bacteria plentiful in farmhouse dairies; laboratory-prepared starter cultures will be used in factory cheesemaking.

These lactic ferments are added to the fresh milk which is heated to 91–95°F (33–35°C), when liquid rennet is added. After 30 minutes the curd is ready to be gently and gradually cut to release the whey and encourage drainage. The pieces of curd should be the size of walnuts. They are then transferred to square moulds measuring 8 x 8 in (20 x 20 cm). The cheese forms are heated in their moulds for 6–7 hours at 73–77°F (23–25°C), being turned at intervals. The mould is removed and the cheese forms are then divided into four so that the surface ratio is increased and micro-organisms can develop and ripen the cheese through to its interior. The cheeses are then dry-salted or salted in brine and ripened in an atmosphere of 90% humidity at 29–41°F (4–6 °C).

Robiola contains 50–52% water, 26–27% fat, 21–22% protein, a good deal of which is broken down during the ripening process.

There is a good selection of Robiola available but the choicest are probably those which come from the districts of Langhe, Alba, Bossolasco, and Roccaverano in Piedmont, and those produced in the valleys of Bergamo in Pavia, and the neighbourhood of Lodi in Lombardy.

Fresh Robiole (*Robiole Fresche*) are also popular; these are mainly acid-curd cheeses, often enriched with cream, and they must be eaten only a few days after they have been made. In composition and cheesemaking methods they resemble the Suisse or Petit Suisse type of French cheese (see page 149).

Robiolini

The diminuitive form of the name Robiola indicates the small size of these little cheeses which also go under the names of *formaggini* (little cheeses) or *caprini* (little goat's cheeses) since goat's milk is often used. They are cylindrical, 1¼–1½ in (3–4 cm) in diameter, 2–2¾ in (5–7 cm) high and weigh 2–2½ oz

(50–70 g). Acid whey and solid rennet are added to raw, whole cow's milk. A curd forms in 4–5 hours at a temperature of 68–71°C (20–22°C). When the curd has been gathered into cheesecloths and drained (without being cut), salt is added and the curd is worked and blended, then shaped into small cylinders which are allowed to ripen for 10–15 days in caves or cellars with 95% humidity at a temperature of 42–59°F (6–15°C). They are traditional specialities of the provinces of Milan, Como and Cuneo.

Romadur

A soft cow's milk cheese which is made in several central European countries (Germany, Czechoslovakia, Austria etc.), oblong-shaped and smooth-textured with the occasional small hole, and covered by a yellowish-brown washed rind. The taste is reminiscent of many surface-ripened cheeses and is full and fruity, becoming strong, with a slightly ammoniacal tinge if overripe.

Romadur is made in much the same way as Limburger and although somewhat similar, is milder. Partially skimmed or whole milk is used. This cheese contains 50–60% water, 10–30% fat and 15–35% protein.

Romano

This is the name adopted in the USA for hard cow's milk cheeses which are made by the Pecorino-Romano technique. The cheeses are drum-shaped, about 9¾ in (25 cm) in diameter and 6 in (15 cm) tall. The paste is even, close-textured, with a thin rind and a

strong taste. Moisture content is 32%, fat 25–27% and protein 32–33%.

Roncal

A Spanish ewe's milk cheese which resembles Manchego, except in size, being smaller and harder.

Produced in the valley from which it takes its name, in Navarra.

Roquefort

This ewe's milk cheese shares the title of the most famous blue cheese with Stilton, and it has been protected by law for a longer time than any other cheese. It is named after Roquefort-sur-Soulzon in the neighbourhood of Saint-Affrique (Aveyron), a hilly and mountainous region of southern France. The approved production zone includes the Larzac plateau and parts of the Gard, Lozère and Tarn departments. The main production season lasts from February to July; the marketing season starts in September but Roquefort is available all the year round nowadays, due to efficient refrigerated transport.

Roquefort is often made at the milk producer's farm but is more often manufactured in creameries sometimes as far away as Sardinia; but the cheeses are always matured in the limestone caves of Cambalou at Roquefort, as has been the custom for over 1200 years.

The cheese starts life when milk exclusively from the Larzac breed of sheep is heated to 75–82°F (24–28°C); rennet is added and the curd is formed in two hours. The curd is then cut and placed in moulds with perforated sides and no base like tall hoops 8 in (20 cm) in diameter and 3½–4 in (9–10 cm) high. The cheese forms weigh 5½–6½ lb (2.5–3 kg). Spores of *Penicillium roqueforti* are added to the curd in the vat or when it is in the moulds. The cheeses are then heated gently at 68–71°F (20–22°C) for two days and then they are dried for two days. The cheeses are matured in the caves where they are dry-salted, first on one side, then on the other; the rind is cleaned to remove any stickiness and the cheeses are skewered to promote the blueing of the paste.

When the cheeses have ripened the skin is orange-yellow and very thin, the paste is creamy white, rich and buttery with even greenish-blue veining. The taste is decided yet subtle with a slight sheep's milk tang to it.

Matured Roquefort are classified as *surchoix*, first, second and third grade, and *rebuts*, and the quality of each cheese is shown by the colour of its foil wrapping.

When ripe, Roquefort contains 36–38% water, 32–36% fat and 22–24% protein.

Roquefort is an aristocrat among cheeses, of ancient lineage. Pliny the Elder refers to it in the chapter *De diversitate caseorum* of his *Naturalis Historia*; it was the Emperor Charlemagne's favourite cheese and several other famous historical figures are known to have thought highly of it, among them, Charles VI, who in 1411 granted the inhabitants of the village of Roquefort the sole rights to ripen their cheeses in the limestone caverns nearby. Air finds its way through the fissures in the rock of these caves and circulates in cool breezes keeping the temperature in the caves at a constant 44–46°F (7–8°C), providing perfectly ventil-

ated natural curing conditions which Roquefort must have to develop its inimitable taste.

Royalp

This semi-hard cheese comes from eastern Switzerland and is made with raw cow's milk. It is wheel-shaped, measuring 10 in (25 cm) in diameter, 2¾–3½ in (7–9 cm) thick and weighing 8¾–11 lb (4–5 kg). The cheese-making technique has much in common with Tilsit and Royalp has a considerable affinity with that cheese. Royalp's rind is moist and reddish-brown and the paste is buttery.

The flavour is mild but delicately aromatic. The moisture content is 38–39% water, 28% fat and 26.5% protein.

Saanenkäse

A hard Swiss cheese which can be served as a sliceable dessert cheese or used for grating. It is a cooked-curd cow's milk cheese.

Milk from two successive milkings goes to make the cheese, which is curdled with powdered rennet at 89°F (32°C). The curd is cut and then cooked at 122–125°F (50–52°C), and then pressed for 24 hours. The cheese forms are dry-salted and matured in cool, damp conditions for as long as 4–5 years, when the paste is dense, without any holes, has a flaking, scaly texture and a fragrant, mellow taste.

It is a very highly-prized cheese, made in small quantities and not at all widely marketed.

Sage Derby

A hard English cheese with green marbling formed by soaking sage leaves in chlorophyll and adding the juice to the curds. The cheese itself is mild with a slightly flaky texture.

Sage cheeses are also made on the East Coast of the USA.

Saingorlon

A soft blue French cheese which resembles Gorgonzola. Cow's milk is used to make the squat cylindrical cheeses weighing 11–22 lb (5–10 kg); their creamy white paste is streaked by blueish mould veins which confer a strong and spicy taste on the cheese. The rind is soft and uneven with surface flora.

Moisture content is 55%, fat 20–21% and protein 20%.

Auvergne is the main producing region but it is also made in other parts of France. Saingorlon was invented during the Second World War when Gorgonzola could not be imported, as a substitute for the Italian cheese.

Sainte-Maure

This soft goat's milk cheese is shaped like an elongated cylinder or log, weighing 7–8 oz (200–230 g) and comes from Sainte-Maure in Touraine although they are also made in Poitou.

The goat's milk is curdled with a small dose of rennet immediately after milking, at a temperature of 59–68°F (15–20°C); after 18–24 hours the curd is firm enough to be ladled into moulds and left to stand for a day. The cheese forms are then unmoulded and salted before being ripened for 3 weeks. The paste is white and creamy with no holes and a smooth, delicate texture. The rind is covered with a thin white bloom.

Saint-Marcellin

Also known as Tomme de S. Marcellin

This soft cheese comes from the Isère valley in France; the farmhouse cheeses are made with goat's milk while the industrial creameries use cow's or mixed milk. It is a disc-shaped cheese, 2¾–3¼ in (7–8 cm) in diameter and only ¾ in (2 cm) thick, weighing 2½–3 oz (70–80 g). The cheeses are ripened in cool, damp conditions for two weeks. The soft paste has no holes and the delicate rind is covered with greenish-blue mould.

Saint-Nectaire

A semi-hard French cow's milk cheese shaped like a flat disc and weighing 1 lb – 4½ lb (500 g – 2 kg).

It is named after the village of Saint-Nectaire in the Auvergne, where the cows graze the high pastures on Mont Dore.

The raw milk is curdled at 82–89°F (28–32°C) and the curd is cut, pressed in moulds and salted. The cheese forms are then cured in cool cellars for 40–60 days, after which the natural crust becomes violet to pink, enclosing a creamy-coloured,

smooth, homogeneous paste with an aromatic flavour. It melts well.

Moisture content is 44–45%, fat 25% and protein 22–23%.

Saint-Paulin

Whole cow's milk cheese which is a descendant of the Port-du-Salut cheese made by the monks of the Abbey of the same name at Entrammes, France. The uncooked, pressed cheese is round and measures 8–8¾ in (20–22 cm) in diameter, stands 1½–2 in (4–5 cm) high and weighs 4½ lb (2 kg).

Pasteurized milk is used for this factory-made product, heated to 89–91°F (32–33°C) and inoculated with a starter culture of lactic bacteria to raise the acidity level and produce the finished cheese's unmistakable flavour. A curd is formed in 15–20 minutes, cut into ⅜–⅝ in (10–15 mm) cubes, the whey is drawn off and the curd is washed with a 1% solution of salt and water. The curd is placed in moulds, pressed, and then salted in brine for a few hours. Curing follows, in cellars at 50–59°F (10–15°C) with 90% humidity.

Saint-Rémy

A soft French cheese made with cow's milk in Lorraine. It is usually

square, weighing 7 oz (200 g), and has a delicate, bloomy rind and smooth, springy yellow paste. These cheeses are matured in damp caves.

Salami

Polish hard cow's milk cheese. The close-textured paste has small eyes and weight is in the region of 2¼–2¾ lb (1–1.2 kg).

Salers

This whole cow's milk cheese comes from the vicinity of Salers in the Auvergne (France). It is a semi-hard, pressed cheese with a soft, dry rind. Made in drum shapes weighing 77–88 lb (35–40 kg), the average moisture content is 40%, fat 27% and protein 25–26%.

This is generally considered to be a particularly good variety of the Cantal type of cheese (see page 106).

Samsø

Named after the Danish island of Samsø, this is a whole cow's milk cheese with an even texture and evenly-distributed medium-sized holes. Shaped like a squat cylinder, 16–18 in (40–45 cm) in diameter, 3–4¾ in (8–12 cm) thick and weighing 26½–33 lb (12–15 kg). The rind is golden yellow and the pressed paste inside has a mild, aromatic flavour.

San Maurin

A small, soft goat's milk cheese from Piedmont in northern Italy, which looks like an elongated cylinder measureing 4–4¾ in (10–12 cm) in length and 1–1¼ in (2.5–3 cm) in diameter. The curd is usually formed by natural souring of the milk and the cheese is white with an acidulated flavour and a typical goat's milk taste.

Sanroch

Another soft goat's milk cheese from Piedmont (Italy) shaped like a small elongated cylinder. The rind is covered with flora and traces of mould. When ripened the taste acquires a certain sharpness.

San Simón

This semi-hard cow's milk cheese is called after San Simón de la Cuesta in the north-west of Spain. It is a pear-shaped cheese and weighs 2¼–4½ lb (1–2 kg).

The milk is coagulated at 87–89°F (31–32°C) and then salt is added; the curd is transferred to the distinctively-shaped moulds. After 24 hours the cheese forms are immersed in hot whey and when they have ripened for 10–15 days, are often smoked.

Sapsago

A very hard Swiss cow's milk cheese which derives its green colouring and pungent, penetrating aroma and taste from a special clover: blue melilot. Sapsago is made in the shape of a truncated cone and makes a good grating cheese. The equivalent of this cheese, called **Schabzieger,** can be found in the United States.

Moisture content is 37%, fat 75% and protein 41%.

Sarusø

Semi-hard cheese named after a Danish island. These squat cylindrical cheeses weigh 30¾ lb (14 kg). The dry rind is golden-brown and the firm paste is liberally scattered with holes the size of large peas. The taste is mild and sweet.

To make Sarusø the milk is curdled at 86–87°F (30–31°C) and the curd is then heated in the whey to 100–102°F (38–39°C). The cheeses are cured for 3–4 weeks at 59–68°F (15–20°C).

Sassenage,
see Bleu de Sassenage

Savaron

Whole cow's milk semi-hard cheese from the Auvergne (France) with a smooth, even texture and soft crust with patches of white rind flora.

Disc-shaped and measuring 8–9½ in (20–21 cm) in diameter, and 1½–2½ in (4–6 cm) in height, it is similar to Saint-Paulin in appearance, taste and the cheesemaking technique followed for its manufacture.

Sbrinz

This traditional Swiss cheese is named after the village of Brienz in the Bernese Oberland, where it has been made since the days of the Roman Empire and probably before. Nowadays it is also made in France, Germany and some parts of Italy. Whole cow's milk is used to make a full-fat cheese, 16–20 in (40–50 cm) in diameter and 4–5½ in (10–14 cm) thick; weight varies from 44–55 lb (20–25 kg). Very fresh milk is heated as soon as possible after milking to 93–100°F (34–38°C), and inoculated with a fermenting whey to introduce lactic-acid-producing bacteria; sufficient rennet is also added to form a curd in 15–20 minutes. The curd is cut until the pieces are the size of wheat grains, then heated to 112–118°F (45–48°C) while being stirred continuously.

A pause ensues to allow the pieces of curd to release more whey and become firmer before the curd is cooked at 129–132°F (54–56°C).

The curd is gathered into cheesecloths or sievecloths, placed in moulds and pressed for 24 hours. The cheese forms are then salted in a 22–24% brine solution for 18–22 days before maturing commences at a temperature of 60–64°F (16–18°C) in 80% humidity.

Sbrinz is mature after 6–12 months but is often aged for a good deal longer. The smooth rind is a yellowish colour, darkening to brown when aged for a long time, and the dense paste is white or very pale straw-yellow, granular in texture and aromatic with a savoury mellow taste.

Sbrinz is very probably the cheese which Pliny referred to as *caseus helveticus* – Swiss cheese. Sbrinz used to be exported to northern Italy on a regular basis in the sixteenth century, being loaded onto the backs of mules for its journey over the St. Gotthard pass, and this is possibly why in the Swiss canton of Ticino, the cheese is also referred to as *sulle spalle* – meaning 'on the shoulders or back' – a name that has been assimilated into German, as **Spalenkäse.**

Apart from its excellent grating and melting qualities, Sbrinz is also shaved into curly slivers with a plane-like knife, and these shavings of cheese are served as appetizers.

Scamorza

A plastic or spun-curd cheese which is somewhat firmer than Mozzarella. The name derives from the southern Italian dialect expression *scamozza* (*capo mozzo* – beheaded) suggesting the appearance of these cheeses, caught in a tightly-tied stranglehold of string or raffia at their apex, leaving a small protruding head. Whole cow's milk is used, sometimes mixed with ewe's milk, and nowadays the milk is usually pasteurized and then inoculated with lactic ferment cultures (*Streptococcus thermophilus* and *Lactobacillus bulgaricus*).

Liquid rennet is used to form a curd at 95–96°F (35–36°C); after 25–30 minutes the curd is firm enough and is cut; the pieces are allowed to fall to the bottom of the vat and most of the whey is drawn off. After 3–4 hours, when the curd has reached the correct

acidity level, it is ready for kneading. First it is cut into slices, just under ½ in (1 cm) thick, and then hot water – heated to a temperature of 192–194°F (89–90°C) – is poured over it; kneading follows and the curd is shaped into spherical pieces weighing 5–9 oz (150–250 g), being drawn out on top to enable a piece of string or raffia to be tied tightly round the 'neck' of the cheese. The cheeses are then cooled in running water, salted in a 18–20% brine solution for 20–30 minutes and often smoked. The Scamorza cheeses are tied together in pairs with plaited raffia or rushes.

These cheeses have the same layered texture as Mozzarella and contain 50–52% water, 23–25% fat, 20–25% protein and 1–1.5% salt. The paste has an even consistency, without holes, a smooth, thin skin without bloom and a fresh lactic flavour.

Schabzieger Glaronnais

A semi-hard Swiss cheese only produced in the Canton of Glarus, made with skimmed cow's milk and pungent herbs.

The cheeses look like truncated cones, and weigh 1½–3½ oz (45–100 g). Sometimes sold ready grated.

Selles-sur-Cher

French whole goat's milk soft cheese which is protected by an *appellation d'origine*. It is made in the provinces of Berry and Orléans. The natural rind is rubbed with powdered charcoal and wood ashes. Selles-sur-Cher cheeses are shaped like a very squat truncated cone.

Selva

This cow's milk cheese is made in the Selva region of Spain. The consistency is soft and the cheeses are cylindrical, weighing about 4½ lb (2 kg). Usually eaten when the cheese is 3–6 weeks old and, depending on the length of curing the cheese has undergone, the paste is either white and granular in texture or smooth, homogenous and a pale straw colour. Selva has a delicate, slightly salty taste.

Serena

A hard, Spanish ewe's milk cheese; the cylindrical forms weigh 2¼–3¼ lb (1–1.5 kg). The rind is dry, enclosing dense yellowish paste without any holes. The milk is coagulated with vegetable rennet and moulded in esparto grass hoops before being salted. Curing lasts for 50 days at room temperature.

Moisture content averages 40%, fat 30% and protein 25–26%.

Serra

A Portuguese cheese made with ewe's milk, sometimes mixed with goat's milk.

The milk is salted and heated to 86°F (30°C) before it is curdled using vegetable rennet – this takes 60–70 minutes. The curd is then cut, pressed and placed in moulds. These cheese forms are ripened for 45 days at 50–57°F (10–14°C). When mature,

Serra has a supple texture and mildly lactic flavour; the rind is smooth and yellow.

The word *serra* in Portuguese means mountain and the best of these cheeses are made in very mountainous country – the Serra da Estrela to the east of Coimbra.

Silter

An Italian cheese from the Camonica valley in the province of Brescia. Cow's milk from two or even three milkings goes into the cheese, which is left to stand and has the cream skimmed off the top.

It is a scalded-curd cheese, shaped like a squat cylinder and varies in size and weight. In the summer season it is made in the herdsmen's alpine huts, while in winter production takes place in the dairies in the valley.

The paste of the cheese is close-textured and hard with occasional cracks and few holes.

Single Gloucester,
see Gloucester

Sobado, see Armada

Stangenkäse

Austrian cow's milk cheese which resembles Tilsit and is bar-shaped, varying in weight.

Steinbuscher

A soft, uncooked-curd German cheese made with whole or partially skimmed cow's milk. It is made and matured in much the same way as Romadur. Shaped like a flat block, it measures 4¾ x 4¾ – 5⅛ x 5⅛ in (12 x 12 – 13 x 13 cm) and is 2 in (5 cm) thick. The skin is yellow and bloomy and the interior is smooth and buttery, with a few small eyes; it has a distinctive taste without being sharp.

Moisture content is 50–55%, fat 17–25% and protein 20–30%.

Stepnoj

This cow's milk cheese is made in the USSR and in other central European countries. It is spherical or oblong, weighing 11–13¼ lb (5–6 kg) and the paste is hard with small holes, covered by a natural, dry rind.

Stepnoj contains 43–45% water, 16–25% fat and 26–35% protein.

Stilton – Blue and White

Stilton is ripe when the paste is a rich creamy yellow that is moist and slightly crumbly. There will be a greater proportion of blue towards the centre than around the edges. Do not judge ripeness by the amount of blue, as this will vary from cheese to cheese.

White Stilton is often available and its somewhat sharp, acidulated taste is recommended by some writers as a substitute for Greek Feta.

Coagulation of the milk (usually unpasteurized) is made at 86°F (30°C): the curd takes 60–70 minutes to form before being drained and put into cylindrical moulds 8 in (20 cm) diameter and 10–12 in (25–30 cm) tall. The cheeses are left in their moulds for 7–8 days at 62–64°F (17–18°C), then matured for about 6 months at 57°F (14°C). The mould is *Penicillium Roqueforti*, which appears in 1–2 months, and each cheese is pierced to encourage veining.

Stracchino, see Crescenza

Stracchino di Gorgonzola,
see Gorgonzola

Suisse, Demi-Suisse, Petit-Suisse

These small fresh cow's milk cheeses, cylindrical in shape, weigh 2 oz (60 g) (Suisse), or 1 oz (30 g) (Petit-Suisse and Demi-Suisse). Pasteurized milk is used and this may be enriched with varying amounts of cream, depending on how rich the end product is to be. The milk and cream are heated to 62–68°F (17–20°C) and a small quantity of rennet is added; 24–48 hours later the curd is gathered and shaped.

Suprême des Ducs

A soft French whole cow's milk cheese which is smooth and creamy when ripe, with either a few scattered holes or rather more tiny, evenly-distributed holes.

The cheese is oval, with its flat surfaces covered in white rind flora, since this is a surface ripening cheese. Suprême des Ducs has a pleasant fragrance and the taste grows more accentuated as the cheese ripens.

Sveciaost

A typical hard Swedish cheese, made with cow's milk. Cylindrical or oblong in shape, varying in weight from 26½–33 lb (12–25 kg). The paste is broken by medium-sized, scattered holes enclosed by a thin yellowish skin. The taste can be mild or very piquant when mature.

Spices are often added to the cheese and it is then called *Kryddsvecia*.

Svenbo

A semi-hard close-textured Danish cow's milk cheese, with large holes and a natural dry rind (or no rind at all, when the factory-produced variety is matured in vacuum plastic packaging). The taste is mild and unobtrusive.

Average moisture content is 42–44%, fat 25% and protein 23–25%.

Swiss

Made in the United States; a hard, cooked-curd cow's milk cheese

shaped like a squat cylinder, weighing 176–220 lb (80–100 kg).

Standarized 3% fat content milk is pasteurized at 158°F (70°C) for 15 seconds and then cooled to 95°F (35°C) when it is inoculated with a starter culture of *Lactobacillus bulgaricus*, *Streptococcus thermophilus* and *Propionibacterium shermanii*. Liquid rennet is added. Once the curd has formed, it is cut, cooked to a temperature of 122–127°F (50–53°C) and stirred while being held at this temperature for a further 30–60 minutes.

The curd is allowed to pitch (fall to the bottom of the vat) and is then lifted out in cheesecloths, placed in moulds, pressed and salted in brine for 2–3 days, then stored at 68–75°F (20–24°C) with 80–85% humidity for 3–6 weeks. It is subsequently cured at 44°F (7°C) for 4–12 months.

Swiss is an efficient imitation of the classic Swiss Emmental, while lacking that cheese's subtlety and distinction. When made in block form, the US Swiss cheese is salted, dried and then vacuum packed in plastic before it is matured at 69–75°F (21–24°C) in wooden containers for 3–6 weeks. While the cheese is maturing gas forms in the paste due to the action of bacteria and the paste of the cheese expands to fill the plastic wrapping very snugly so that no rind is formed.

The cylindrical cheeses have smooth, shiny golden-brown rinds and a springy interior.

Taffel

Semi-hard cheese from Austria, made with cow's milk. It has no rind and the paste is close-textured with medium-sized holes. The cheeses weigh about 22 lb (10 kg).

Moisture content averages 45%, fat 24% and protein 22–23%.

Taleggio

This is the most widely-used name for the soft, uncooked-curd Italian cheeses which are also known as **Stracchino** since the start of the cheesemaking season coincided with the cows' descent from the high Alpine pastures, and the milk was taken from the animals when they were tired – *stracche* in Lombard dialect – after their long journey down from the moutains.

The cheeses which came from the Taleggio valley were so buttery, soft and delicate that they became extremely popular and consumer demand helped to ensure that the officially recognized production zone was extended to cover the neighbouring regions where cheeses of this type were made.

Taleggio is one of the most ancient soft cheeses. It was already being made on a small scale by families in the area for their own used in the eleventh century, and today it is manufactured in medium-sized and large industrial creameries in the provinces of Milan, Padua, Bergamo, Brescia, Como and Cremona throughout the year.

Taleggio is classified into two distinct varieties: the first is the traditional cheese, made with raw milk, which has a thin, soft, slightly crumpled skin and a soft reddish colour with grey patches of mould on the surface. Near the crust the paste is pale straw-yellow, velvety and melting; closer to the centre it is more dense, white, firmer, and more friable with a very few tiny holes or no holes at all. The taste is delicate with a hint of acidulation towards the middle.

Cooked-curd Taleggio, however, bears much more of a resemblance to the Italico type of quick-ripening soft cheeses. The grey rind is thin and encloses an even-textured evenly-coloured pale straw-yellow paste with relatively little development of micro-organisms on the surface.

Uncooked-curd Taleggio is a typical surface-ripened cheese; the presence of yeasts, moulds and schizomycetes on the rind produces enzymes which feed on the acid in the cheese, making the taste sweeter, and breaking down the casein (cheese protein) and fats, giving a softer, smoother and more digestible cheese. As their action spreads inwards, the heart of the cheese will still be slightly chalky when the rest of the cheese is ripe enough to eat.

As soon as possible after milking, the fresh milk is heated to 89–95°F (32–35°C) in cauldrons or small vats; liquid rennet is added and when a layer of whey is observed covering the curd, and the curd has become firm enough to leave a small space down the inside of the vat sides, it is time to cut it into 1¾–2¼ in (2–3 cm) pieces.

The curd is left to stand for a while, turned, and cut once more by which time the granules have become opaque, very pale straw-yellow, and elastic. The curd is then placed in square moulds without bases, supported on racks which facilitate drainage of the whey. The next stage is to heat the curd in the moulds for 8–24 hours at 71–77°F (22–25°C), the exact time and temperature depending on the quality of the milk, the speed with which the curd reaches the correct acidity level, and the length of time the whey takes to drain. Farmhouse Taleggio cheeses are dry-salted, whereas industrial producers salt in brine.

Taleggio needs 90% humidity to ripen and a temperature of 39–42°F (4–6°C) for 30–40 days. The cheeses are turned often and wiped with cloths to control the surface moulds.

Telemea

An oblong Romanian cheese made with ewe's milk which was traditionally raw but is now pasteurized.

Pasteurization of the milk at 154°F (68°C) is followed by cooling to 87–95°F (31–35°C); powdered rennet is added, and the curd takes an hour to form. The curd is cut, placed in cheesecloths, drained, pressed and cut into square blocks which are dry-salted. The cheeses are matured at 57–64°F (14–18°C) for 30 days in barrels, immersed in acid whey and salt. The cheese can be stored in this way for as long as a year at 41–50°F (5–10°C).

Telemea has no rind and the surface has a pure white, glazed appearance; the white paste sometimes has cumin seeds added to it for extra flavour.

Moisture content is usually 50%, fat 25% and protein 20%.

Tête de Moine

These semi-hard Swiss cheeses, shaped like little drums, are made during the summer months in the Bernese Jura and marketed during the autumn and winter when the cheeses have been cured for 3–5 months. They have an unmistakable bouquet.

Tetilla

Also known as Perilla

A soft Spanish cheese shaped rather like a pear which weighs 2¼–3¼ lb (1–1.5 kg). Cow's milk is coagulated at a temperature of 68°F (20°C), taking 1–1½ hours. The curd is then cut, the whey drawn off and salt added before the curd is placed in moulds and cured for two months at 50–59°F (10–15°C). The texture is soft with small eyes, and the white paste has an agreeable, slightly sour, salty flavour.

Tetilla is composed of 50% water, 22% fat and 20–22% protein.

Tilsit, Tilsiter

This cow's milk cheese is produced in several central European countries in cylindrical or oblong shapes, the weight varying from 6½–11 lb (3–5 kg). It is a semi-hard cheese with a few cracks in the paste and, occasionally, a few medium-sized holes.

Either raw or pasteurized milk is used, inoculated with lactic ferment starter cultures and curdled with liquid rennet at a temperature of 84–86°F (29–30°C). The curd is cut, cooked at 109–113°F (43–45°C), then transferred to perforated moulds and turned frequently without being pressed. The cheese forms are dry-salted and salted in brine before being ripened in cool, damp conditions; the washed rind has a dry bloom.

Tilsit contains 45–50% water and 10–30% fat, depending on what quality milk is used. Protein content varies also, again depending on how rich the milk is.

Toggenburger Ploderkäse
see Ploderkäse

Toma

Small creameries in Piedmont, the Aosta Valley and Savoy account for the bulk of production of Toma. Its name stems from one of the steps in making the cheese, *tuma* being a dialect word for fall or precipitation of the casein (milk protein) during coagulation of the milk.

Whole or partially skimmed milk is used, from cows pastured on high Alpine meadows rich in sweet-smelling herbs and flowers. The cheese is shaped like a thick disc, 4¾–8 in (12–20 cm) in diameter and 2–3 in (5–8 cm) high; weight up to 8¾ lb (4 kg).

The cheesemaking process starts with the milk being heated to 93–96°F (34–36°C) and curdled with liquid rennet. After 2 hours the curd is firm enough and is cut and put into cheese moulds. When the cheese forms have drained and taken shape they are dry-salted or salted in brine and then matured in cool curing rooms for 30–40 days or longer.

This uncooked cheese is quick ripening or may be cured for a short period; the thin yellowish crust covers a pale yellow paste with small holes and a robust, appetizing flavour. When aged, Toma's rind is rough and the yellow interior is dense with a sharp, salty taste.

Whole milk Toma contains 42–45% water, 25–27% fat and 22–24% protein; partially-skimmed milk cheeses (the milk is left to stand and some of the cream removed from the surface) have an average moisture content of 40%, 40% protein and 18% fat *in dry matter*.

Tomino

Piedmont and the Aosta Valley produce this uncooked quick-ripening cow's milk cheese, and the name stems from the same dialect word (*tuma*), referring to the precipitation of the casein (milk protein) after rennet is added to the milk.

Nowadays pasteurized milk is used (often enriched with added butterfat), acidified by the addition of a lactic bacteria starter culture, and curdled with liquid rennet at 95°F (35°C). The curd is cut into 1¼–2 in (3–5 cm) cubes and shaped and drained in perforated moulds 2½–2¾ in (6–7 cm) in diameter. When the cheese forms are firm enough to hold their shape, they are salted (usually dry-salted but they are sometimes salted in brine) for 15–20 minutes, allowed to dry, and are then wrapped in vegetable parchment.

Semi-fat Tomini are made with partially skimmed milk curdled with liquid rennet. The curd is allowed to stand for 8–12 hours and not cut before it is put into perforated moulds to drain. Once these cheese forms have been salted, the cheese is ready for consumption.

Tomini are also made into *Cremini*, following the same method, but 8–10 hours after the curd has formed it is blended, salted and pressed in cylindrical tube moulds which shape the cheeses into small elongated cylinders, 1–1¼ in (2–3 cm) in diameter and 6–8 in (15–20 cm) in length.

Tomini cheeses have no rind and are delicate cheeses with a pleasantly lactic flavour when fresh; the texture of the white paste is soft, friable and smooth. When fresh and ripened they make good dessert cheeses or, dressed with oil and pepper, can be eaten as an hors d'oeuvre.

Tomme de Saint-Marcellin,
see Saint-Marcellin

Tomme de Savoie

A semi-hard cow's milk cheese, shaped like a squat cylinder, approximately 8 in (20 cm) in diameter, 4¾ in (12 cm) high and weighing 2¾–3¼ lb (1.2–1.5 kg).

These cheeses are made in Haute-Savoie (France) and over the border on the Italian Alpine slopes, the two products being very alike. The taste is lactic and appetizingly aromatic.

Tomme Vaudoise

A small soft Swiss cheese from the Vaud and Jura cantons. They weigh about 3½ oz (100 g) and are cylindrical or oblong in shape. The rind is covered with white flora and the interior is dense, without holes. The taste is mild when the cheeses are fresh, becoming savoury and fragrant after 10 days' ripening.

Tomme Vaudoise is normally made with whole cow's milk.

Torta del Casar

This soft Spanish ewe's milk cheese is shaped like a flat disc and has a thin, soft crust; the paste is ivory-white with a few small holes.

Vegetable rennet is usually employed to curdle the milk; the curd is then cut, slowly drained and pressed in moulds before being salted. Curing lasts for 30 days at temperatures ranging between 69–77°F (20–25°C) with low humidity.

Toscanello

Central Italy (Tuscany) and Sardinia are the main producers of this semi-hard ewe's milk cheese, weighing 6 lb (2.7 kg) and shaped like a cylinder.

The milk is first heated to 98–102°F (37–39°C) and coagulated with calf's rennet; the curd is then cut and drained for 6 hours. The cheese forms are salted in brine and matured for 3–4 months within a temperature range of 50–59°F (10–15°C).

The rind is smooth and white shading to pale straw-yellow; the white paste is dense and homogeneous, though it sometimes has a few scattered holes, and it has a muted flavour, mild or slightly sharp, as befits its ewe's milk origins.

Trappisten, Trappiste

A semi-hard cow's milk cheese which bears a close resemblance to the cheese originally produced by the Trappist monks of the Abbey of Port-du-Salut, France.

It is disc-shaped, 10 in (25 cm) in diameter, 2 in (5 cm) thick, and 3¼–6½ lb (1.5–3 kg) in weight. Moisture content is 44–46%, fat 24–26% and protein 21–23%. The smooth, close-textured paste has a few small holes

and is covered by a soft, bloomy rind.

In the nineteenth century this type of cheese was being made by the monks of Benjaluka in Bosnia, now part of Yugoslavia, and nowadays production is carried on in Austria, South Germany, Yugoslavia, Czechoslovakia and Hungary.

The cheese is closely associated with the monastic order founded at La Trappe in Normandy and monks

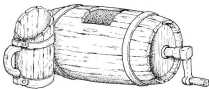

make it all over the world, which accounts for slight variations in flavour and cheesemaking techniques.

Trecce di Bufala,
see Mozzarella di Bufala

Tronchón, see Aragón

Trou de Sottai

A soft cylindrical Belgian cheese made with cow's milk, and weighing 10½–14 oz (300–400 g). The paste is smooth and buttery, covered with a golden-yellow rind.

Troyes, see Barberey

Tupi

This Spanish product is not strictly speaking a cheese, but cheese forms the main ingredient. Aged cheese is

finely grated or ground, and blended with oil and alcohol; when smooth and well-mixed the paste is stored in glass jars and left to mature for 2–3 months.

The resulting taste is strong, aromatic and alcoholic; it is spread on plain fresh bread and eaten with salad or honey.

Twaróg, Twrog

The USSR and Poland both make this acid-curd cow's milk cheese. It is even-textured with no rind, and packaged in sizes varying in weight from 7 oz – 2¼ lb (200 g – 1 kg).

Average moisture content is 65–75%, fat 10–12% and protein 20–22%.

Tybo

A close relative of Samsø, this cow's milk cheese comes from the Thay district in Denmark. It is brick-shaped and weighs 4½–8¾ lb (2–4 kg); the paste is supple with widely-scattered medium-sized or large holes, and is covered with a thin yellow rind.

Tyroler Alpenkäse

A cooked cow's milk cheese made in small wheels weighing 25½–30¾ lb (12–14 kg).

Matured for 2–3 months, it has medium-sized to large holes and a mild, slightly sweet taste.

Tyroler Graukäse

Lactic ferment cultures are added to cow's milk to raise its acidity level and the soured milk eventually forms a curd which is cut and heated to 122°F (50°C).

Curing lasts for 10–20 days at a temperature and humidity level which promotes the growth of greenish-grey mould over the surface.

Ulloa

A semi-hard Spanish cow's milk cheese which resembles Tetilla. The disc-shaped cheeses weigh about 2¼ lb (1 kg).

Ulzama

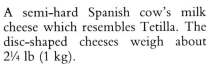

This cheese comes from Navarra in north-eastern Spain and is made with ewe's milk. Cylindrical in shape and weighing 3¼–4½ lb (1.5–2 kg), the cheeses have a chestnut coloured rind, enclosing a white, dense paste with small holes which has a strong, decided flavour.

Uova di Bufala,
see Mozzarella di Bufala

Urbia, see Idiazabal

Vacherin des Beauges

In the Haute-Savoie region of France these soft cheeses are made with cow's milk and shaped like large, flat discs with a diameter of 10 in (25 cm), 1½ in (4 cm) thick, and weighing 4½ lb (2 kg). The delicate crust is grey or brown and the cheeses are ripened in cool damp conditions, bound with a strip of spruce bark which permeates the cheese with its subtle resinous aroma.

Vacherin Fribourgeois,
see Freiburger Vacherin

Vacherin Mont-d'Or

A soft Swiss cheese (from the Canton of Vaud) made with cow's milk in a disc shape which varies in size and weighs from 10½ oz – 6½ lb (300g – 3 kg). The paste, when ripe and ready to eat, is velvety and buttery with small holes. The taste remains deliciously creamy and delicate.

Vacherol du Port-du-Salut de la Trappe

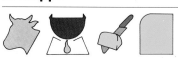

A semi-hard French cow's milk cheese shaped like a squat cylinder

and usually weighing 6½–11 lb (3–5 kg). The interior of the cheese is yellow and the skin a reddish-yellow.

The cheesemaking technique is the same as that followed for Saint-Paulin.

Valais Raclette

Made in the Alpine region of the Swiss Canton of Valais with whole cow's milk, this wheel-shaped cheese measures 14 in (35 cm) in diameter and weighs 13¼–15½ lb (6–7 kg) in weight. The paste has very few holes and is pale and creamy. This is one of the Raclette cheeses which, when exposed to direct heat, melts into a delicious rich, buttery, velvety mass. Raclette is a Valais specialty, a very tasty Swiss dish almost as famous as fondue.

Valdeteja

A semi-hard Spanish goat's milk cheese, shaped like a long cylinder; the paste is white with occasional holes and the rind is dry and smooth, rubbed with olive oil. Cured for 10–15 days in a dry, cool atmosphere.

Val di Muggio

Swiss uncooked cow's milk cheese with a rather subtle, delicate taste and a smooth skin.

Valençay

This French goat's milk cheese comes from the province of Berry. The soft interior is enclosed by a crust which is covered with wood ash. It looks like a truncated pyramid in shape and weighs about 10½ oz (300 g).

Västerbottenost

A Swedish cow's milk cheese shaped like a squat cylinder. The weight of this hard cheese varies between 35¼–44 lb (16–20 kg).

Pasteurized milk is inoculated with a starter culture of heat-loving lactic bacteria and the milk is then curdled with liquid rennet at a temperature of 86–89°F (30–32°C). The curd is cut, heated to 104–107°F (40–42°C) and kept at this temperature while being stirred for some time; the scalded curd is then lifted out of the vat and pressed. The cheese forms are salted and matured for 7–8 months at 53–60°F (12–16°C).

Västerbottenost's texture is dense and firm with small holes.

Venaco

Small Corsican goat's milk cheese, weighing at most 10½–14 oz (300–400 g). The cylindrical cheeses are only made at certain times of the year; the texture is supple. The milk is curdled with rennet.

Cured for 30–50 days in naturally cool, damp conditions which favour the growth of a crust covered in micro-organisms which give a greenish-grey or white appearance.

Véritable Nantais, see Nantais

Vezzena

Scalded-curd cow's milk cheese made with milk which has been allowed to stand and had its top layer of cream skimmed off. The cheese takes its name from the neighbourhood of Vezzena on the high plateau which divides the Veneto region from the Trentino in Italy, and is made during the summer in Alpine huts high up in the mountain valleys.

The milk is left to stand while the cream rises to the surface. This is skimmed off and the milk is curdled with powdered rennet at a temperature of 91–98°F (33–37°C). The curd is cut into pieces measuring ⅛–¼ in (3–5 mm), heated to 107–114°F (42–48°C) and then ladled into round moulds 14–18 in (35–45 cm) in diameter and 5½–6¼ in (14–16 cm) deep. The cheese forms are dry-salted and matured for six months (for sliceable table cheese) or for a year for grating cheese.

Villalón

also known as Pata de Mulo

A fresh Spanish ewe's milk cheese which originated in the countryside around Valladolid in Old Castile, near the Portuguese border. Nowa-days it is made throughout the region known as Tierra de Campos, in the provinces of León, Zamora, Valladolid and Palencia.

Villalon looks like an elongated cylinder in appearance, oval in section and with rounded ends; it is also called Pata de Mulo (mule's hoof). The white paste is even-textured and rindless. It contains 53–55% water, 25–27% fat and 15–16% protein.

When minor details of the cheese-making process are modified (such as in the salting method) a hard cheese will result and is called **Cincho**.

Vivaro

This is a scalded-curd cheese, made with cow's milk in the countryside around Vivaro in the Italian province of Friuli. The technique is much the same as that followed for Montasio.

The colour of the paste is a lustrous pale straw-yellow, supple and creamy with very few holes. The taste is mild and pleasing. The golden-brown rind is hard and smooth.

Walliser

The generic term for scalded-curd cow's milk cheese with dry, bloomy rinds and mild pastes broken by the occasional hole which are produced in the Valais region of Switzerland. These are superb melting cheeses and as such are used for the Swiss specialty Raclette. Walliser cheeses, which mature for 2–3 months, are wheel shaped.

Washed Curd

A Canadian product which borrows some of its production techniques from the Cheddar method; the Canadian process differs in that the curd is cut up very finely in the vat without any whey, and is covered with cold water for 5–30 minutes. This lowers the acid content of the cheese and the texture is coarser with a softer body.

The cheeses are ripened for 1–2 months at 50°F (10°C).

Weichkäse

The generic term for a family of soft German cheeses with a very high moisture content and which have a bloomy thin rind or are covered with white rind flora. They all have close-textured pastes, sometimes with small holes, and taste fresh and delicate.

Weisslacker

A German cow's milk cheese which is oblong and weighs 6½–8¾ lb (3–4 kg). It is heavily salted which makes the colour of the paste snowy white. The taste is sharp and strong and the surface is covered in the flora which ripens the cheese from the outside towards the middle.

Wensleydale – White and Blue

White Wensleydale is made in a flat disc weighing about 8 lbs (3½ kg) and its highly-pressed white paste matures rapidly to give a mellow, honey-like flavour, unrivalled as an accompaniment to apple pie. Even though made with milk from successive milkings the curd is not allowed to develop acidity and any Wensleydale cheese that is sour or yellow is over-aged.

Drum-shaped Blue Wensleydale is smoother and less veined than Stilton and tastes not unlike it; but the un-soured curd will sometimes develop a richer flavour.

The milk for both cheeses is heated to 86°F (30°C) and inoculated with a small amount of fermenting whey. After the curd has formed in 50–60 minutes it is drained, salted and pressed. Blue is matured for 4–6 months; White for 3–4 weeks.

Wine with cheese

European Wine Partners for World Cheeses

Cheese	Wine	Alternative wines
Alpsbergkäse	Hermitage	Chianti Classico, Barsac
Asiago	Bardolino	Beaujolais Villages, Valrolicella
Beaufort	Apremont	Mondeuse, Jurançon Sec
Bel Paese	Rosé de Provence	Chiaretto del Garda, Anjou Rosé
Bleu d'Avergne	Côte de Brouilly	Gigondas, Coteaux du Languedoc
Bleu des Causses	Saint-Emilion	Barsac, Gigondas
Brie	Médoc	Volnay, Chablis
Bûche de Chèvre	Graves	Muscadet, Sancevre
Caciocavallo	Collio Cabernet	Pommard, Pauillac
Caciotta	Rosé de Touraine	Rosé de Provence, Grignolino
Caerphilly	Nuits-Saint-Georges	Nebbiolo, Pommard
Camembert	Saint-Emilion	Moulin-à-Vent, Bourgogne Blanc
Cantal	Bordeaux	Chinon, Graves Blanc
Caprino	Soave	Bordeaux Blanc, Muscadet
Caprino Stagionato	Sangiovese	Barsac, Saint-Emilion
Carré de l'Est	Pinot d'Alsace	Riesling, Saint-Estèphe
Cheddar	Brunello di Montalcino	Saint-Emilion, Rioja
Cheshire	Juliénas	Valpolicella, Rosé de Touraine
Coulommiers	Pomerol	Côte Rôtie, Nuits-Saint-Georges
Derby	Rosé de Provence	Chiaretto del Garda, Beaujolais Villages
Dorset Blue	Port	Marsala, Madeira
Double Gloucester	Pommard	Chianti, Médoc
Dunlop	Cabernet	Médoc, Barolo
Edam	Pinot Noir	Médoc, Chianti
Edelpilzkäse	Juliénas	Beaujolais Villages, Saint Emilion
Emmental	Jura Blanc	Seyssel, Chiroubles
Feta	Cabernet	Pinot Noir, Bordeaux Rouge
Fontal	Chianti	Dão, Beaujolais Villages
Fourme d'Ambert	Cornas	Fitou, Saint-Emilion
Gloucester, Single Gloucester	Médoc	Pommard, Chianti
Gorgonzola	Marsala	Port, Sauternes
Gouda	Beaujolais Nouveau	Juliénas, Bardolino
Grana Padano	Barolo	Pommard, Châteauneuf-du-Pape
Gruyère	Dôle du Mont	Valpolicella, Pauillac
Kefalotiri	Othello	Sangiovese, Rully
Lancashire	Pauillac	Barbaresco, St Julian
Leicester	Pommard	Chianti, Médoc
Livarot	Châteauneuf-du-Pape	Juliénas, Gewürztraminer
Maroilles	Monthélie	Meursault, Pomerol
Mascarpone	Muscadet	Cortese di Gavi, Bordeaux Blanc
Mimolette	Côtes de Provence	Corbières, Saint-Veran
Mozzarella di Bufala	Frascati	Muscadet, Bordeaux Blanc
Munster	Chénas	Hermitage, Sauternes
Neufchâtel	Crozes Hermitage	Côtes du Rhône Villages, Nebbiolo

Wine with cheese

Cheese	Wine	Alternative wines
Nieheimer	Cabernet d'Anjou	Coyvo Rosso, Barbaresco
Pannerone	Collio Cabernet	Moulin-à-Vent, Beaujolais Villages
Parmigiano Reggiano	Barbaresco	Chianti, Saint-Emilion
Pecorino Romano	Chianti	Côtes de Poussillon, Médoc
Pont l'Évêque	Pommard	Pauillac, Madiran
Provolone	Dolcetto d'Alba	Franciacorta, Rosso, Irancy
Reblochon	Listrac	Nuits-Saint-Georges, Pouilly-Fuissé
Ricotta	Muscadet	Bourgogne Blanc, Arbois Rosé
Romadur	Pomerol	Chianti, Margaux
Roquefort	Saint-Emilion	Barsac, Fitou
Sage Derby	Crozes Hermitage	Médoc, Chianti
Sainte-Maure	Chignin	Apremont, Côtes du Luberon
Saint-Nectaire	Tavel	Côtes-du-Rhône, Montravel
Saint-Paulin	Côte de Beaune	Bergerac, Pouilly-Vinzelles
Stilton, Blue	Port	Marsala, Muscat de Baumes de Vluise
Stilton, White	Beaujolais Villages	Volnay, Barolo
Taleggio	Barbaresco	Pauillac, Beaujolais Villages
Tilsit	Saint-Emilion	Chianti, Bordeaux Rouge
Tomme de Savoie	Fendant	Costières du Gard, Mondeuse
Wensleydale	Dão	Rioja, Jumilla

American Wine Partners for World Cheeses

Bel Paese	Mondavi Gamay Rosé; Mirassou Gamay Beaujolais
Brie	Cabernet Sauvignon: Heitz, Phelps, Sonoma
Caciocavallo	Beaulieu Cabernet Sauvignon; Mondavi Pinot Noir
Caerphilly	Phelps Syrah; most Zinfandel
Camembert	Merlot: Stag's Leap, Rutherford Hill
Cheddar	Zinfandel: Pedroncelli, Martini, Masson
Double Gloucester	Giumarra Ruby Cabernet; Parducci Petite Syrah
Feta	Mondavi Fumé Blanc; Sterling Sauvignon Blanc
Gorgonzola	Estrella River Muscat; Ficklin Port
Gouda	Monterey Gamay Beaujolais; Martini Gewürztraminer
Gruyère	Chardonnay: Mondavi, Jekel, Gallo
Pecorino and Parmesan	Cabernet Sauvignon: Clos du Val, Charles Krug
Ricotta	Sauvignon Blanc: Cakebread, Gallo, Spring Mountain
Roquefort	Ridge or Clos du Val Zinfandel; Sebastiani Barbera
Blue Stilton	Phelps Late Harvest Riesling; Krug Moscata di Canelli

South African Wine Partners for World Cheeses

Blue Cheeses	Laborie Red; Hazendal Freudenlese Special Late Harvest
Brie	KWV Steen; Blaauwklippen Pinot Noir
Camembert	Fairview Sauvignon Blanc; Overgaauw Trio Corda
Cheddar	Bertrams Shiraz; Chateau Libertas Dry Red
Cheshire	Kanonkop Cabernet Sauvignon; Le Bonheur Blanc Fumé
Cottage and Fresh Cheeses	Simonsig Rosé; Uiterwyk Chenin Blanc
Feta	Twee Jongegezellen TJ39; Goede Hoop Red Wine
Goats' Milk Cheeses	Hamilton Russell Blanc de Blanc; Mont Blois White Muscadel
Gorgonzola	Alto Rouge; Delheim Noble Late Harvest
Gruyère, Comté and Emmental	Boplaas Vin Blanc; Uitkyk Carlsheim

Cheese	Wine
Mozzarella	Backsberg Rosé; Culemborg Pinotage
Munster	Neethlingshof Gewürztraminer; Rust-en-Vrede Shiraz
Parmesan and Pecorino	Groot Constantia Blanc de Blanc; De Wetshof Sauvignon Blanc
Pont l'Evêque	Oude Nektar Furmint; L'Ormarins Sauvignon Blanc
Roquefort	Weltevrede Noble Harvest; Rietvallei Red Muscadel
Saint-Paulin	Rustenberg Classic; Boschendal Shiraz
Stilton	Simonsig Noble Late Harvest; Fairview Special Late Harvest

Australian Wine Partners for World Cheeses

Cheese	Wine
Blue Cheeses	Bailey's Muscat; Taltarni Shiraz
Brie	Balgownie Cabernet; Brown Bros Chardonnay
Camembert	Bleasdale Shiraz; Huntingdon Estate Semillon
Cantal	Seaview Sauvignon; Valencia Chenin Blanc
Cheddar	Brokenwood Shiraz; d'Arenberg Burgundy
Cheshire	Seppelt Hermitage-Cabernet; Stanley Cabernet Sauvignon
Cottage and Fresh Cheeses	Gramp Steingarten; Hardy's Old Castle Riesling
Feta	Ryecroft Shiraz; Moss Wood Cabernet
Goats' Milk Cheeses	Tulloch Dry Red; McWilliams Lexia
Gorgonzola	Chambers' Rosewood Flame Tokay; All Saints Muscat
Gouda	Vasse Felix Cabernet Sauvignon; Quelltaler Semillon
Gruyère, Comté and Emmental	Hardy's St Thomas Burgundy; Lake's Folly Chardonnay
Mozzarella	Gramp Barossa Pearl; Arrowfield Rhine Riesling
Munster	Chateau Tahbilk Cabernet; Rothbury Hermitage
Parmesan and Pecorino	Tyrrell Pinot Noir; Evans and Tate Reds
Pont l'Evêque	Petaluma Chardonnay; Mount Mary Pinot Noir
Roquefort	Morris Liqueur Muscat; Smith's Yalumba 'Galway Pipe' Port
Saint-Paulin	Bowen Estate Cabernet Sauvignon; Houghton White Burgundy
Stilton	Westfield Verdelho; Penfold's Grandfather Port

New Zealand Wine Partners for World Cheeses

Cheese	Wine
Blue Cheeses	Corbans Auslese; Penfolds Autumn Riesling
Brie	Matawhero Gewürztraminer; Montana Cabernet
Camembert	Nobilo's Pinot Noir; Corbans Chenin Blanc
Cantal	Villa Maria Sauvignon Blanc; Matua Valley Muscat Blanc
Cheddar	Nobilo's Pinotage; Te Mata Cabernet
Cheshire	Penfolds Cabernet; Glenvale Red Wines
Feta	Penfolds Pinotage; Glenvale Red Wines
Goats' Milk Cheeses	Villa Maria Riesling-Sylvaner; Mission Tokay d'Alsace
Gorgonzola	Cooks Te Kauwhata Gewürztraminer; Totara Chenin Blanc
Gouda	Cooks Chasselas; Corbans Chenin Blanc
Gruyère, Comté and Emmental	Matwhero Chardonnay; Cooks Chenin Blanc
Mozzarella	Cooks Pinot Meunier; McWilliams Cresta Doré
Munster	Montana Cabernet; Te Mata Chardonnay
Parmesan and Pecorino	Cooks Cabernet; McWilliams Baco Noir
Pont l'Evêque	Montana Marlborough Sauvignon Blanc; Hunter's Müller-Thurgau Dry
Roquefort	Delegats Reserve Bin Müller-Thurgau Auslese; Cooks Vintage Port
Saint-Paulin	Montana Marlborough Pinot Noir; Matua Valley Fumé Blanc
Stilton	Matua Valley Vintage Port; Delegat Late Harvest Selected Vintage Müller-Thurgau; Cooks Late-Picked Riesling

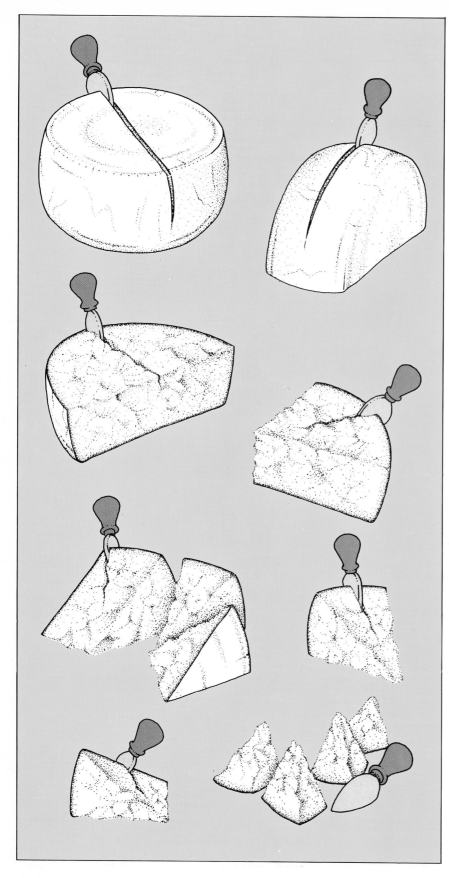

Cutting Cheese

Cutting a cheese correctly is extremely important, not only to keep it looking attractive and presentable, but also to ensure that it keeps successfully. The way a cheese is cut can even affect the taste, in that certain parts of a cheese will have a slightly different flavour from other parts; texture, too, will vary in much the same way, depending on how close to the rind or how creamy the portion is, how much veining the portion contains if it is a piece of blue cheese, and so on.

Cutting a whole Parmesan

In some cases (such as when opening a whole Parmesan cheese) the process calls for expertise and long experience. The stages of this difficult operation are shown in the drawings on the left of this page. A special almond-shaped knife is always used to split open a whole Parmesan and this preserves its characteristic granular quality. The point of the knife is first used to cut a line dividing the cheese in half, and the rind is then cut through along this line to a depth of ½–¾ inch (1–2 cm), working across the diameter, down the convex walls until it is time to insert the knife at the juncture of flat surface and flank. Two knives are usually inserted and each will be used as a lever, being pulled apart until the cheese splits into two halves.

The same procedure is followed to divide the cheese further, into quarters and smaller sections, taking care that a consistent ratio is maintained between rind and cheese.

Cutting different shaped cheeses

1. Large, hard or firm wheel-shaped cheeses are cut from the centre towards the outside edge in triangular wedges just like a pie or a cake; these large sections can then be cut into smaller pieces, working from the middle to the crust.
2. Large, soft wheel-shaped cheeses such as Brie are also sliced into triangular pieces like the harder, larger cheeses but the soft cheese pieces should be cut lengthwise for each individual serving.
3. Small, cylindrical shaped cheeses should be sliced into rounds, rather like slicing a salami sausage.
4. Very small cheeses (especially goat's milk cheeses) need simply to be cut in half, or served whole.
5. Very large, cylindrical cheeses such as Provolone are sliced off in large rounds which are then cut up into triangular portions.
6. Square or rectangular soft or buttery cheeses are best cut following the method shown in the nearer of the two drawings: this means that if only a certain amount of the cheese is eaten the two cut faces can be pushed gently together and the soft cheese will not run out of the crust. If the cheese is not one of the varieties which will run out of the crust when cut and collapse if left for any length of time, then the second method illustrated can be adopted, trying to cut the pieces with equal proportions of rind and cheese.
7. Pyramid-shaped goat's cheeses are usually simply cut into neat quarters.

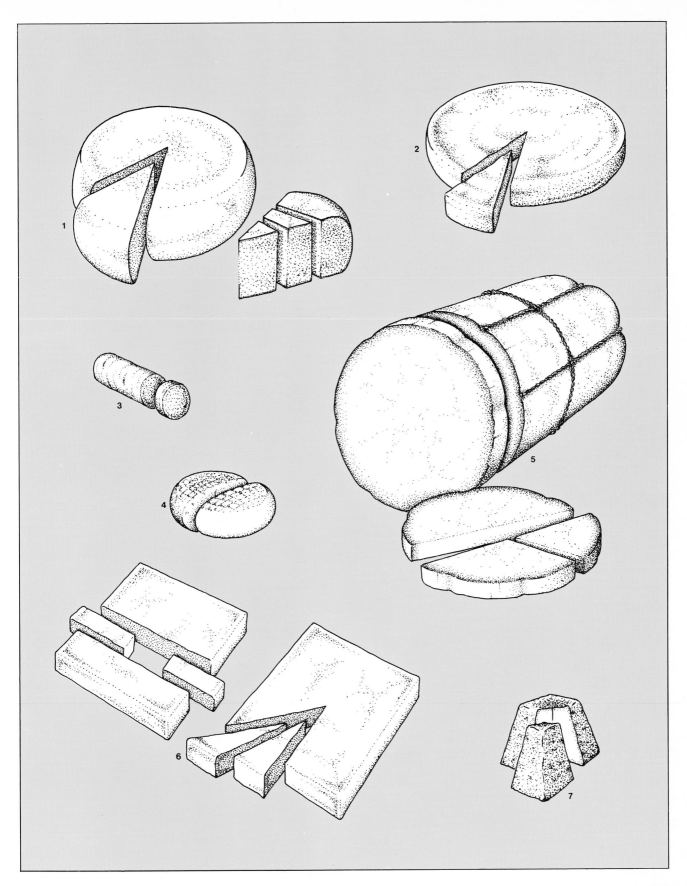

Cheese Defects

Industrialisation of cheesemaking and the resulting standardization of procedures, close control throughout the cheesemaking process, as well as improved hygiene in milking parlours and monitoring of the milk's progress from the cow or other animal through to its transformation into cheese, have all greatly reduced the likelihood of cheese developing faults, whether these be of consistency, texture, taste or appearance.

But when something does go wrong during the chemical and biological reactions which physically alter the nature of milk, then these cannot fail to appear in the finished cheese. Whether the cheese is fresh or soft, ripened for a short time, or well-aged as in the case of semi-hard and hard cheeses – these faults are instantly identifiable to the trained eye and may affect one or more features of a cheese. In factory-produced or large creamery cheese production, however, these defects are usually minor and hardly affect the eating qualities of the cheese, let alone prove harmful to the consumer, but the cheese may look less appetizing and may well be sold off as a second-grade cheese.

Once a cheese has been put in an ageing-room or cellar it is still subject to strict quality control and this is usually carried out by very experienced experts who tap, smell and sometimes taste a sample from a batch of cheeses to see how they are progressing. Defects in composition (too high or too low a moisture content in the cheese, or an excessive salt or fat content) are rare, while faults in texture and development of the correct micro-organisms are more frequently encountered. The rind, or crust, which should be thin or firm or missing in certain cheeses (such as Mozzarella) can be too rumpled, crumpled and rough, too dry or too sticky; cracks may form in the surface when they should not be present, through which undesirable bacteria may penetrate and adversely affect the texture, appearance and taste of that part of the cheese closest to the crust or rind.

Cheeses which should be smooth, homogenous and unbroken may develop medium-sized or large holes, fissures or cracks. Here the micro-organisms (for each cheese is an enclosed world which is very much alive, and even if the external conditions are favourable much can go wrong inside) may have developed abnormally or unevenly or the curd or paste has inherent faults. If the cheese has holes (often desirable in certain varieties) these are usually produced by bacterial action inside the cheese; the gas which is given off forms bubbles which are trapped in the paste and whether the holes are large, small, round, regular or irregular will depend on the texture of the paste. Fairly large fissures are caused when the cheese cracks internally due to a lack of suppleness and elasticity; the cheese may have been cured in too dry an atmosphere or bacteria inside the cheese may be producing gases which could cause these cracks. These anomalies will usually lead to some impairment of taste and aroma. The cheese may become acid, sharp-tasting, bitter or may well develop a repugnant smell.

Many cheeses develop the wrong type of consistency or texture through faulty storing or curing; fresh cheeses (Mozzarella in particular) deteriorate rapidly and their texture undergoes marked deterioration if stored improperly or for too long (even under cool, moist conditions). The taste changes, the cheeses develop acidity and sharpness and may become mushy or slimy. Deterioration in taste is also caused by bacteria which are harmful to cheese gaining a hold because the cheese has not been correctly handled, and their action – or reaction – with the cheese may cause it to give off unpleasant odours.

Slightly different shades of colour are quite normal and acceptable as milk varies in richness throughout the year (for example, the colour will be brighter straw-yellow when the cows have been fed on green forage rich in carotene), so there is no need to worry about that.

Soured Milk Products

When milk is soured, the lactose or milk sugar it contains has been fermented by several species of bacteria, leading to the formation of lactic acid, and in some cases alcohol. This bacterial activity precipitates a curd which can be firm or watery (sometimes ropey, stringy or slimy) and it is difficult to draw a hard and fast line or make a categorical distinction between soured milk and cheese. However, the ideal bacteria for producing such products as yogurt do vary from those which are commonly used for making cheese.

Sour milk products can be made with whole, partially or wholly skimmed, milk or the milk can be enriched and concentrated by adding powdered milk. Yogurts and soured milks are the oldest milk derivatives known to man and have been made all over the world, originating in hot countries where the heat-loving bacterium *streptococcus thermophilus* which thrives at 104–113°F (40–45°C) can develop without any artificial aids.

These milk foods can be classified in the following groups:

a) Very acid soured milk such as yogurt;

b) Soured milk with low acidity content, such as cultured milk;

c) Soured alcoholic milk drinks, such as kéfir; this originated in the Caucasus and is only slightly alcoholic. Koumiss also comes under this heading: it has a higher alcoholic content and is made from mare's milk (still common in the Soviet Union);

d) Sour milk with low acidity and a ropey consistency, such as Scandinavian rangmjolk, which is also called long milk;

e) Soured milk products which can be kept for some time, having good keeping qualities, such as labneh or labna.

Yogurt

This is milk which has first been heated is cooled to 104–113°F (40–45°C and a special starter culture is added. The acidity level of yogurt usually varies between 0.7 and 1.1%. Depending of the process adopted in making yogurt, one of two types will be produced: one setting as an unbroken curd in containers and the other involving cutting the curd when it has soured in large vats and transferring it into the cartons or pots in which it will be marketed. The latter method is the most commonly used on a commercial scale and produces a homogenous, velvety texture with no whey separation, the taste being fresh and mildly acid and the smell delicate and appetizing.

The main bacterial starter culture which is used for yogurt is made up of *Streptococcus thermophilus* and *Lactobacillus bulgaricus*, although others are sometimes included, particularly in the USA. The amount of starter employed and its age determine how acid the resulting yogurt will be (since the starter culture becomes more acid all the time as it ages); also dependant on the starter to a certain extent will be the thickness of the yogurt, its taste and texture. Yogurt can be kept at a temperature of approximately 41°F (5°C) for about a fortnight without deteriorating.

Acidophilus Milk

This product is made by souring milk with only one species of lactic bacteria, *Lactobacillus acidophilus* which develops slowly in milk at a temperature of 99°F (37°C) producing a lactic acid content of 0.6–0.8%. The flavour differs markedly from yogurt.

It is supposed to be one of the most beneficial of all soured milk products. *Lactobacillus acidophilus* is a common inhabitant of the human gut, but will flourish only if it is given milk or milk sugar to grow on. Acidophilus milk is very digestible, and is credited with neutralizing organisms responsible for putrefaction, as well as pathogens (disease-producing agents).

Cultured Milk

Cultured milk is produced by souring the milk with moisture-loving lactic bacteria at a temperature of approximately 68°F (20°C). It has a low acidity content (0.45–0.60% lactic acid) and a clean fresh acidulated taste.

163

Cultured buttermilk and soured cream are closely-related products. Cultured buttermilk is generally made with the by-product of butter-making, which is then soured. This drink has a very decided flavour with a very low fat content and low sugar (lactose) content; in some countries it is mixed with acidophilus milk. In most countries the product sold as buttermilk is actually skimmed milk.

Kéfir

This is one of the most widely-known and widely-consumed alcoholic soured milk drinks and it is particularly popular in Middle Eastern countries and in the Soviet Union.

It is made from cows' milk usually, and kéfir grains are used as the starter – known popularly as 'the prophet's millet' – which are soaked in warm water until swollen to twice their original size, and then placed in the milk, producing a complex chemical reaction which sours the milk and causes it to ferment.

Kéfir has a lactic acid content of between 0.6% and 0.9% and an alcohol content varying from 0.2% to 0.8%; it has a slightly effervescent quality about it, producing a tingling sensation when drunk, and at the same time it is a smooth, thick and creamy liquid.

When drunk fresh it is considered an effective germ destroyer helping to cure infections of the digestive tract. It is widely-used in the Soviet Union to treat gastro-intestinal infections and disturbances.

Koumiss is very similar to kéfir but was originally made from mare's milk. It usually has a higher alcoholic content than kéfir and when mare's milk is used it is unmistakable in appearance, due to its low casein content (much lower than in cows' milk); this also makes it eminently digestible.

In the USSR this product has long been valued for its therapeutic properties and koumiss cures are often prescribed for patients suffering from gastro-intestinal problems.

Labneh or labna

This is, effectively, a Middle Eastern cream cheese, made from yogurt which has had part of the whey drained off. It is consumed on a large scale in Arab countries where milk is soured by heat-loving lactic bacteria and yeasts. The very light, soft, creamy white curd cheese is shaped into small balls about 1¼ in (3 cm) in diameter and which are then rolled in olive oil and herbs or paprika or stored in oil for eating with bread. Labneh keeps well.

Laktofil

This originated in Sweden, a concentrated cultured milk which has had enough whey drained off to reduce the volume by half. Once the whey has been drawn off, the concentrated milk is enriched with cream until it has a fat content of 5% and is then homogenized and packaged.

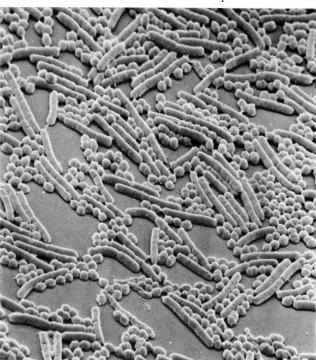

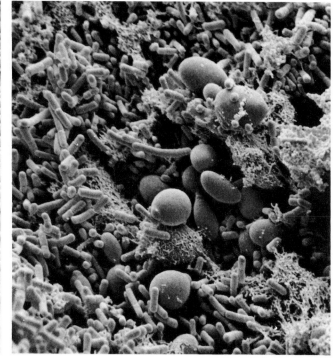

GLOSSARY

Blue cheeses Cheeses develop internal moulds by the introduction of *Penicillium glaucum* or *Penicillium roqueforti* spores. There are two basic types of blue-veined cheese: one has a naturally-formed dry rind and the other has almost no rind or its rind is so thin as to be almost transparent, and in this case the surface is slightly sticky. A new variety gaining enormous popularity is soft cream cheese with blue veins and a white-mould surface – looking like a Blue Brie. The British make Lymeswold, called Westminster when exported, the Germans sell Bavarian Blue and the Danes make a delicious smaller version called Castello.

Butter If cream is shaken, churned or beaten the fat globules adhere to one another leaving behind the watery substance called buttermilk. Butter contains a minimum of 82% fat and a maximum of 16% water. The residual percentage is accounted for by buttermilk and freshly-made butter is usually washed several times to get rid of this sharp-tasting by-product.

Buttermilk The residue left when milk has been churned to make butter; it has lost most of the fat and some of the other milk solids which have coalesced to form the butter. Buttermilk proper is sharp, as opposed to skimmed milk which has a sweeter taste. In modern commerce, buttermilk and cultured buttermilk are often skim milk and cultured skim milk respectively.

Coagulation The fundamental process by which milk starts its transformation into cheese. The casein or milk protein is coagulated or precipitated, with consequent release and separation of the whey, when a number of conditions are favourable to cause this reaction: the temperature and acidity level of the milk must both be right if the added rennet is to curdle the casein; milk salts must also be present in the correct proportion.

Colostrum The first milk produced by a cow after calving. Often referred to as 'beestings': it is thick and albuminous, vital for the newborn calf if it is to thrive.

Cracking or splitting When internal fractures form in very hard dense cheeses which should have an even texture, this defect indicates that the cheese has insufficient elasticity, and the paste has possibly dried out too much.

Cream This is the less dense, fatty part of the milk which will rise to the top of the milk if it is left to stand. It is less dense because it is composed of the larger fat globules which float because they are lighter than water. Cream can be obtained by skimming the surface of raw milk which has been left to stand 4–6 in (10–15 cm) deep for 6–12 hours. A more modern method is to remove the cream with a separator, which spins the milk and concentrates the cream by centrifugal force. British standards for the fat content in cream specify that single cream must contain 18% fat, whipping cream 35% and double cream 48%. Cream can be pasteurized or sterilized, depending on the degree to which the temperature is raised.

Draining Once the casein or cheese protein has coagulated and formed a curd, whey will be released and this process of release and drainage of the whey from the curd is accelerated by cutting the curd. The curd may be heated, when it will contract and expel yet more whey, or the whey will separate spontaneously from the curd. Acid curds retain far more moisture than curds formed by the addition of starter cultures or rennet, since they contract less.

Enzymes These organisms play a vital part in the development of cheese and belong to a group of catalytic proteins that are produced by living cells: they mediate and promote certain chemical processes without themselves being destroyed or altered. In order to play out their role the ambient temperature must be within certain limits, and other conditions must also be favourable – such as the correct degree of acidity. They are present to a degree in milk but flourish in cheese since during the phases of coagulation and ripening micro-organisms develop which release enzymes in large numbers. Pepsin and rennin are also enzymes, helping to bring about curdling of milk.

Enzymes also play a vital part in developing and determining the taste, aroma and consistency of a cheese.

Eyes This is a commonly used term to describe the holes which are formed by gas trapped in the paste of a cheese while it is ripening. If there are no eyes or holes present in the paste of a cheese, it is often – logically enough – described as blind.

Fermentation This is a complex process by which micro-organisms break down certain organic compounds and transform substances in the cheese as it ripens, by the action of enzymes as catalysts. In fresh cheeses lactic fermentation will take place, while in soft cheeses casein fermentation occurs. Propionic fermentation in hard cheeses accounts for the holes, sometimes very large, which occur when the gases produced by the bacterial action cannot escape. Fermentation has an alkalizing effect on soft cheeses, neutralizing the lactic acid. In soft cheeses the process will lead to the breaking down of the casein or cheese protein and, in hard cheeses, as already mentioned, carbon dioxide will break down fat, forming holes or eyes.

Fermentation is a vital process through which most of the components of cheese and fermented milk products are formed.

Homogenized milk When milk is homogenized the fat globules are broken down to a very small size (less than one-thousandth of one millimetre: a micron) and this stops the cream rising to the top of the milk. The milk is forced through small nozzles at great pressure – 60–200 times atmospheric pressure. The taste of the milk becomes uniformly richer and more digestible, and where cheesemaking is involved, the texture of the cheese is likely to be smoother and more even.

Milk acidity Fresh cow's milk (to chose the most commonly used milk as an illustration) has a pH value which varies between 6.5 and 6.8, making it very slightly acid, accounted for by the substances which are found in solution in milk (including lactic acid, citric acid, citrates etc.) while caseinogen, the chief protein, is in colloidal suspension. As the milk ripens or sours, bacteria feed on the milk and convert the lactose (milk sugar) into lactic acid. When the acidity of the milk reaches a certain level it will curdle easily. At the other end of the cheesemaking process, during the ripening of the cheese, enzymes and bacteria will feed on the acid, thus reducing the acidity of the cheese and making it take on a sweeter taste, sometimes accompanied by softening brought about by the enzymes in the moulds of surface ripened cheeses.

Mould This is the container into which the curd is placed to be shaped; the old English word is *chessit* which is probably less confusing as cheese mould has a second meaning – that of the specific bacteria which act on cheeses to give them individual flavours and textures. Cheese moulds or chessits are normally made with holes or perforated so that the curd can drain while it is being shaped.

Mould and bacterial colonies The layer which may form on the surface or crust of a cheese as it matures. Not all cheeses develop surface blooms or microflora. The type of mould varies according to the variety of the cheese's paste and rind, and is also determined by the level of humidity, the prevailing temperature and the treatment of the cheese while it is being cured: they are often white, as with Brie or Camembert. The bacteriological cultures which grow on washed rind cheeses may be yellow, orange, brown or red, varying in intensity and coverage depending on which micro-organisms are present in the greatest numbers on the surface of the cheese.

Pasteurization In order to kill germs in milk without altering the flavour, the milk is heated to 145°F (63°C) for 30 minutes or to 167°F (75°C) for 15 seconds. This process eliminates the possibility of disease being transmitted through milk, but also destroys the naturally-occuring organisms which promote cheesemaking in raw milk. These have to be replaced by lactic starter cultures.

Plastic or spun-curd cheese At the outset the curd will be very elastic due to strong acidity; the natural tendency is for this acidity to reduce. In the case of plastic or kneaded/spun curd-cheeses the curd is washed several times in hot whey which reduces its calcium content, and it can then be easily drawn out into strings. The soured curd is heated in water to 137°F (57°C) until it becomes plastic and can be stretched and kneaded. Mozzarella and Provolone are good examples of this type of cheese.

Processed cheeses These cheeses have their ripening process arrested at a given point by heat treatment. Several cheeses, which may be of different varieties or qualities, are finely ground and blended together by heating and stirring. An emulsifying agent is then added and the mixture is transformed into a homogenous plastic mass. Only certain types of cheese are suitable for this treatment and lactic, citric, acetic or phosphoric acid or small amounts of cream, water, salt, colouring and spices etc. may be added. Processed cheese was pioneered by the Swiss in the early years of this century; its manufacture has now spread to all parts of the industrialized world.

Rennet This substance is extracted from the stomach lining of such unweaned animals as calves, kids and lambs and it contains substances which coagulate milk (such as pepsin and rennin); it may also contain lipase, an enzyme that catalyzes the hydrolysis of fats.

Washed rind The rinds of certain cheeses are washed regularly during the ripening process: this is to keep the cheese moist and supple and to improve the taste of the cheese by inhibiting growths of certain moulds but encouraging certain bacterial cultures. Salt water, spiced brine, spirits and beer etc. may be used.

Waxed The rinds of many cheeses are given a protective (and incidentally decorative) coating of paraffin wax; the cheese is dipped into hot wax; this process improves its keeping qualities.

Whey This is a by-product of the coagulation of milk: it is the watery part containing albumin and a little fat left behind from the precipitation of the casein. It accounts for about 90% of the total volume of the milk used in cheesemaking, and besides albumin, contains lactose, globulin and mineral salts.

Index

Aarey 93
Abgesottener 93
acid-curd 11, 29, 34, 165
acidophilus milk 163
Ädelost 36, 93
Agrafa 93
Agrini 93
Alcobaça 93
Alicante 93
Alpin 94
Alpsbergkäse 68, 94
Altay 94
Altenburger 94
Alvorca 94
American cheeses 38–9 *and see under individual names*
Ancien Impérial 94
Appenzell 15, 16, 17, 62, 94, 142
Applewood 24
Aragackij 95
Aragón 86, 95
Armada 95
Asiago d'Allevo 95
Asiago Grasso Monte 95
Asiago Pressato 56, 96
Aura 96
Australian cheeses 39–40 *and see under individual names*
Austrian cheeses 17 *and see under individual names*
Azul 96

Babybel 46, 96
Bagozzo 96, 120
Bakers' 96
Balaton 96
Banbury 24
Barac 23
Barberey 97
Battelmatt 97, 98
Bavarian Blue 165
Beaufort 97
Beaumont 97
Beda 97
Beenleigh Blue 24
Belfermière 97
Bellos 98
Bel Paese 54, 98, 101
Bergader 68, 98
Bergkäse 72, 98
Bergues 98
Berkeley 24
Beyaz Peynir 98
Bijeni Sir 98
Bitto 98
Bjalo Sirene 99
Bleu d'Auvergne 37, 48, 99
Bleu de Corse 99
Bleu de Gex 99
Bleu de Laqueuille 100
Bleu de Sassenage 100
Bleu des Causses 100
Bleu du Haut-Jura 100
Bleu du Quercy 100
blue cheeses 20, 21–2, 35, 165
Blue Vein 37, 39, 40
Bondon 100
Bou de Fagne 74, 100
Boulette d'Avesnes 100
Bouquet des Moines 74, 100
Bra 100, 142
Branzi 101
Brenne 17
Brick 37, 38, 101
Brie 16, 17, 31, 32, 33, 36, 37, 38, 46, 101–2, 166
Brie de Meaux 22, 27, 37, 102, 149
Brie de Melun 102
Brinza 102

Brinza de Moldauer 102
British cheeses 16, 18, 20–4 *and see under individual names*
Broccio 102
Brucialepre 102
Bruscion 66, 103
Bûche de Chèvre 44, 103
buffalo mild 18, 26 *and see under individual cheeses*
Burgos 88, 103
butter 36, 165
Butterkäse 72, 103
buttermilk 163, 165

Caboc 23
Cabrales 86, 103
Caciocavallo 37, 56, 103, 123
Caciofiore 103
Cacioricotta 104
Caciotta 104
Caciotta di Pecora 56, 104
Cadiz 104
Caerphilly 20, 23, 24, 84, 104–5
Calcagno 105
Cambridge 23
Camembert 16, 20, 27, 31, 32, 36, 37, 38, 39, 44, 105, 134, 166
Camerano 105
Canadian cheeses 37–8 *and see under individual names*
Cancoillotte 17
Canestrato 52, 105–6
Cantal 17, 42, 106, 146
Caprice des Dieux 48, 106
Caprino a Pasta Cruda 106
Caprino Semicotto 106
Carnia 106
Carré de l'Est 106–7
Casanova 107
Casatella 107
casein 11, 25, 26, 30, 31, 32, 165
Castello 165
Castelmagno 58, 107
Castelo Branco 107
Castigliano 88, 107
Cebrero 107
Cécil 107
certification of type and origin 36–7
Chabi 108
Chabichou 66, 108
Chamois d'Or 50, 108
Chaource 108
Charnwood 24
Charolais 108
Cheddar 16, 20, 22, 24, 32, 36, 84, 108, 112, 156; American 38, 90, 108; Australian 39, 108; Canadian 37, 108; New Zealand 40
Cheedam 39
Cheshire, Red, White and Blue 20, 21, 23, 36, 39, 84, 109
Chester 109
Cheviot 24
Chevrotin des Aravis 42, 109
Chittlehamholt White 24
classifying cheeses 33–6
coagulation 11–12, 25, 27, 29–30, 165
Colby 37, 38, 40, 109, 130
colostrum 165
Colwick 23
Comté 17, 30, 37. *See also* Gruyère
Coon 38
Cornhusker 38
Cotherstone 32
Cotswold 24
Cottage cheese 38, 90, 109–10
Cottenham 24
Coulommiers 24, 48, 110
cow, breeds of 16, 18

cow's milk 12, 14, 16, 17, 18, 24, 26, 166
cracks, cracking 32, 165
cream 36, 165
cream cheese 15, 110
Crédioux aux Noix 50, 110
Crescenza 60, 110
Crotonese 110
Crottin de Chavignol 37, 110
Crowdie 23
cultured milk 163, 164
curd cheese 34
curds 11, 26, 27, 29, 30, 165
cutting cheese 160

Danablu 35, 36, 78, 110–11
Danbo 36, 40, 78, 111, 113
Danish cheeses 18, 20 *and see under individual names*
Dariworld 111
defects of cheese 162
Demi-Sel 111
Derby 23, 84, 111
Devon Garland 24
Domiati 111
Doppelrahmstufe 70, 111
Dorset Blue 23, 111
Double Gloucester 23, 24, 39, 84, 90, 111–12
Drabant 82, 112
Dreux 112
Dunlop 23, 84, 112
Dutch Cheese 38
Dutch cheeses 17 *and see under individual names*

Echtermainzerkäse 70, 112
Edam 18, 39, 40, 72, 76, 82, 112, 130, 136
Edelblankkäse 72, 112
Edelpilzkäse 70, 112
Egmont 40
Elbo 78, 113
Emmental, Emmentaler 17, 19, 30, 32, 36, 38, 62, 68, 72, 113, 126, 150
enzymes 11, 27, 28, 29, 165
Époisses 113
Eremita 113
Erimys Peynir 113
Erkentaler 113
Esrom 80, 113–14
Essex 24
Estonskij Syr 114
Euda 114
ewe's milk 12, 14, 16, 18, 21, 23, 24, 26 *and see under individual cheeses*
eyes 165

Farmhouse Cheddar 22, 27, 31, 108
Färsk Getost 114
fat content 32–3
fermentation 165
Feta 24, 30, 37, 39, 40, 90, 114
Fior di Latte 60, 114–15, 131
Fiore Sardo 52, 115
Flotemysost 115
Folies de Béguines 74, 115
Fontal 54, 115
Fontina 39, 54, 98, 101, 116
Formaggella della Val Bavona 66, 116
Formaggella Ticinese 116
Formaggio Bianco 116
Fourme d'Ambert 50, 116
Freiburger Vacherin 64, 117
French cheeses 17–18 *and see under individual names*
Friese 36, 76, 117

Friulano 54, 117
Fromage des Pyrénées 117
Fynbo 36, 80, 117

Gammelost 18, 117
Geheimratskäse 70, 118
Gervais 20, 118
Getmesost, Gjetost 27, 118
Getost 118
Giuncata 118
Gloucester 20, 23, 118. See also Double Gloucester
goat's milk 12, 13, 14, 17, 18, 23, 24, 26, 35 *and see under individual cheeses*
Gorgonzola 16, 30, 35, 37, 54, 107, 118–19, 145, 166
Gorgonzola a Due Paste 119
Gouda 32–3, 36, 37, 39, 40, 76, 12, 119–20, 136
Gournay 120
Gournay Affiné 120
Graddost 82, 120
Grana, Grana Padano 52, 120–21, 135, 136
Grana Lodigiano 58, 121
Granular 38
Grazelema 121
Green Fade 20
Grevéost 121
Gruyère, Greyerzer 17, 32, 36, 37, 38, 40, 62, 93, 97, 98, 121, 135
Gruyère de Beaufort 121
Gruyère de Comté 42, 121
Gudbrandsdalsost 122
Guildford 24

Halloumi 122
Haminiog 24
Handkäse 112, 122
Havarti 35, 36, 80, 122
Herrgårdsost 82, 122
Hervé 122
homogenized milk 166
Huntsman 2
Hushållsost 82, 123

Idiazabal 88, 123
Ilchester 24
Islay 23
Italian cheeses 16, 17 *and see under individual names*
Italico 103, 123

Jarlsberg 123
Jerome 123
Jowa 37

Kachkaval 123
Kasar 123
Kasseri 124
Kefaloteri 124
Kéfir 163
Kernhem 76, 124
Klosterkäse 68, 124
Kopanisti 124
Korbkäse 124
Koumiss 163, 164
Kümmelkäse 124

Labna, Labneh 24, 164
lactic acid 11, 24, 27, 29, 34
lactose 11, 19, 26, 27, 163
Laguiole 124
Laktofil 164

Index

Lancashire 21, 23, 84, 124
Langres 125
Latteria 125
Leicester 23, 84, 125
Lemoine 37
León 125
Levroux 125
Leyden 76, 125
Liederkranz 38, 125
Limbourg, Limburger 38, 70, 125–6, 144
lipase 166
Lipids 27
Liptauer 126
Livarot 35, 37, 126
Llangloffan 24
Lou Palou 50, 126
Lymeswold 165

Maasdam 76, 126
Mahón 86, 126
Mainauer 126–7
Malaga 127
Mamirolle 127
Manchego 90, 127, 134, 144
Manteca 127
Margotin 48, 127
Maribo 80, 127
Marmora 128
Maroilles 17, 42, 125, 128
Marzolino 16
Mascarpone 60, 128
Masnor 129
Meshanger 129
Mesost 129
milk, acidity of 166; composition of 26–7; heating techniques 18; preparation of 27–9; types of 26
Mimolette 129
Minas 129
Minas Frescal 129
minerals 27
Misch 129
Mischling 129
Molbo 80, 129–30
Moldavian 130
Moncenisio 130
Mondseer 130
Montafa 20
Montasio 58, 98, 106, 125, 130, 131, 155
Monterey 38, 130–1
Morbier 131
Morlacco 131
mould (bacteria) 27, 31, 166
Mt St Benoit 37
Mozzarella 34, 37, 38, 39, 58, 60, 114, 131, 135, 138, 139, 148, 162, 166
Munster 31, 37, 42, 101, 132
Murazzano 132
Murbodner 132
Murol 132
Mycella 132
Mysost 115

Nantais 132
Neufchâtel 37, 132–3
Newmarket 24
New Zealand cheeses 40 and see under individual names
Nieheimer 133
Niolo 133
Niva 133
Njeguski 133
Nøkkelost 18, 133

Normanna 133
North Wiltshire 24
Norvegia 134
Nutwood 24

Oaxaca 134
Oka 37, 134
Olivet 134
Olmützer Quargel 134
Orduna 134
Orkney 23
Oropesa 134
Ovci Hrudkovy 134

Pannerone 58, 134–5
Pannonia 135
Păpuşi de Caş 135
Parenica 135
Parmesan (Parmigiano Reggiano) 16, 30, 32, 35, 37, 39, 40, 52, 121, 135–6; to cut 160
Parmesão 135
Pasiego Prensado 136
Passe l'An 136
Passendale 74, 136
pasteurisation 27, 166
Pastorello 39
Patagrás 136
Pecorino 24, 30, 35, 37, 39, 40, 115, 136–7, 166
Pecorino Foggiano 136–7
Pecorino Romano 56, 137, 144
Pecorino Siciliano 52, 137
Pedroches 137
Petit-Suisse 20, 133
Pikantinij 137
Pineapple 38
Pinzgauer Bergkäse 36
Piora 66, 137
Pizza Cheese 37, 38, 90, 131, 138
plastic or spun-curd cheese 34, 166
plastic-wrapped cheeses 31, 32
Plateau 138
Ploderkäse 138
Pont l'Evêque 31, 37, 42, 138
Pont-Moutier 46, 138
Port-du-Salut 134, 138, 139, 146, 153
Port-Salut 42, 82, 97, 101, 134, 138–9
Port Salutost 82
Poshekhonskij 139
Pot Cheese 38
Poligny-Saint-Pierre 139
Prästost 82, 139
Prato 139
Prince-Jean 74, 139
processed cheese 36, 38, 39, 40, 166
Provola 139
Provolone 52, 134, 139–40, 166
Pultost 140
Puzol 140
Pyramide 44, 50, 140

Quark 27, 29, 34, 140–1
Quartirolo 54, 141
Queso Blanco 141
Queso de Cabra 141

Ragusano 52, 141
Rahm Brie 68, 141
Rahm Camembert 68, 141
Rahmfrischkäse 142
Rance, Patrick 21
Raschera 142

Rässkäse 142
Reading Yellow 24
Reblochon 34, 37, 44, 142
Red Leicester 39
rennet 11, 20, 29, 165, 166
rennet-curd cheeses 34
Requeijão 142
Ricotta 24, 27, 34, 60, 128, 142–3
Ricotta Salata Moliterna 143
Riddar 82, 143
Rigatello 143
Rigottes 143
rind 31
rindless cheeses 32
ripening 27, 30–2
Robiola 60, 143–4
Robiolini 60, 144
Romadur 35, 72, 124, 125, 144, 149
Romano 40, 144
Roncal 86, 144
Roquefort 17, 21, 35, 37, 44, 133, 144–5
Royalp 145
Rutland 24

Saanenkäse 64, 145
Sage Derby 39, 145
sage-flavoured cheeses 23, 38–9
Sage Lancashire 124
Saingorlon 145
Sainte-Maure 42, 103, 145–6
Saint-Marcellin 146
Saint-Nectaire 37, 146
Saint-Paulin 30, 34, 36, 37, 98, 146, 147, 153
Saint-Rémy 146
Salami 146
Salers 146
salting 18, 27, 30
Samsø 36, 78, 113, 117, 146, 153
San Maurin 147
Sanroch 147
San Simón 88, 147
Sapsago 147
Sarusø 147
Sauerkäse 17
Savaron 147
Sbrinz 17, 62, 147–8
Scamorza 37, 58, 148
Scandinavian cheeses 18 and see under individual names
Schabzieger 147
Schabzieger Glaronnais 64, 148
Scottish cheeses 23 and see under individual names
Selles-sur-Cher 148
Selva 88, 148
Serena 148
Serra 148
Sherwood 24
Shropshire Blue 20
Silter 149
Slipcote 23
Soaked-Curd 38
soured cream 163
soured milk products 163–4
Stangenkäse 149
Steinbuscher 149
Stepnoj 149
Stilton 20, 21–2, 23, 35, 84, 144, 149, 156
Stirred-Curd 38
Suffolk 24
Suisse, Demi-Suisse, Petit-Suisse 29, 144, 149
Suprême des Ducs 46, 149–50

surface-ripened cheeses 31, 34, 166
Suries 37
Svecia 36, 82, 150
Svenbo 150
Swaledale 23
Swiss 38, 150
Swiss cheeses 15, 17, 18, 19 and see under individual cheeses
Swiss style cheeses (Australian) 39

Taffel 150
Taleggio 54, 141, 150–1
Telemea 90, 151
Tête-de-Moine 64, 151
Tetilla 88, 151, 154
Tillamook 38
Tilsit, Tilsiter 35, 72, 101, 145, 149, 151
Toma 58, 152
Tomino 60, 152
Tomme de Savoie 44, 152
Tomme Vaudoise 66, 152
Torta del Casar 88, 152–3
Toscanello 56, 153
Trappinsten, Trappiste 153
Trou de Sottai 74, 153
Tupi 88, 153
Twaróg, Twrog 153
Tybo 18, 78, 153
Tyroler Alpenkäse 153
Tyroler Graukäse 154

Ulloa 154
Ulzama 154

Vacherin des Beauges 154
Vacherin Mont-d'Or 64, 94, 154
Vacherol du Pont-du-Salut de la Trappe 48, 154
Valais Raclette 154
Valdeteja 154
Val di Muggio 66, 154
Valençay 125, 155
Vaquinha 37
Västerbottenost 82, 155
Venaco 155
Vermont Sage 39
Vezzena 155
Villalón 86, 155
vitamins 26, 27, 32
Vivario 155

Walliser 62, 98, 155
Walton 24
Warwickshire 24
Washed-Curd 38, 156
washed-rind cheeses 32, 166
Waxed rind cheeses 166
Weichkäse 68, 156
Weichkäse mit Champignons 70
Weissläcker 156
Welsh cheeses 20, 23, 24 and see under individual names
Wensleydale, White and Blue 21, 23, 39, 156
Westminster (Lymeswold) 165
whey 11, 25, 27, 29, 30, 36, 166
Windsor Red 24
wines to serve with cheeses 157–9

yogurt 26, 29, 163